CARMARTHENSH... ART
LIBRARY

D0234842

Problems and Solutions in Marital and Family Therapy

To Judith
J.

Problems and Solutions in Marital and Family Therapy

John Carpenter and Andy Treacher

Basil Blackwell

Copyright © John Carpenter and Andy Treacher 1989

First published 1989

Basil Blackwell Ltd
108 Cowley Road, Oxford, OX4 1JF, UK

Basil Blackwell Inc.
432 Park Avenue South, Suite 1503
New York, NY 10016, USA

All rights reserved. Except for the quotation of short passages for the purposes of criticism and review, no part of this publication may be reproduced, stored in a retrieval system, or transmitted, in any form or by any means, electronic, mechanical, photocopying, recording or otherwise, without the prior permission of the publisher.

Except in the United States of America, this book is sold subject to the condition that it shall not, by way of trade or otherwise, be lent, re-sold, hired out, or otherwise circulated without the publisher's prior consent in any form of binding or cover other than that in which it is published and without a similar condition including this condition being imposed on the subsequent purchaser.

British Library Cataloguing in Publication Data

Carpenter, John, 1952–
    Problems and solutions in marital and
    family therapy
    1. Welfare work. Family therapy
    I. Title   II. Treacher, Andrew
    362.8′286

    ISBN 0–631–15556–0

Library of Congress Cataloging in Publication Data

Carpenter, John, 1952–
    Problems and solutions in marital and family therapy / John Carpenter and Andy Treacher.
        p.   cm.
    Bibliography: p.
    ISBN 0–631–15556–2 (pbk.)
    1. Marital psychotherapy.   2. Family psychotherapy.   I. Treacher, Andrew.   II. Title.
RC488.5.C365 1989
616.89′156––dc 19   88–23238
                                                                        CIP

Typeset in 11 on 12½ pt Sabon
by Photo·Graphics, Honiton, Devon
Printed in Great Britain by Billing and Sons Ltd, Worcester

Contents

Foreword

With the proliferation of marital and family therapy literature in recent years, any further publications must have some clear justification. What is it therefore that Carpenter and Treacher offer in this text that justifies its production and demands its purchase? Quite simply it is one of the very best books to have been written on marital and family therapy. In a field that is swamped with competing and often contradictory theories and techniques – some presented with a dogma and determination reminiscent of fundamental religion, and others presented with a language that makes them alien to all but the initiated – this book stands out for its clarity and pragmatism.

The authors' eminently practical approach to understanding and treating families will be of value and interest to anyone involved in such work. They have achieved this by keeping their feet firmly on the ground. No sacred cows are worshipped, and no dogma goes unchallenged. Ideas, theories, problems, dilemmas and techniques are all most carefully explored, explained and analysed. The very skills required of an effective therapist – perceptual, conceptual and executive – are demonstrated in each chapter. So whether the topic is convening or ending, secrets or violence, the family's or the therapist's 'stuckness', Carpenter and Treacher guide us in a clear, practical, and objective way through each step in the process.

Beginners and the relatively inexperienced will learn more from this book than probably any others on the market, whilst intermediate and experienced therapists will be pleasantly surprised by how much more they have gained. And even if they do not agree with all the authors' conclusions they will have to admit that each side of every argument has been properly considered.

Carpenter and Treacher are very well known and respected family therapists in Britain, having contributed an enormous amount to the practice, teaching and promotion of family therapy. In this work they have done themselves proud, whilst at the same time showing how much they value what they have learned from others. In this book they generously acknowledge that debt whilst at the same time providing an invaluable addition to the literature. It is my privilege to have been one of the first to read it, and to recommend it to everyone in the field. No student nor colleague of mine will be allowed to miss it.

Bryan Lask
Editor, *Journal of Family Therapy*
Consultant Psychiatrist, The Hospitals for Sick Children,
Great Ormond Street, London

Acknowledgements

To our colleagues in a variety of agencies and to all the couples and families who have helped us to find solutions to the problems of therapy.

To *The Australian and New Zealand Journal of Family Therapy* for permission to include the cartoon by Brian Cade from vol. 7 (1) 1986, p. 54.

To Brunner/Mazel Publishing Co. for permission to include figure 1.1 ('Interaction within the person of the therapist of the three social systems – personal, professional and patient/client family') from the chapter by A. C. R. Skynner, 'An Open-systems group-analytic approach to family therapy' in A. S. Gurman and D. P. Kniskern (eds) *Handbook of Family Therapy* (1981).

To the *Journal of Family Therapy* for permission to include extracts from the following papers: vol. 4 pps. 15–34, 285–305; vol. 5 pps. 81–96, 337–58.

To Margaret Hardwidge for her many valuable comments in addition to her excellent work in typing and preparing the manuscript, and compiling the indexes.

1

Problems and Solutions

One common way to think about therapy is to consider it as a form of combat. Thus, the therapist, an heroic figure, pits himself (the pronoun is always male) against the many-headed monster 'resistance' and, by dint of subtle strategy and tremendous technique, eventually succeeds in becoming its master. Alternatively, it is like a game of chess, of move and counter-move, in which one side attempts to outwit the other and so force surrender.

Certainly, therapy is often difficult – for clients as well as for therapists. It can provide a most compelling challenge to the participants' skill and creativity and, especially for the clients, to the values and assumptions which govern their lives. However, to agree that therapy is both difficult and challenging is not to concede that it need be a contest between therapist and client. Indeed, it is our contention that to view therapy in this way is to make it more, not less, difficult, to create problems rather than to solve them. Yet much of the writing and discussion about marital and family therapy is ostensibly based on the premise that, despite the apparent evidence to the contrary, couples and families do not really want to change, preferring rather to hang on to the status quo and thereby thwart their therapist. Problems in therapy, whether the reluctance of a family member to attend, the questioning of the therapist's competence or the failure to complete an agreed task, are consequently seen as an expression of the couple's or family's resistance. The therapist's solution becomes one of developing more and more sophisticated strategies with which to overcome these 'resistant' clients. Such solutions include using the clients' 'resistance to change' against them, apparently tricking them into giving up their symptom or problem. The failure of therapy is similarly attributed to a lack of motivation or a high degree of resistance.

In this book we set out to describe a way of understanding problems in marital and family therapy which does not assume that these are caused by resistance, on the part of either the couple or family on the one hand, or the therapist on the other. In earlier work (Treacher and Carpenter, 1982; Carpenter et al., 1983) we suggested that the term 'stuckness' should be used to describe such problems in therapy. Stuckness is an ugly word, but valuable since it stresses that it is both the family (or the couple) *and* the therapist who are stuck; the problem lies in the *therapeutic system*, that is, the family plus the therapist, rather than with the family or therapist alone. We assume that there are many reasons why therapy becomes stuck and that these include difficulties in the process of therapy as well as the context in which it takes place. In our experience, the search for solutions to these problems begins with a careful analysis of their nature: our first responsibility is to determine where and how we and the family are stuck. Our second responsibility is to avoid the kind of contest which serves only to entrench our positions, and either to re-engage the family members in an effort to find a solution, or, alternatively, to cease therapy. The succeeding chapters in this book describe our approach in practice, but our first concern is to discuss how our theoretical framework attempts to escape the strictures of existing literature concerning resistance and change. We will do this by considering the following questions:

1 How has the concept of resistance been developed in marital and family therapy?
2 Why do couples and families find change difficult?
3 How can marital and family therapy be effective in facilitating change?

The Concept of Resistance in Marital and Family Therapy

In seeking to understand the use of the concept of resistance in marital and family therapy, it is important to remember the dual influences of the medical model and of psychoanalysis. We are so familiar with the language of therapy that it is easy to overlook the medical origin of such terms as 'identified patient', 'diagnosis' and 'symptom'. Much less obvious, but equally important in shaping our thinking are the underlying assumptions about human motivation which derive from psychoanalysis.

Doctors have long had a problem with resistance. Patients through the ages have, from time to time, stubbornly and irritatingly declined to comply with their doctors' instructions. The doctor may have been totally convinced that a patient's cure lies in a particular treatment, but the patient has thought differently. The problem for the doctor in this situation was to make the patient 'comply' and to take the prescribed treatment whether it be medication, a change of diet or a change of lifestyle. Further, even if the treatment was begun, there was no guarantee that the patient would continue with it, or report back to the doctor so that its effects could be monitored. The study of this phenomenon has not surprisingly become a major focus for medical research under the heading of 'patient compliance' (for example, Haynes et al., 1979).

Given its partly medical heritage, it was only to be expected that the literature and the practice of marital and family therapy would reflect a concern with 'getting people to do what is best for them'. The therapist, who had probably been trained as a doctor or, if not, most likely worked in a medical setting, easily assumed the mantle of expert and with it the expectation that the patients should comply. (Indeed, following the diagnosis of the identified patient's symptom, the therapist would, and in many places still does, proceed with the issuing of a 'prescription'.) If the patients did not comply then they were naturally construed to be 'resisting'.

In marital and family therapy there has been a particular problem of compliance with the therapist's request to include in therapy other members of the family in addition to the person complaining of the problem. Therapists have worked hard to engage the husbands, wives or partners of their patients, to recruit reluctant fathers and to persuade parents to bring their rebellious adolescents. The literature reflects these efforts, with such titles as 'A note on luring a resistant spouse into marital therapy' (Berger, 1975), 'Involving the reluctant father in family therapy' (Doherty, 1981) and 'Helping parents to get resistant adolescents into family therapy' (Fisher, 1981).

The implication of the terms compliance and resistance is that the problem is the unreasonable behaviour of the patient, but just as researchers in the field of 'patient compliance' are moving towards a more sophisticated, interactional understanding (Doherty and Baird, 1983), so have marital and family therapists preceded them. For example, Skynner (1976) pointed out that therapists as well as families can be resistant. He suggested that those who described low socio-economic families as typically 'unmotivated' should more appropriately ascribe that label to themselves. Certainly, for a variety of reasons, some therapists are unmotivated to work with some families but the end result is a product of the interaction between family and therapist. This can be partially clarified by drawing up a two-by-two table (table 1.1).

Table 1.1 Family's and therapist's motivation and the outcome of therapy

Therapist's position	Family's position	
	Motivated	Unmotivated
Motivated	Therapeutic change likely to occur	Possibly stuck
Unmotivated	Probably stuck	Very stuck

However, the outcome is also very likely to be affected by the attitude of the therapist's employing agency. If the agency does not encourage therapeutic activity on the part of its workers, or even hinders them by refusing to provide time or space, even strongly-motivated families and therapists will find it hard to prosper (table 1.2).

Table 1.2 Therapist's and agency's motivation and the outcome of therapy

Therapist's position	Attitude of the therapist's agency to the outcome of the therapy	
	Motivated	Unmotivated
Motivated	Therapeutic change possible	Possibly stuck
Unmotivated	Probably stuck	Therapeutic change probably impossible

The problem of drawing up such tables is, of course, that we can only compare two variables at a time. In real life many factors interpenetrate in a bewilderingly complex fashion, so that if we are to discuss them productively we are forced to make a systematic, multidimensional analysis of each concrete situation. Skynner (1981)

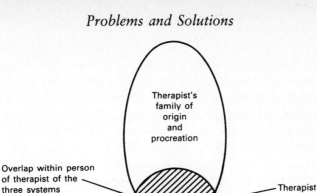

Figure 1.1 Interaction within the person of the therapist of the three social systems — personal, professional and patient/client family

has contributed a useful diagram (figure 1.1) which provides a starting point for getting to grips with such analyses.

In discussing this diagram Skynner makes a basic point about its value in assessing whether or not therapy can be effective (1981, p. 57):

> All three systems – the family being treated and their network; the therapist's personal life, his or her family of origin, family of procreation, and other personal relationships; and the therapist's professional life, colleagues and professional world – must interact within the person of the therapist in an optimal way if she is to be as effective as possible professionally and grow and learn from her experience.

Skynner's approach is clearly of value, but we feel that his position is still not sufficiently elaborated. For example, he correctly points out the significance of the co-therapist, the supervisory team, institution and professional colleague network; but in many cases it is essential (as Palazzoli et al., 1980a, have pointed out) to examine the significance of the referrer and the agency in which she works.* Often the agency providing therapy and the referring agency may not be working to the same plan, so therapy flounders. Skynner, despite labelling his approach an 'open systems' one, does not systematically analyse other important systems. For example, although he includes the therapist's work (or 'professional') system in his analysis (as we have already noted), he does not take the work-systems of his client's family into consideration. Equally important systems (such as other caring agencies, schools, courts, the police, etc.) will have to be included in our analysis if we are to take a comprehensive systems approach to the problem. As Kingston (1979) has pointed out, family therapists generally fail to widen their analysis to include such systems, preferring instead to concentrate on the nuclear family and occasionally its wider family networks.

More recently, Anderson and Stewart (1983) in a lengthy and detailed text entitled *Mastering Resistance* have attempted to gather together a variety of unhelpful influences on the process and outcome of therapy under the general heading of resistance. They argue that it is not only families and therapists which can be described as resistant, but agencies too (1983, p. 24):

> Resistance can be defined as all those behaviours in the therapeutic system which interact to prevent the therapeutic system from achieving the family's goals for therapy. The therapeutic system includes family members, the therapist, and the context in which therapy takes place, that is, the agency or institution in which it occurs. Resistance is most likely to be successful, that is, to result in the termination or failure of family therapy, when resistances are present and interacting synergistically in all three components of the therapeutic system.

Anderson and Stewart acknowledge that to label all behaviours which impede family therapy as 'resistance' may not be strictly accurate, but defend such an approach on the grounds that these behaviours all function in the same way and can therefore be considered as part of a 'pragmatic' approach to therapy. They go

---

* We use the feminine pronoun throughout this book in recognition of the fact that most marital and family therapists are female and also to avoid the clumsy use of 'he/she', 'his/ her' etc.

on to consider three types of resistance which interact with each other: family-based, therapist-based and institution-based.

We welcome both Anderson and Stewart's extended model of resistance and their stress on the interaction between resistances, but we are concerned that the labelling of all impediments as 'resistance' will inadvertently serve to increase, rather than decrease, the difficulties in coming to terms with these problems. Such labelling carries with it the explicit assumption that the resistances must be 'mastered' – a disappointingly 'macho' expression in itself, which again conjures up the vision of the heroic therapist struggling against the odds. This creates a very misleading impression and, as we have said earlier, is the reason why we have preferred the use of the term 'stuckness' to describe the process in which family and therapist have become embroiled. This approach flows more directly from systems theory and is clearly depicted by Hoffman (1981) in her book *Foundations of Family Therapy* in which she outlines the significance of Bateson's thinking for therapy (1981, p. 8):

> The therapist can no longer be seen as 'impacting' on the client or family through personality, craft or technique. The therapist is not an agent and the client is not a subject. Both are part of a larger field in which the therapist, family, and any number of other elements act and react upon each other in unpredictable ways, because each action and reaction continually changes the nature of the field in which the elements of this new therapeutic system reside.

Hoffman herself later comments (1981, p. 348) that 'It is more accurate to describe resistance as the place where the therapist and client or family intersect. Resistance is merely an artefact of that time and place.' But, of course, that time and place is also where change takes place: it is not just the client or family which changes but also their *relationship* with their therapist and, indeed, the therapist herself. This is hardly a new insight, since psychoanalysts have long recognized that changes in the relationship over time are the essence of therapy. It is, however, being discovered by both family therapists and behaviour therapists as a necessary corrective to the overly manipulative scientistic approach. Thus Liddle (1985, p. 176) declares:

Replacing the notion of a therapist applying a model or technique to a patient-family is the still-developing idea of therapist and patient-family as a coevolving, changing system. That is, therapist and family in the course of their therapeutic contact (and perhaps beyond) constitute an organic system, and it is the functioning of this therapeutic system that changes – in rules, structure, organisation, and so on – in therapy.

The concept of resistance and an emphasis on its 'mastery' also fails to give due credence to the fact that clients, whether individuals or members of families, *think* and amongst their thoughts are those about the process of therapy in which they are engaged. This point is delightfully made by Brian Cade in a cartoon published in the *Australian and New Zealand Journal of Family Therapy*. He depicts a father talking to his family during an interval in a family therapy session whilst the therapist is out of the room conferring with his colleagues about the team's intervention. It is clear from what the father says that he has learned much about the team's peculiar style and unusual way of thinking. What is also striking about the father's statement is his recommendation of a strategy to 'counter' the therapist's expected intervention. Therapy is a battle for him, too.

To sum up, we consider that to label problems in marital and family therapy as being the result of resistance is unhelpful. Problems and their solutions need to be understood in terms of the many contexts in which clients and therapists come together, along with the developing relationship between the parties. To treat difficulties as problems of compliance with the therapy, as in the crude medical model, is quite inappropriate. There is, though, another sense in which families and couples have been considered to 'resist' change and this is more deeply embedded in the way in which therapists think about problems. It derives in essence from the legacy of psychoanalysis.

Why do Couples and Families 'Resist' Change?

The systems approach to working with families developed principally from research into and practice with families with schizophrenic members (see Nichols, 1984, pp. 42–64, in which he describes the contributions of Jackson, Weakland, Haley, Bowen, Whitaker and Boszormenyi-Nagy). The family was described as a system, the

'My hypothesis is that our therapist is sacrificing himself in the belief that it will help his team stay together. His apparent incompetence has the effect that his colleagues feel more competent, and also helps them avoid dealing with the covert supervisor/supervisee dysfunction in the team. I think he will come in, pose us with a dilemma, and give us a no change prescription. I suggest we counter it with a split family message that makes overt their covert problems'.

components of which acted in such a way as to maintain an emotional equilibrium. Of particular interest was the way in which symptomatic behaviour acted as a kind of balance. As Hoffman (1981, p. 18) recalls, therapists were impressed by the frequent observation that if the schizophrenic patient got better, someone else in the family usually got worse. Jackson (1957) in a truly seminal paper, 'The question of family homeostasis', described this tendency to resist change as being analogous to the operation of a homeostat controlling, for example, the temperature of a central-heating system.

Unfortunately, the early emphasis on studying families with chronic problems and the compelling description of homeostasis as the most characteristic feature of these family systems had the effect of skewing the development of theory and practice. The emphasis settled on stability rather than change and the question became: Why do families *resist* change? The answer given to this question has sometimes been the tautological one: families resist change *because of* homeostasis. It is, of course, rarely presented so crudely, but our observations of some therapists in action suggest that they really do believe that 'homeostasis' exists. They take it for granted that families 'resist' change and automatically assume that defiance-based techniques, such as no-change paradoxes, must be used in order to induce it.

But why should couples and families hang on to their problems or symptoms? Why do some couples remain locked in apparently mutually destructive combat? Why do some families cling on to the symptoms of one of their members as if they really did not want him or her to get better? The only possible conclusion must surely be that they get something out of it, whether it be some sort of sado-masochistic gratification, or the satisfaction of preserving the status quo. This approach enshrines the doctrine that the symptom must have a 'function within or for the system' and it has been of considerable importance in the practice of family therapy. For example, Papp (1983, p. 18) in a recent book on 'systemic' family therapy suggests that the first two questions to be kept in mind when gathering information about a family are:

1   What function does the symptom serve in stabilizing the family?
2   How does the family function in stabilizing the symptom?

Earlier in her book Papp states her central premise that the symptom (note the use of the medical term) and the system (by which she means the *family* system) are '... *connected* and defined as *serving one another*' (1983, p. 10). She continues:

> The question is often raised as to whether a symptom always serves a function in the system or whether it may be a reaction to a situation outside the family, such as work, school, or social relationships. Although the origins of a symptom may be rooted in an outside event, its persistence would indicate it is being *used* by the family in some ongoing transaction. For example: If a husband is laid off from his job because of an economic recession, he may become depressed as a result of being unemployed. The depression will most likely disappear when he obtains another job. However, if in the meantime he begins to use his depression as a weapon in an ongoing power struggle between him and his wife, the depression is likely to

become chronic, because it will be serving a function in the marital relationship.

A major problem with this kind of thinking (which links symptoms and systems in the service of each other) is that it makes the family system into a kind of 'thing'. Wilden, in his introduction to an important collection of essays on the use of systems theory, warns against the use of invalid 'system analogies' such as the analogy of the family as a kind of 'mind' as in 'the family thinks that . . .' or 'the family system acts in order to restore homeostasis.' The 'family' of course does no such thing, although its members may share certain thoughts or act in concert to achieve a particular goal. Similarly, the family, unlike its individual members, has no needs, whether for accommodation or for emotional equilibrium (Wilden, 1980, p. xxxviii). The danger of this reification is that when the family system is perceived as an *object to be changed*, all kinds of methods can be justified as appropriate in achieving this goal (Treacher, 1986). The family members cease to be people in their own right, but rather become part of a system – cogs in a machine – and any distress or discomfort caused by the therapist's efforts to change the system can be overlooked. (The ethical consequences of this are explored in Carpenter, 1987a.) From a practical point of view, exponents of this way of thinking about families ignore the potential for change available in the therapeutic relationship, readily lose a focus on the agreements and understandings by which family members have entered into therapy and, instead, fall into a combative relationship with members of the family they are trying to 'help'. As we have discussed earlier, this notion of the therapist 'acting on' the family cannot be part of a systems perspective. It is also most likely to increase the 'resistance' experienced by the therapist.

What then is the origin of this notion of symptoms serving a function? In a brief but persuasive comment on resistance in family therapy, Ransom (1982) argues that it is an unwitting inheritance of the principle of unconscious purposiveness from psychoanalysis. Freud believed that patients' symptoms were the method by which they maintained a dynamic equilibrium when their psyche was under threat. Ransom proposes that the model of the family as a system 'is little more than the Freudian equilibrium model in disguise, applied at the level of "family" instead of "personality" organisation'. Psychoanalysis took a sceptical stance towards what patients said and did, and focused attention on unconscious purposes which contradicted conscious intentions. Unfortunately, family therapy followed a similar path by which the unconscious motives of the individual patient were replaced by the unconscious imperative of the family system in order to maintain its homeostasis.

In psychoanalytic practice the analyst typically aims to uncover the patient's resistances so that he can be made aware of these unresolved intra-psychic conflicts. As Ransom points out, it is an essentially adversarial position – one which has been uncritically adopted by family therapists. The consequences of this for the practice of therapy are spelt out by Ransom (1982, p. 7) as follows:

> . . . when the therapist's behavior is guided by an underlying idea that an unconscious purposivism or covert design is at work, *and* when that purposivism or design is believed to be governed by principles that direct behavior toward seeking gratification and/or maintaining the status quo, a suspicious, accusatory tone inevitably informs and pervades the therapy process. Family members will react defensively to the suggestion or implication that they are getting something out of the problem, that they have hidden agendas, or that they do not really want to change. Efforts to force or trick them into changing will, for obvious reasons, also be met with resistance. Participants will very likely feel misunderstood, invalidated, or manipulated. The most likely (and I would add 'healthy') response will be to resist such approaches.

Families and Change – an Alternative Approach

The early studies of chronic problems such as schizophrenia led family theorists to emphasize stability rather than change. However, families with chronic problems are unusual in that they appear to be stuck in a 'time warp', at a stage of family development which they should long ago have passed, typically that of 'leaving home'. Most people, on the other hand, come to therapeutic agencies because of *change*, either change that has recently taken place, or change that is in prospect.

Many people come for help at a time of crisis. The crisis may have been provoked by something that happened to a member of the family, such as death or sudden illness, or it may have been the impact of some external event such as redundancy or emigration. In a crisis, change will have *already* taken place: what the family members now require is assistance in adapting to these changes, the implications of which are just becoming apparent. As every textbook on crisis intervention reminds us, the Chinese pictogram for crisis indicates both a time of danger and a time of opportunity. The task for the therapist is to *work with* (not against) individuals, couples and families in order to help them to adapt and to make use of the opportunity. A model of therapy which is based on medicine and psychoanalysis, symptoms and unconscious processes, resistance and an adversarial stance, is therefore inappropriate and unhelpful.

Similarly, when families come to therapy for help with the consequences or prospects of developmental change, such as at adolescence and re-marriage, it is change rather than stability which should be at the forefront of the therapist's mind. It is pointless the therapist attacking the family's supposed resistance to change, when they are already caught up in the process of change.

Even in the case of chronic family problems, we can shift from a focus on what is staying the same to considering what is changing. For example, if the members of such a family are asking for help, why are they doing so now, rather than last month or last year? Almost certainly, change will have occurred or will be anticipated, if not in the family, then in their relationship with other people or agencies. Once again, the therapist's task is to help in the adjustment to this change. If the therapist then meets 'resistance', we would suggest that she recognizes this as 'stuckness' – a problem not 'in' the family but rather in the working of the therapeutic relationship.

Rather than thinking of stability and resistance to change as the norm for marriages and families, we feel more comfortable in thinking of families as constantly changing in ways both large and small. Everyday experience of family life confirms this view. Families change as their individual members grow older and develop new abilities, interests and ideas. They also change as the world changes around them, and as they change that world. In 'systems talk', the family is an 'open' not a 'closed' system and cannot therefore be treated like the proverbial central-heating system.

Some family systems theorists, notably Speer (1970) and Hoffman (1981), have followed Maruyama (1968) in proposing an 'evolutionary' model for systems change. Maruyama, according to Hoffman

(1981), suggested that the survival of any living system depended on its capacity for both 'morphostasis' and 'morphogenesis'. Morphostasis is the capacity to maintain constancy in the face of environmental fluctuations. Morphogenesis refers to the capacity of a system to change its basic structure, as in the case of a genetic mutation in a species which allows adaption to changes in the environment – hence the evolutionary analogy. De Shazer (1984), in discussing this idea, suggests that, since therapy is concerned with *change*, the 'organizing concept' for the study of therapeutic systems should therefore be morphogenesis rather than homeostasis. In our work with families, we should be concerned not with what is keeping things the same but with what is changing. The emphasis should be not on how clients resist change but on how they co-operate with the therapist.

De Shazer cites Haley's observations of the highly influential Milton Erickson in support of his recommendation that the therapist approach each patient with an expectation that change is not only possible but inevitable. In describing Erickson's working method, Haley remarked: 'There is a sureness which exudes from him, although he can be unsure if he wishes, and an attitude of confidence as if it would surprise him if change did not occur' (Haley, 1967, p. 535). As de Shazer remarks, 'The therapist's stance is not *if* change will occur, but rather *when*, or *where* or *what type of* changing will occur' (1984, p. 16). A concern with resistance within this framework would merely hinder the therapist because it implies that change is not inevitable. We would add that the kind of contest which is called resistance is also much less likely with this emphasis on co-operation. If the therapist is looking out for signs of co-operation rather than signs of resistance then she is more likely to find it and be in a position to encourage it. Furthermore, in our experience, therapists too often fail to recognize change, even when it is happening in front of them. Because they have been trained in theories of pathology they see problems rather than strengths; they see what is still going wrong rather than what is now going right.

The evolutionary perspective has been further developed by Dell (1982) who borrows from ecology the concept of 'fit'. In the study of ecology the concept of causality, 'circular' or otherwise, is unnecessary since organisms simply exist in an environment in which each influences the other. Similarly, Dell suggests that causation is an unnecessary concept in the study of family systems. He proposes 'fit' as an alternative which '...simply posits that the behaviours occurring in the family system have a general complementarity; they fit together' (Dell, 1982). There is, however, a serious problem with this ecological analogy when it comes to the practice of therapy. It is well illustrated in the kind of popular television documentary on the lives of animals in a particular ecology, for example the Serengeti: the viewer is invited to watch, with scientific detachment, the killing of an antelope by a lion. The cameraman does not interfere to save the life; the task is to demonstrate part of the ecological relationship, not to alter the law of the jungle, however unjust the law might appear to the individual antelope. There is no question that the lion is more powerful than the antelope, even though the antelope occasionally outwits or outruns the lion; and even though the lion from time to time goes hungry and suffers real pain it still has most of the advantages. In the same way as the complementary behaviour of the lion and the antelope fit together in the same ecology, so does the behaviour of members of a family system, for in both *power* is a factor.

Over the last few years there has been a growing feminist critique of marital and family therapy (e.g. Goldner, 1985; Hare-Mustin, 1978; Osborne, 1983; Magagna and Black, 1985; Pilalis and Anderton, 1986) which forces a re-evaluation of such easy statements as 'power is a metaphor'. There are, of course, many different aspects of power in family life and it is a mistake to confuse them: the power of decision-making is different, for example, from the power to regulate intimacy. Nevertheless, what is often lost in generalizations about 'the marriage' or 'the family' is an awareness that power is distributed unequally within the marriage or family. The relationships and behaviour may fit together as parts of a system, but that fit may be to the considerable disadvantage of some of the system's members. The implications of this point for the practice of therapy are, we consider, of great importance.

Palazzoli (1983), in a discussion of her work in consulting to organizations such as schools, stressed that it was the faction which was *losing*, not the one which was winning, in a power struggle which invited the consultant. The same is true of marriages and families: it is generally the loser, not the winner, who seeks help from an outsider to restore his or her position and who is the most likely 'customer' for change. Conversely, it is the winner, the person or persons who fear they have least to gain, or most to lose, who are the reluctant attenders, the least likely customers. What is immediately apparent to anyone working in marital and family therapy is that most of the losers are women and most of the winners are men. It is, on the whole, women who are depressed, battered and left, and who want change; it is the winners, men, who from the therapist's point of view are most often 'the problem'.

In our approach to marital and family therapy, therefore, we are concerned to remember that marriages and families are made up of people – women, men and children – with their own individual needs, wants and aspirations. An over-emphasis on a marriage or family *as a system* tends to obscure the significant differences between people as *individuals*. In particular, changes that have taken place or which are in prospect when members of a family come for help will carry different advantages and disadvantages for the members involved. For example, there may be many advantages for a man who has recently moved with his family to a new area in order to take up a job. He may enjoy the challenge of his new work, the company of his work-mates and the quietness of his new home. His wife, on the other hand, may be very unhappy at having given up her old job, leaving her family and friends and finding herself living in a dull and lonely new estate. The change that she may want is for a greater marital intimacy – a change he fears will disadvantage *him* in that it will curtail the time he has available to spend in establishing his position at work and with his new colleagues.

The Dilemma of Change

We have been suggesting that any change has its advantages and disadvantages and that these will be different for the different people involved. What is perhaps the most useful contribution of a systems approach is its focus on the corresponding changes in all parts of the system. This focus acts to prevent what Keeney (1983) has called 'ecological ignorance'. For example, if one partner in a marriage acts to make a change in her life, we know that not only will that change affect her partner and her children, but also her own mother and father, her mother-in-law, her best friend, and so on. The requirement for the therapist working within this framework is that she helps to articulate the possible repercussions and to evaluate, with the family, their advantages and disadvantages. We would stress the word 'evaluate' because it is people's fears about the consequences of change that hinder them, fears which are often ill grounded and thus the apparent dilemma is false. This brings forward an answer to the question of why families and couples become 'stuck' and live in considerable psychological discomfort with distressing symptoms. It also provides a sound reason why families should not simply comply and do what their therapist tells them.

Following Watzlawick and his colleagues, we take the view that no matter how painful or peculiar the behaviour of family members, it represents the best possible 'solution' they have been able to find so far to the dilemmas they experience (Watzlawick et al., 1974). Furthermore, it is at least familiar and '. . . as bad as they are, these known patterns [of behaviour] may be better than any else the family members can envisage' (Greenberg et al., 1964). They persist in (apparently) irrational or self-destructive behaviour because they believe that if they were to stop, matters really would get worse. It is important for the therapist to treat these fears as genuine, but without falling into the same trap as the client and seeing only one possible (bad) consequence or a grossly restricted choice. For example, the husband who believes he has to 'choose between' his wife and his mother has not allowed the possibility of his maintaining a relationship with both. The daughter who fears that she cannot leave home because her mother will be lonely without her, has not allowed the possibility that her mother can develop her own, independent life.

Bogdan (1984), in an important paper, proposes a cognitive model of family functioning in which each member's definition of a situation leads him or her to behave in ways which confirm the ideas held by other members. He assumes that individuals are 'cognitively conservative': frequently-used ideas become unconscious habits and we assume their essential truth — that is how the world is for us. Ideas which are shared implicitly with other members of our family are consequently more difficult for us to revise and change, even when there is abundant evidence that they are too restricted or even wrong.

A primary task of therapy, therefore, is to challenge clients' assumptions and ideas, to help them anticipate consequences, evaluate advantages and disadvantages and to seek out alternatives.

The process of therapy, as Hoffman (1981, p. 324) reminds us, is frequently one in which the 'solution' to the problem which brought the couple or family into therapy is followed by the emergence of a new difficulty. For example, the children's behaviour improves and with it comes a realization by the parents of difficulties in their marriage. These difficulties too can be solved, or the marriage itself may break up, which may be the consequence that is most feared. The question 'What will happen if the problem which brought the couple or family into therapy is solved?' is, therefore, one of the most useful to ask when therapy is stuck.

To sum up, what we are recommending here is a stance which does not assume that families or marriages *need* problems for their survival but rather that such problems are just as distressing as the family members say they are. People who fear the consequences of change, or the prospect of change, do so for reasons which are understandable but restricted in vision. The therapist should assume that change has taken and will take place. Her concern should be to help the family members understand the repercussions of change and to evaluate the advantages and disadvantages. In understanding 'stuckness' the therapist should re-evaluate her beliefs and those of the couple or family about the advantages and disadvantages of change and, in particular, of what would happen if the goal of therapy were to be achieved.

Problems and Solutions

In discussing the relationship between couple, family, therapist and agency earlier, we drew on Skynner's 'open systems' approach (Skynner, 1981). An understanding of problems in their context and at different levels is the hallmark of the systems approach. The context for the family or couple's problems may appropriately be understood as the economic and social conditions in which they live – conditions which in turn reflect the world's political and economic structure. As one of us has discussed elsewhere with reference to India, a systems analysis of problems at this level is highly relevant (Carpenter, 1987b), but it is important to make a distinction between such social problems and the kind of problems which fall within a therapist's remit.

Social problems, mass unemployment, urban decay, poverty and racism, for example, are evident in society in a broad sense and can be effectively addressed only through social-policy measures and large-scale social programmes. Individual clients and their families are unlikely to conceive of themselves as having a 'social problem' in this sense, but they do typically experience specific problems in their interaction with a limited number of other people such as their neighbours, and agencies and institutions like the courts, the income-maintenance system, schools and so on. The family and other systems which interact to produce the problem can be termed the 'problem system' – it revolves around the client's concern and is limited to those people and agencies directly involved in maintaining the problem (Carpenter, 1984a, p. 26).

Thus, in assessing problems in marital and family therapy we need to determine who is involved and how they are involved, to identify the participants in the problem system and to clarify how those participants interact to maintain the problematic behaviour. This is likely to require extensive knowledge about the couple and family as well as the many systems which may be presumed to impinge upon them. Although not all these systems are certain to play significant roles in contributing to the problems of any given family, a comprehensive assessment in cases of stuckness will pay dividends – not just in analysing the source of the problem, which might otherwise be overlooked, but also in identifying possible resources for alternative solutions.

As we stressed in our previous book, the usefulness of a systems approach in working with couples and families is, first, that it does not assume that the family is 'the problem' and second, that it illustrates the many possible targets for a worker's intervention (Treacher and Carpenter (eds), 1984, p. 4). We observed that, in many cases, it is the relationship between the family and the agencies which impinge on it which proves to be of crucial importance: if therapeutic interventions are to be effective then an understanding of the function of the agency and of the expectations of its clients is essential. (The same point is made in a collection of papers by Berger, Jurkovic et al. (1984) describing the practice of family therapy in agencies in the United States.)

Thus, for example, the 'clients' of social services departments in Britain and child welfare organizations in the United States do not expect a therapeutic service. The functions of such agencies include the provision of resources such as day-care places for children and elderly people, advocacy in relation to housing services and electricity suppliers, the investigation of child abuse and neglect and so on. In the probation service the primary task is the supervision of offenders, and not the provision of therapy. Even in agencies which are more therapeutically orientated, there is a variety of other functions which have to be fulfilled: child guidance clinics have to make assessment for special education; residential homes have to

deter children from running away; psychiatrists and social workers
have to make decisions about the compulsory admission of people
to hospitals. These functions may make the practice of therapy
more difficult, although we will also discuss how the therapist's
official position, access to resources and influence with other
agencies can have positive advantages if used as part of a systems
approach.

We will be particularly concerned with the question of whether
there is a 'customer' for change. Fisch and his colleagues at the
Mental Research Institute Brief Therapy Centre in Palo Alto,
California, have proposed that if family therapy is to be successful,
then at least one member *must* be a 'customer' for help. They define
a customer as being someone who communicates three basic
statements (Segal and Watzlawick, 1985, p. 83):

1 I have a problem regarding the behaviour of myself or another,
   which distresses me;
2 I have tried to solve this problem alone or with the help of others,
   and these problem-solving attempts have been unsuccessful;
3 I am asking for your help.

We have found that, in spite of its unfortunate materialist
connotations, this concept of customer is of particular value both
in analysing stuckness and in influencing the way we approach the
pre-contract phase of therapy. As we will discuss later, the lack of
a customer is one of the most important causes of problems and
failure in marital and family therapy. It is a major hazard of work
in agencies whose clients do not come on a voluntary basis. For
example, an education department may refer a family because one
of the children is not attending school. From the parents' point of
view this may not be a problem (they consider education to be
irrelevant or a waste of time), except that it provokes the unwelcome
attention of the education department (which is threatening to
prosecute). In this instance – and here we extend the use of the
concept – the education department are the more likely 'customers'
for the agency's services. The parents, however, feel obliged to
attend the agency since this saves them from being taken to court.

The trap that the therapist can fall into is in assuming that the
parents have the same goal as the education department (that of
returning their child to school), and, when they fail to co-operate,
in labelling them as 'resistant'. The therapist's task in working with

the parents is, rather, to understand the problem from their point of view and, if necessary and appropriate, to help them appreciate the consequences of their actions. For example, the therapist may establish that the parents' perception of their problem is that they are being victimized by the education department. What they want is to 'get the Department off our backs', and to an extent they can achieve this by attending for therapy since they can then claim to be tackling the problem even though they have no intention of sending their child to school. It would certainly be a mistake in this instance to persist in offering family therapy, since the parents do not believe that their family relationships are problematic. However, the therapist can point out that attending the clinic will not be a long-term solution to their problem with the education department and can anticipate with them the department's future options, including prosecution and the removal of their child into the care of the local authority. If the parents acknowledge the likely failure of their efforts, they are then potential 'customers' for the therapist's help in achieving their goal. Only once this stage has been reached can the therapist profitably discuss how the problem might be tackled – for example by the therapist acting as a conciliator between the two parties. (Since the education department is a customer too, this approach might well be effective.)

To sum up: our perspectives therefore in understanding problems in marital and family therapy will include assessing the wider context in which the therapy is taking place, and paying close attention to identifying accurately both the problem system and the customers for change.

Intervening at Different Levels

It is worth re-stating that marital and family therapy is not a panacea. Troubled relationships are not the only cause of problems in marriages and families and, conversely, changes in relationships may sometimes best be effected by interventions at different systems levels. A particularly poignant example of the former was included in our original stuckness paper.

□ One of us had struggled with a depressed, under-achieving girl aged thirteen and her family, adopting the hypothesis that the problem hinged around unresolved mourning for her father who had died the previous year. After several months during which no change had taken place, there was a rapid deterioration in her condition. Referral to an educational psychologist and thence for a neurological examination led to the diagnosis of sub-acute panencephalitis, a persistent infection of the brain cells by the measles virus. This is a rare disease (with an annual incidence in the UK of one per million children: *British Medical Journal*, 1979), and very sadly the infection proved fatal. □

Similarly, a therapist who has got caught up in therapy with a family who eke out an existence crowded into two rooms of a damp and decaying flat at the top of a tower block with no working lifts, will do best to help them find somewhere else to live. The method of intervention here will not be therapy but advocacy, or perhaps encouraging the parents to join a housing action group designed to put pressure on the housing department.

It seems probable that the more serious problems experienced by the clients of psychiatric and social welfare services, problems such as severe mental illness and child abuse, will be helped effectively only by interventions at more than one systems level (Carpenter, 1987b). For example, in describing a programme for schizophrenic patients and their families, Falloon and his colleagues include neuroleptic drug therapy and social rehabilitation as well as problem-solving family therapy (Falloon et al., 1984). Similarly, Minuchin, by any account one of the most influential family therapists, describes as standard a series of intervention methods with anorexic patients and their families, at individual, marital and family levels (Minuchin et al., 1978). Again, in working with child abuse Dale et al. (1986) discuss the use of network meetings, individually-focused work and multiple family meetings as part of their programme.

The range of interventions open to the therapist will, of course, be determined by her own skills and abilities as well as by the terms of reference laid down by the agency for which she works and her own profession: a social worker has no sanction to prescribe medication and few psychiatrists will have the skills to intervene in the welfare network. In this book we will purposely restrict the range to intervention at the level of the individual, the marriage, the family and the problem system. We will not be concerned with either consultations to larger systems (for example, schools) or with the therapy of individuals isolated from their families. On the other hand, we will place rather more emphasis on how individual members think about themselves in relation to their families and to the process of therapy than is the usual case in books on marital and family therapy.

A Model for Therapy

In the succeeding chapters of this book we hope to demonstrate how the values and assumptions we have outlined so far can inform an effective approach to marital and family therapy. We wish to show how a respectful and co-operative approach can help avoid the pitfalls encountered by adversarial methods which too easily end up in bewilderment, mutual recrimination and drop-out. More particularly, we will identify and analyse the most common problems experienced by therapists in working with couples and families and suggest solutions to those problems. But first, we owe it to our readers to outline, in brief, our therapeutic model and to do so we need to add one further assumption.

We agree with Scheflen (1978) that, although usually presented as opposing truths, the different theoretical approaches to marital and family therapy are all useful and valid. In fact, there is a great deal in common between various 'schools' (see, for example, Dryden and Hunt, 1985), and various writers have used the similarities to build integrative models. For example, Stanton (1980) has proposed a 'structural/strategic' approach to family therapy and offered guidelines on when to use techniques derived from each of these two influential schools. Similarly, Crowe (1985) uses structural and strategic family therapy techniques to extend an approach based on behavioural marital therapy. He suggests a hierarchy of techniques and recommends moving from straightforward ones (such as communication training) to more elaborate and less direct methods (such as strategic) only if the former fail. Not surprisingly our preference, too, is to be direct and open with the couple or family and to begin simply. Our initial emphasis, therefore, is on understanding the problems from the clients' own points of view, learning their goals and seeking their ideas on what might be helpful and unhelpful. What we take care to avoid is offering our own opinions and solutions until we have understood, and shown that we understand, theirs. This approach, which forms the first stage too of the MRI Brief Therapy Model (Fisch et al., 1982), can be summed up by the dictum: 'starting where the client is'. As a corollary, which we will discuss in chapter 7, many of the problems in therapy originate in the therapist and client starting in different places with different assumptions about problems, goals and solutions.

The most important process in this initial stage of therapy is the formation of an effective therapeutic alliance between therapist and clients (Bordin, 1979; Dryden and Hunt, 1985) or, in family therapy jargon, to create a therapeutic system. Minuchin (1974) graphically describes the necessity for joining every family member and yet accommodating to the family's overall style. We discuss problems in this phase in chapter 3.

A Contractual Approach

In order to stress our aim of a co-operative rather than an adversarial relationship with clients we prefer to formalize the relationship in an agreement or 'contract' to meet and discuss agreed problems and to work towards solutions. These contracts may be more or less specific, ranging from detailed, mandatory contracts in the case of statutory work with child-abusing parents, to interim agreements to meet from time to time – for example, to review the progress of a schizophrenic patient discharged from hospital to his family's care.

The use of contracts has been advocated in social work by theorists such as Maluccio and Marlow (1974) and more recently in marital therapy by Barker (1984). Surprisingly, as Anderson and Stewart (1983, p. 76) remark, there is so little written about contracts in the literature on family therapy that it could easily be assumed that they are not part of the approach. Nevertheless, most therapists proceed on the assumption that it is their task to set the 'ground rules' – such as who should meet, where, for how long and what they should talk about. If the couple or family return, it could be said that they have implicitly agreed to the therapist's rules and entered into a contract. Because we think that there is considerable potential for misunderstanding in this implicit approach we prefer a more explicit discussion and negotiation of the therapeutic contract.

The advantage of a contract is first, and most importantly, that it stresses the co-operative nature of the work and the clients' participation, rather than that the expert knows best and will provide a solution. Secondly, it can help the therapist to maintain a focus for her work in terms of the agreed problems and goals. If therapy flounders, she can return to the contract and examine the ways in which it is not being met. In some cases the contract will need to be re-negotiated because different and more pressing problems have emerged or the goals have to be changed. What is important is not that the contract itself is sacrosanct but that it exists as an explicit agreement between therapist and clients.

Some therapists fight shy of contracts because they fear giving too much power to the clients by revealing their own ideas; this is an example of the adversarial method. In any case, the principal elements of the contract contain the ground rules about attendance etc., and agreements about the problems and goals. It is not usual for the therapist to spell out her own theories of causation, except in very general terms, or to outline her therapeutic plan; she should, however, be open to discussion with her clients on the assumption that they want to co-operate with rather than resist her efforts. The following example will help to make this clear.

□ Paul, a 25-year-old man, was referred with his parents to a family clinic in a psychiatric unit following his discharge from compulsory detainment in a hospital in another city. He had been diagnosed as '. . . either suffering from a psychotic illness exacerbated by the use of drugs or from a drug-induced psychosis'. His gross delusional behaviour had by this time disappeared.

The man's father was a retired senior personnel officer who defined the problem as his son's lack of motivation: what he needed was a demanding job and the way to it was via a psychological assessment of his capabilities at a prestigious institute. His mother, on the other hand, thought that her son's apathy was a product of his illness and that he required further psychiatric treatment; in the meantime, she would continue to look after him at home and ensure that he would not become 'stressed'. While these statements were being made, the son indicated his opinion non-verbally by raising his eyebrows, sighing and slouching in his chair. The problem as far as he was concerned was that his parents would not let him lead his own (quiet) life. □

The first element in the contract is an agreed definition of the problem – an over-arching definition which must necessarily encompass the different views of the family members. Usually this will be a simple statement of disagreement or worry. In this example, the therapist offered the following statement.

☐ 'After all that's happened, not least Paul's detention in hospital, you're naturally all concerned about his future. But it's clear that you have different ideas about where to go from here. I think it would be useful to discuss these, do you agree?' ☐

It is important to note that the therapist resisted any temptation to diagnose a 'family' problem by highlighting the parents' intrusiveness, the obvious 'detouring' of conflict through the son or the latter's contribution to the process through his provocatively immature behaviour. Whilst all these factors, and others, could be observed, the therapist's pointing them out would merely offend the family members. The skill at this stage in therapy is to find an area of agreement acceptable to all and so create a working agenda. Note too, the second part of the therapist's statement which proposes a discussion of goals as the next step forward and, explicity, asks for their agreement.

☐ At the therapist's suggestion, first the father and then the mother discussed their hopes for Paul with him – or, more accurately, they each stated their views in the expectation that he should and would agree with them. As before, Paul indicated his dissent. Once again, the therapist, seeking agreement, proposed an over-arching goal:
   'You both want Paul to be responsible and grown-up in his behaviour. Paul wants to take his own decisions and have responsibility for his own life. It seems that there is room for agreement here, is that right?' ☐

Note here that the therapist takes the side of change (morphogenesis rather than homeostasis) by pointing out that they all want Paul to be responsible. Note also that this initial goal is limited to Paul; the therapist might believe that a change in the marital relationship is desirable, but this will remain a matter for later negotiation, when and if the parents consider that it is a problem to them.

As a conclusion to this first meeting, the therapist proposed various details about when, where and how often they should meet. This is an important part of contract making and is often overlooked by therapists who are more interested in their own ideas about the pace of change and/or their own convenience! As we will discuss in chapter 2, lack of attention to the clients' views and circumstances is a common cause of failure to convene meetings.

The essential elements in contract making are summarized in figure 1.2. The example we have chosen to illustrate contract building is, in the interests of clarity, intentionally straightforward. It does not, in particular, include the important case in which the therapist has a statutory responsibility in relation to the clients and must therefore make her own goals part of the contract. Such goals may include a requirement that a member of the family refrain from violence or stop offending. As we discuss later, the consequences of failing to abide by the contract need to be spelt out, consequences which in some circumstances might include returning to court or a child being removed from home.

Therapeutic Interventions

Our initial work with a couple or a family begins at the simplest level of clarifying communication between participants and enabling each to hear and be heard; this sets the stage for re-negotiating behaviour, roles and relationships, and rules and beliefs. As many theorists have discussed, therapeutic 'interventions' can be made at a number of different levels, and different schools tend to emphasize one or more of these. A simple working classification of levels is as follows:

Level 1 Intrapersonal – how individuals think, feel and act.
Level 2 Interpersonal behaviour – the patterns or sequences of behaviour between members of a system (for example, couple or family), especially those around the problem or symptom including their attempts to solve it.
Level 3 Interpersonal relationships – the pattern of intimacy and distance, dominance and submission, coalitions and alliances.
Level 4 Shared beliefs, values and assumptions held by members of the system which define, and are defined by, the way in which they live together.

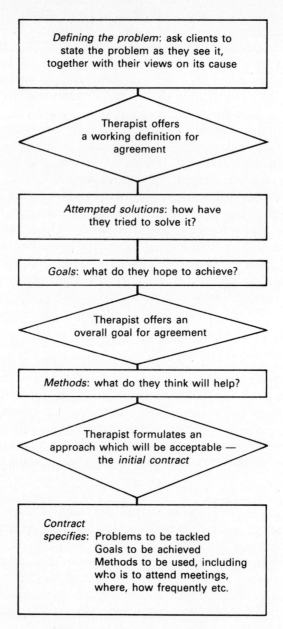

Figure 1.2 Contract building

Our position is that any and all of these levels will be appropriate foci for work with a couple or family or with individual members. The choice of level will be negotiated implicitly or explicitly with the clients during the course of therapy. For example, if a couple come for help because of one partner's depression, the initial focus might be on interpersonal aspects of the depressed person's behaviour; for example, what the other members of the family do when he is feeling 'low', how he responds to their efforts, and so on (level 2). However, this might well be replaced by a discussion about intimacy in the marriage (level 3) and an attempt made to help the couple re-structure their relationship both with each other and in relation to their children. Should this attempt fail, perhaps because the couple remained entrenched in their behaviour, a switch to level 4 would be indicated in which the partners' values and assumptions about marriage were explored and challenged. Again, if one partner remained stuck, the genesis of these beliefs might be analysed, using a genogram, in terms of the individual's family of origin (Lieberman, 1979), or his thought patterns uncovered and challenged through cognitive therapy (Beck et al., 1979). Finally, the focus might return to level 3 and the couple to re-negotiating other aspects of their relationship. (See Treacher, 1985, for a detailed discussion of multi-level work with a depressed couple, and Treacher, 1988, for a similar approach to a family.)

We must reiterate that the agenda and process of therapy is not, and should not be, determined by the therapist alone. In our view, successful therapy is based on the relationship between therapist and couple or family, or to put it another way, on the health of the co-evolving therapeutic system. As the family changes, so too must the therapist in response to the feedback they give about the impact of her interventions and the pace of change. Change is best accomplished when people feel challenged *and* supported.

This emphasis on the relationship between therapist and clients is not very fashionable amongst some family therapy practitioners, who prefer to emphasize a more detached, impersonal approach. Yet it is the ability to establish a positive relationship with family members which has received consistent support as the most important aspect of the therapist's behaviour in determining the outcome of therapy (Gurman and Kniskern, 1987a, b). Gurman and Kniskern (1978b) also report that more detailed studies of therapist empathy, warmth and genuineness indicate that these variables are very important in keeping families in therapy beyond

Problems and Solutions

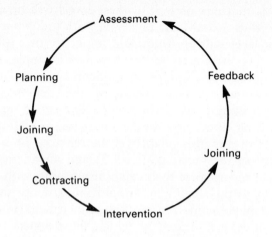

Figure 1.3 Therapy as a cyclical process

the first interview (Shapiro, 1974; Shapiro and Budman, 1973). Further, Kniskern and Gurman add that relationship skills appear to be related to positive outcome irrespective of the theoretical position taken by the therapist.

We assume that it is the therapist's ability to relate to her clients which facilitates and maintains the therapeutic alliance – the process of joining. Joining, therefore, is not simply a matter for the beginning of therapy, but rather a process which requires attention throughout, most particularly before and after the therapist's interventions. This is a continuous, circular process which can be indicated as shown in figure 1.3. It must be acknowledged, however, that this picture does not do justice to the complexity of the processes involved. Thus, as Liddle (1985) remarks, reading feedback is a 'tricky business'; it involves the selection of information and its interpretation. Much of it is available as feelings in the therapist – feelings of discomfort, powerlessness, irritation and so on. It must also be correctly attributed, so that the therapist does not, for example, read her anxiety as being her clients' and thereby slow down the rate of change to accommodate her needs rather than theirs.

The emphasis on therapy as a cyclical process is essential, we consider, in order to correct the tendency to think of therapy as the application of a series of therapeutic interventions. Thus, we are guided by the theoretical insights of many of the schools classified under the general rubric of 'systems approach', and are prepared to use techniques of assessment and intervention derived from them. We have, however, been particularly influenced by Minuchin's structural family therapy (especially as elaborated in Minuchin and Fishman's *Family Therapy Techniques*, 1981) which gives a central place to joining and discusses a range of therapeutic techniques at different levels. Nevertheless, we can do well to heed Minuchin and Fishman's powerful warning against the limitations of technique (1981, p. 1):

> If the therapist becomes wedded to technique, remaining a craftsman, his contact with patients will be objective, detached, and clean, but also superficial, manipulative for the sake of personal power, and ultimately not highly effective.

This caution applies just as well to the solutions to the problems in therapy that we propose in the remaining chapters of this book. They are not intended as a set of techniques to be followed slavishly but are, rather, suggested guidelines. Each 'problem' is analysed and discussed using the available clinical and research literature and our own experience. Examples are given from our own practice or from the people we have supervised. The solutions proposed are those which have worked for us, but we must stress that every therapeutic endeavour is unique because it is founded on a unique relationship between the therapist and her clients. In finding solutions to problems in marital and family therapy the therapist must first take care to analyse each problem in terms of her developing relationship with each unique individual, couple or family. Then, having attempted to resolve the problem, she must re-tune carefully to the feedback they will give her. And so the process may continue.

Further Reading

Anderson, C. M. and S. Stewart (1983), *Mastering Resistance*. Chapter 1: an overview of concepts of resistance in psychological therapies in general and family therapies in particular. Proposes an inclusive definition of resistance and concludes with a down-to-earth discussion of responsibility for change.

Bogdan, J. L. (1984), 'Family organisation as an ecology of ideas: an alternative to the reification of family systems', *Family Process*, 23, 375–388. Bogdan, citing Bateson, argues that there is no need to create a new entity – the family's organization – to account for interpersonal behaviour which can be more economically explained. He proposes a cognitive model, described as an ecology of ideas, in which each family member's definition of a situation leads him to behave in ways that confirm the ideas held by other members.

Coyne, J. and T. Widiger (1978), 'Towards a participatory model of psychotherapy', *Professional Psychology*, 700–710. As an alternative to the prevailing model which emphasizes the therapist's control and responsibility, this paper proposes a participatory model which stresses 'sceptical' efforts by the client to be informed and to share responsibility.

Goldner, V. (1985), 'Feminism and family therapy', *Family Process*, 24, 31–4. An important critique of systems theory and therapeutic techniques in work with families and couples.

Lask, B. (1987), 'Cybernetico-epistobabble, the emperor's new clothes and other sacred cows', *Journal of Family Therapy*, 9, 207–215; and Speed, B. (1987), 'Over the top in the theory and practice of family therapy', *Journal of Family Therapy*, 9, 231–240. Recent reflections on the state of family therapy which 'debunk' some of its claims.

2

Anyone for Change?

Having outlined our approach, we will now begin to explore the major areas of difficulty that confront marital and family therapists. But where precisely should we begin? Most textbooks, especially those on family therapy, curiously ignore the earliest phases of therapy and plump instead for a discussion of the first interview. But if no referrals are received or the clients don't come, then even the most skilled therapist will be left kicking her heels.

Convening

The literature on convening families and couples to attend sessions is rather limited, but there is a small number of studies including those by Teismann (1980) and Stanton and Todd (1981) which are extremely useful in solving convening problems. Different theories of family therapy adopt different attitudes to convening. The 'minimalist' position is held by the Mental Research Institute (MRI, Palo Alto, California) group who are content to work with anybody who turns up (Fisch, Weakland and Segal, 1982) while the 'maximalist' position is held by Palazzoli et al. (1978) who will send family members away (even if they have travelled hundreds of miles) if a single family member fails to attend.

Our own position on convening will become clearer in the course of exploring several common convening problems; we tend to take a median path between these two extremes. Our preference is to convene at least the household of the presented client because this enables us to be in personal contact with some of the most salient people in the client's life. Rather than relying on reports from other people we can directly question household members and at the same time mobilize joining skills in order to create a viable therapeutic alliance.

Problem 1   The Empty Waiting Room

Analysis

One possible reason for referrals being few and far between is that the agency, team or individual therapist has what the advertisers call an 'image problem'. An agency certainly creates an image for itself (consciously and unconsciously) and clients, referrers and other agencies construct their own images of it. Needless to say these different images do not necessarily coincide. The following example helps to clarify some of the issues that may be involved.

☐ A fourteen-year-old girl was, unusually, referred to a hospital instead of the local child guidance clinic. She attended a private boarding school within the clinic's catchment area but her GP did not make the referral because four years previously he had been told that the clinic was only interested in seeing children who were living with their families. The GP had built up an image of the clinic as dogmatic, unhelpful and inflexible. In point of fact over the years the clinic had become much more flexible in its policy and would have been willing and able to offer an appointment to the girl in question – all that was needed to change the situation was for somebody to act as a go-between. ☐

This example illustrates how a professional myth can be easily built up – the GP was not in touch with the changes that had occurred at the clinic and the latter had not made any clear attempt to update its referrers about its policies. Every agency has a unique history and set of relationships with other local agencies and with its referrers which are important to understand.

Solutions

Ideally, every agency needs periodically to collect information from its clients, its referrers and its related agencies so that it can assess how others see it. Professional workers are, in our experience, extraordinarily insensitive to the issue of agency image – for example, how many psychiatrists and other professionals who work in adult mental health agencies actually understand how painful it is for their clients to admit that they need help and therefore need to go to an outpatient clinic or day hospital? How many child and marriage guidance workers are aware of how stigmatizing it is to attend their centres? The limited research on stigma demonstrates this clearly (Lindow, 1986).

At a practical level it is possible to develop policies designed to make the centre more approachable. Examples of these policies are as follows:

1 Devise and distribute a leaflet for both referrers and clients so that they can be fully informed of the way the centre works.
2 Make sure that the 'climate' of the centre is as informal as possible so that clients actually feel welcomed.
3 Encourage couples and families to attend the centre but be flexible enough to offer home visits to those who feel intimidated by coming to the centre for the first time.
4 Develop a walk-in service – potential clients can then explore the *possibilities* offered by the centre before having to make a commitment to the therapeutic contract.
5 Instigate outreach policies so that a 'de-centralized' service can be offered in other less stigmatizing agency settings such as health clinics and schools. Here clients can make low-key, non-threatening contacts with staff as a prelude for attending the centre itself.
6 Make a special videotape which introduces the couple or family to the way you expect to work with them. A pioneering project by Pam Pimpernell, a probation officer in Wiltshire, illustrates what can be done. Using volunteers Pimpernell made a role-played videotape of a family that had previously undertaken family therapy sessions with her. The viewer is able to understand not just the process of therapy but also the reluctance that the original family showed at the point that it entered therapy. By the end of therapy, family members' attitudes had changed markedly and this comes over well from the videotape. It has proved successful in helping many reluctant families to commit themselves to therapy. (For a more extensive discussion of the tape and its uses see Pimpernell and Treacher, in preparation.)

Problem 2   We Don't do Therapy Here

Analysis

The majority of practitioners using marital and family therapy work in agencies in which therapy is not the accepted or established approach. It is precisely in such situations that convening skills are at a premium because the very structure of the agency and the way that it 'processes' its clients is often directly antipathetic to the development of marital and family work.

As Kingston (1979) has pointed out, one of the facts of life for many people in the helping professions is that they are employed by state organizations. To some extent at least these organizations are agents of social control and, although the inclusion of control does not mean the exclusion of caring and responsibility, it is essential not to gloss over the fact. For example, a social worker intervening in a suspected case of child abuse must never forget that her primary responsibility as defined by law is to safeguard the child: her role is to investigate and 'supervise' (police). Whilst she might subsequently negotiate and take on a therapeutic role, her *primary* responsibility remains to act in the interests of the child and on behalf of the state.

Agency settings differ not just in terms of clientele: at a more complex level, each agency has sets of expectations and rules which influence its relationships with its clients. Clients in turn do not merely passively accept what the agency offers them – they have complex expectations (Lorion, 1978; Dryden and Hunt, 1985) that must be taken into consideration when devising convening methods.

Solutions

We will explore three typical starting points for convening:

1 Intake or assessment interviews. In many agencies, from psychiatric out-patient departments to social services district teams, the first contact is made with part of the family, often an individual. Family or couple therapy is not usually the form of intervention that the client or clients expect to be offered. The worker, for her part, must consider what duties and responsibilities she has and what would be the most appropriate

course of action. (This may or may not include 'therapy' and may even be a decision to do nothing.)

2 Taking over a case from another worker. Many 'clients' are well known to the agency, if not to the worker. Their expectations may therefore be very different from or even in direct opposition to those of the new worker who must be very careful in 'selling' her new approach.

3 'Conversion' – negotiating a 'therapeutic' role in addition to a statutory one. The worker moves from working solely in a statutorily determined way with a family to one in which a statutory function is maintained but concomitant therapy is also undertaken on a contractually negotiated basis.

1 Intake or assessment interviews

The goals of such an interview can be defined as follows: to join with the client; to obtain a wide-angled picture of what is happening; to hold on to one's role (as defined by the agency) and to keep one's options open; and to make a preliminary contract regarding the approach to be taken. The next steps are to contact and negotiate with other agencies (as appropriate) and to convene a meeting of the family and other relevant parties.

In order to achieve these ends we have devised the following structured interview. In large part it is derived from the work of the MRI Brief Therapy Centre group (see Fisch et al., 1982, chapters 2 and 3). As we reported in chapter 1, we find their concern to define 'the problem', 'the customer' and his or her 'position' on the problem and on treatment particularly helpful. However, our aim is also to obtain a wider understanding of the context of the problem and therefore to convene a larger system; we have therefore had to modify and extend this model. As with any such interview, its usefulness depends on the user's ability to establish a relationship with her client and on her sensitivity, pace and timing. The interview is in four stages.

Joining phase Before beginning the structured part of the interview it is obviously best to spend time letting clients tell their story in the way they want to. Having established an empathic bridge to the client(s) it is then possible to move on to ask a series of very specific questions.

Exploration This is essentially a series of limited questions which should be elaborated as appropriate:

1 (a) What precisely is (are) the problem(s)? that is, *who* is doing *what* to *whom*?
   (b) How is what you have just said a problem to you and to other family members? (Obtain an answer from each person present and postulated answers for any who are absent.)*
2 (a) Whose idea was it that you approach my agency? (for example, extended family, neighbours, professional agencies).
   (b) What did you think of their suggestion?
   (c) Who in the family was most (and least) keen? †
3 (a) Have you approached any other agency for help?
   (b) Are you receiving help from any other agency for any other problems you may have?
4 (a) What prompted you to approach my agency now?
   (b) Have you experienced this problem before? What did you do to try and deal with the problem?
   (c) What was helpful and unhelpful to you?
   (d) What have you tried so far to solve your current problem?
5 (a) What is your understanding of the cause of your current problem?
   (b) What do other people think is the cause of your problem?
6 (a) What is your understanding of how you can deal with your problem?
   (b) What is your understanding of how other people (family members, agencies, neighbours, etc.) can help?
   (c) How do you think that my agency can help you with the problem?
7 Are there any other issues you would like to talk to me about before I consider (with my colleagues) how my agency might best be able to help?

Planning an approach and selling it It is essential to take a break in the session at this point (retreating into the kitchen or an adjacent room if the interview is at home; in an office setting it may

---

* The answers to these questions may indicate that the worker has certain agency or statutory responsibilities; for example, the answer 'I'm afraid I'm going to hurt my child' may require the worker to investigate and intervene on behalf of the child and not necessarily the client.
† The answers may reveal that the 'client' is under duress or is merely being polite to a referrer.

be possible to consult with colleagues, etc.). If the interview has progressed satisfactorily, the worker should by now have established a working relationship with the client and have a good understanding of the context of the problem and the various views on how it should be tackled. She will not have taken sides or committed herself to any particular action. She must now propose an approach which, whilst being in accord with her agency duty and responsibilities, is also acceptable to the client. In addition, she must decide which agencies to contact and whom to convene, and she should obtain her client's agreement.

Convening the other family members Given that all these questions in the structured interview are asked of *all* the members of the family present (obviously excluding children when appropriate) and that answers are also obtained for all absent members, it becomes easier to convene absent members because the interview succeeds in establishing the message that everybody's point of view is important and should be heard before getting down to the brass tacks of achieving some change. Obviously, the most effective way to get everyone to come to a meeting is to establish that no real 'work' can be done until the absent member's views have also been heard.

2 Taking over a case from another worker

Whitaker (in Haley and Hoffman, 1967) has stated that he likes to 'get the field sterile so that I can work. Otherwise there's no sense in starting' (1967, p. 268). We dislike the use of surgical terminology but it is important to stress that in many agencies cases are frequently not 'clean' and 'fresh': a new worker must not assume her client or clients are as eager to participate in therapy as she is. The approach offered by their previous worker may have been well suited to their needs as they defined them. Frequently, that worker will have occupied a supporting role in coalition with one member of a sub-system of the family. The family for their part will expect the new worker to take on the same role and will (appropriately) be very cautious about any suggestion that the rest of the family become involved. (Alternatively, the previous worker may even visit, unofficially, for 'old times'' sake.)

In this instance it is crucial that the new worker strives to retain her 'manoeuvrability'. It is advisable to set up a meeting with the 'executive' members of the family (usually the parents) in order to discuss how best the worker might be able to help. The questions for intake or assessment interviews (above) will provide a good basis for exploration and contract building and of course special attention should be given to what they found helpful and unhelpful in the previous worker's approach.

Similarly, other agencies will have expectations of the new worker. In many cases it will be crucial to contact and negotiate with them and/or to convene a case conference of all those involved.

3   Conversion – negotiating a therapeutic role in addition to a statutory one

This is perhaps the most complex situation from a convening point of view. The statutory control that the worker has in relation to the family may help to solve convening problems; nevertheless, the family needs to be well motivated to work on a series of goals which are to do with the overall functioning of the family and not just one of its members. Achieving these goals in many cases may, in the long term, lead directly to the discharging of the worker's statutory role, but the family must feel comfortable (and not coerced) in undertaking such changes if success is to be achieved.

Dungworth (1982) has explored this issue in relation to work in social services departments. He suggests that a co-worker be brought in – to mark the change in the focus of work; he notes that this can be useful not only for the family, but also for the initial worker who can find herself stuck in the old role. Alternatively, the therapeutic and statutory roles can be split between two workers. One is involved in a purely therapeutic contract with the family whilst the other agrees to manage the statutory involvement. Given such clarity the second worker can convene a family meeting with a clear, 'therapeutic' brief.

Problem 3   The Others Won't Come

Analysis

Many therapists complain that because individuals are referred it is difficult to convene the rest of the family. The first question we need to tackle here is: Why should therapists bother so much about successful convening? As we have already noted, some writers argue that only 'customers' (that is, those family members who seek change) need to be convened and that it is not necessary for anybody else to attend (Fisch, Weakland and Segal, 1982). However, we do have serious reservations about this position, which in practice discriminates against women. Women are forced, whether they like it or not, to be the principal child carers and it is women who typically find marriage most unsatisfactory. Thus, if we were to adopt the policy of working with the 'customer' only, then we would more or less exclude men from therapy and burden women with the major task of producing change in families that they are already finding burdensome. Family therapists are renowned for their insensitivity to gender issues (Goldner, 1985) and we would suspect that the highly instrumental and pragmatic approach of the brief therapists is in practice an extremely male-orientated way of undertaking therapy – an approach which avoids tackling the crucial issues of power that lurk beneath the surface of most of the presenting problems that clients bring to therapy.

We tend to take a more stringent attitude to convening than the MRI group, but it is important to stress that different families require different approaches. Whitaker's much-quoted statement that there is a 'battle for structure' (Napier and Whitaker, 1978) between the therapist and the family when they first meet needs, like all aphorisms, to be carefully debated. To win the first battle by insisting that they all attend may be to lose the war because some family members may find the initial session too intense. Alternatively, some individuals can be so destructive that their inclusion in sessions is highly problematic. Weitzman (1985), in a hard-hitting discussion of methods for engaging severely dysfunctional families (which will be reviewed in the next chapter), points out just how unhelpful the literature can be to the average practitioner working in an ordinary community clinic.

Weitzman himself advises extreme caution in insisting from the outset that all family members should attend the initial session. This demand is, in fact, a very high-level intervention as far as a highly dysfunctional family is concerned because such a family will rarely, if ever, actually meet as a family. His policy with regard to convening is summarized in the following passage (1985, p. 244):

> Accepting the family 'as is' appears to be a useful strategy . . .
> even at the expense of initially losing the 'battle for structure'
> . . . For, as Barragan (1976) stated, 'we are essentially trying
> to change ways in which family members deal with one

another, as long as we are pledged to changing the family
system of interaction, problems such as who is in the room are
subordinate to the primary undertaking.'

We would accept Weitzman's position in relation to highly
dysfunctional families. Such families do require a gentle yet persistent
approach, but according to Teismann (1980) there are three major
reasons why, with the majority of families, we should encourage
all family members to attend: (a) an adequate systemic assessment
requires the presence of the whole family; (b) full convening
symbolically stresses the systemic nature of the problem and its
treatment; (c) it is often difficult to bring in absent family members
after therapy has begun.

Solutions

Of course some families are easier to convene than others, and it
is at this point that we will refer to Stanton and Todd's (1981)
study of drug abusers and their families. Such families are notoriously
difficult to convene and it seems reasonable to assume that what
works with them will work with other families. Stanton and Todd's
discussion is meticulously detailed so we have summarized their
approach under a number of headings. As will be apparent, these
principles are most relevant to families where an adult member has
been referred; families who present with child-focused problems
require a slightly modified approach.

First contacts

1 The therapist should decide which family members need to be
   included and not leave this decision to the referred client or any
   other family member.
2 Wherever possible, one or more family members should be
   encouraged to attend the initial or intake interview if a fully
   convened initial session cannot be arranged.
3 Do not expect the person referred to bring in the family on his
   own.
4 Obtain permission from the presented client to contact his or
   her family and then get in touch with them, whenever possible,
   during the interview.

These four principles effectively summarize one major point – that it is *the therapist* who must take responsibility both for negotiating who attends the family sessions and ensuring that they do attend. Stanton and Todd advocate a direct approach to the rest of the family, while Teismann (1980) suggests that coaching family members to get other members to attend can be used in an alternative fashion. In our experience, the most successful method is a 'belt and braces' approach – a combination of the two. Telephoning during the session is extremely effective and often overlooked. We should, however, stress that the initial phase of therapy with certain families may be very protracted, with the therapist consciously delaying full convening of the family until she is certain that enough trust has been built up between key family members and herself. This approach is a half-way house between the MRI position and the Whitaker position. Whether full convening ever takes place is a question that must be evaluated afresh for every family.

Get in at the beginning

5 The closer the therapist's first contact to the time of intake and the earlier she enters a potential chain of therapists, the greater are the chances of recruiting other family members.
6 The sooner the family is contacted the more likely are they to be engaged.
7 The therapist must negotiate her way past the presented client and directly contact key family members since if, prior to the first session, she can obtain from them an agreement to participate, the chances of their actually attending are increased markedly.

In general it appears that failure to contact a family rapidly at the point of referral of one of its members may cause all sorts of systemic effects to occur. The family may well engage in 'closure' (Scott and Ashworth, 1967) at the point at which referral to (or contact with) an agency occurs. 'Closure' is a term used by Scott to describe the fact that the family may wish to extrude and scapegoat the presented client, and therefore shun contact with the agency on the basis that 'he is the problem'. However, it is better to assume that closure is only one of the possible alternative approaches exhibited by the family; some families may be more open to respond at the point at which contact with an agency is made.

Use the crisis

8 Viewing the family recruitment effort as crisis-inducing can help the therapist in her engagement efforts.

This principle, which surprisingly is not given much prominence by Stanton and Todd, is potentially the most important as it invites the therapist to empathize with family members as they come under pressure. The whole recruitment process is, as Stanton and Todd point out, 'an intervention that shifts responsibility for the problem to the total system of intimate others. These people are told that they are important – if not generating the problem, then in helping to alleviate it' (1981, p. 269). Such an implicit statement may be a threat to the family, but as we have already noted just getting the family to consider who is to come is itself a major intervention. Equally, the act of coming to therapy may represent the first time that the family has acted collectively.

Nobody is to blame

9 The therapist must approach the family with a rationale for therapy that is non-pejorative, non-judgemental and that in no way blames them for the problem.
10 The primary focus should be on helping the presented client rather than the family.
11 The rationale for family therapy should be presented in such a way that, in order to oppose it, family members would have to state openly that they want to keep their problems.

It is important not to shift from an initial focus on helping the referred client with the problems that are presented at the beginning of therapy. A too-rapid shift to other issues carries with it the risk of unsettling other family members, who may feel that they are being criticized or intimidated. Similarly, the therapist should accept the family's goals for treatment rather than pressing them to accept her own, which may initially be too threatening to the family.

Clearly, principle 11 is problematic and should only be used when a more direct, open-handed approach has failed.

Increasing the therapist's credibility

12   The chances for successful family recruitment are increased if the therapist does the recruiting.
13   The therapist should be the primary therapist of the presented client and the family.

These two principles are perhaps so obvious that they do not need much discussion. Convening often breaks down if a family is passed from one therapist, who undertakes an assessment interview with them, to another who is to undertake therapy with them. In complex situations where a family may have both a statutory worker and a family therapist, it is best to convene the former to attend the family sessions (so that the statutory function can be discharged during the session). If this proves impossible then the statutory worker must be prepared to co-ordinate her work with the family therapist in such a way that the family is not able to play one worker off against the other.

Therapist and agency factors

14   The therapist must show interest in the family through her willingness to expend considerable effort in engaging them.
15   A mechanical approach to recruitment is insufficient to guarantee success – flexibility and skill are crucial if the therapist is to avoid getting deadlocked.
16   The agency must have flexible policies and back up the recruitment effort through committing tangible resources.

Successful convening requires skill and dedication on behalf of the therapist. The right professional milieu (that is, one which treats the recruitment of families as a serious business) enhances a therapist's ability to achieve successful convening.

We have presented Stanton and Todd's principles not as rules that must be slavishly followed, but as prompts to provoke thinking about convening issues. The fact that they usually start their convening by meeting the identified client and then convening the rest of the family means that some of the principles may need to be modified. For example, when convening begins with meeting a concerned mother who wishes to have help for her drug-abusing son, then the approach will be different from when the son is the first point of contact with the family.

Stanton and Todd's discussion is so rich and detailed that it would be impossible (for reasons of space) to illustrate each of their methods. However, the following brief examples give a flavour of the approach:

☐ A sixteen-year-old daughter had run away from home and her parents had lost contact with her. They knew that she worked on a stall at a nearby fairground but had made no effort to contact her there. After discussion with the couple the therapist decided to visit the stall to see what would happen – he failed to meet the girl but left a message saying that her parents were worried about her and that they would like her to contact home. Three weeks later she did so and reluctantly agreed to attend the session on the basis that the therapist was anxious to hear her side of things. At the session she expressed surprise that the therapist had been so interested in her as to visit the fairground. ☐

☐ A sixteen-year-old boy was referred by a probation officer because he was being violent to his mother. The probation officer and therapist visited the family at home, interviewing the parents downstairs while the boy barricaded himself in his bedroom. Careful questioning of the parents revealed that he had good relationships with a close friend and an ex-school master. A brief interview with the boy took place through his bedroom door – he agreed to come to a meeting if his 'supporters' also came. Letters were duly written to both of them – they were happy to attend the session which was successful in achieving a contract for family therapy to begin. ☐

Problem 4   One Partner Arrives at the Session but the Other Does Not

Analysis

This common problem in marital therapy is of such importance that we have chosen to deal with it in this separate section although it should (logically) be dealt with as an example of convening failure. Therapists deal with this issue in different ways depending on their theoretical stance, and many marital therapists are prepared to work just with the partner who attends the session.

Our own position on this issue is guided more by ethical considerations than 'scientific' findings about conjoint or 'individual' marital therapy (the term that is used to describe such a method of working). Recently there was a spirited dispute in the pages of *Family Process* about the reviews of marital therapy research by Gurman and Kniskern (1978b, 1981) which claim that conjoint marital work is clearly superior to individual marital therapy. Like many disputes between researchers it leaves the clinician somewhat befuddled, but our reading of the situation is as follows: Gurman and Kniskern argue that individual marital therapy (that is, working with one partner only) is 'an (essentially) untested method, and since conjoint marital therapy is a well-tested method with demonstrably positive effects, there is ample warrant for the position that conjoint therapy can, for now, be considered the treatment of choice for marital problems' (1986, p. 59).

In our opinion there is a very simple reason why therapists should seek to undertake conjoint therapy – namely, that it is mostly women who are, at least initially, prepared to take their relationship problem to therapists. If such therapists adopt an individual marital therapy position they are, in effect, accepting (in the majority of cases) men's ability to escape working on relationship problems, hence perpetuating the implicit culturally-imposed agreement which insists that it is the woman's task to keep marriages and relationships functioning.

Obviously, the reality we are dealing with is infinitely complex and there is another interesting implication that immediately arises if the individual marital therapy position is adopted. If we are right in assuming that individual marital therapy in practice involves a large majority of women and tiny minority of men, then there is a peculiar sense in which it is likely that such work, unless it is extremely skillful, has a built-in tendency to view *men* rather than the relationship as the problem. Such a situation may well arise all the more easily if the therapist is a woman (a common situation in marriage guidance centres where the number of male counsellors is very small).

Alongside our ethical grounds for preferring conjoint work there are a number of basic theoretical and practical reasons why joint work is likely to be more effective. Convening one partner inevitably activates a triangle in which two people have met and inevitably discussed (among other things) the behaviour of the third (the non-convened partner). Such a triangle is scarcely benign – the non-convened partner is an unknown quantity as far as the therapist is concerned, but it is equally (and obviously) true that the absent partner will have difficulty in being part of the therapy if he or she is absent. There are ways of dealing with the situation if the non-convened member does turn up to a later session, but a sustained absence means that the therapist has a real difficulty since all the information she has at her disposal is derived from one partner. The absent partner's views can be explored by asking the convened partner what they are likely to be, but of course the information collected is the *partner's* view of what the non-convened partner would say – nothing comes straight from the horse's mouth.

Finally, it is important to point out that there is an essential continuity between marital or couples work and spouse- (or partner-) aided therapy. Hafner et al. (1983) have demonstrated that spouse-aided therapy proved superior to individual therapy with a client group suffering from persisting psychiatric disorders. Not unexpectedly, Hafner found that individual therapy did produce improvement in some symptoms but marital dissatisfaction actually increased, with both partners being more depressed at a three-month follow-up.

Nevertheless, we are prepared to work with an individual on their marital problem, but only if we find a *specific* indication for doing so: for example, if one partner, either male or female, is extremely dominant while the other lacks confidence and feels very vulnerable. The rationale for working with them in this way is simply that it is easier to build their confidence away from the hothouse of the marital relationship. Many marital partners are at their most vulnerable with one another, since those who love us also instinctively know where our vulnerabilities lie, and are therefore able (wittingly or unwittingly) to demolish us.

Solutions

In our experience it is usually women who turn up to conjoint sessions without their partner. Our own policy in such situations is as follows: we immediately signal our disappointment that the partner has not turned up and ask permission from the convened client to place a chair next to her in order to symbolize her absent partner. We then explore the reasons for not attending and make a decision about whether or not to proceed with the interview. Usually it is possible to win our client over to our basic position – that is, that couple therapy for ethical and technical (as well as personal) reasons is best carried out with both partners present. If this position is acceptable then we spend the rest of the session (preferably shortened) in devising a method of convening the partner. This may involve composing a letter (guided by the convened partner) or arranging to make a phone call to home (or work if this is possible). The session ends with an agreement to carry out this policy, but we are careful to monitor our client's response to see whether she feels put off by not being seen alone. For a minority of clients this seems to be the hidden agenda of coming so it is important to be sympathetic to this position.

If the client is adamant that her partner will not come then we accept her position and carry out an initial interview, but we gain permission to use the empty chair in order to garner information about the husband's point of view. For example, we will say: 'Supposing John was sitting there, what would he have to say about what you've just said?' This method of interviewing keeps the partner 'alive' and can often result in the client being more open to suggestions (at the end of the interview) about how to get him to come. The following example illustrates the benefits to be gained from persuading reluctant partners to attend family therapy sessions:

☐ The 'S' family consisted of Mr and Mrs S and their four children. Their nine-year-old Ian was bed-wetting and his parents found it difficult to discipline him. Mrs S came to the initial session with two of the children, but agreed to bring all four to subsequent sessions. However, she said that Mr S did not wish to attend any sessions; he did not mind her attending but he did not think therapy would help in any way and was not sure he could be of assistance to his son. A number of interventions were devised in order to facilitate Mr S's attendance, but these proved unproductive. Eventually the therapist adopted a policy of writing detailed letters to Mr S. These summarized the sessions that were being held and requested him to participate in homework tasks. Eventually Mr S attended a session – his initial motivation seemed to hinge on his desire to share with the therapist how angry he was about what happened in the sessions and about the tasks he was requested to undertake. Eventually the discord in the marital relationship began to emerge and both partners were willing to work on the underlying issues which were causing them concern. The initial presenting problems disappeared dramatically as soon as Mr S attended and there were no reported difficulties on follow-up six months after the completion of the therapy contract. □

Problem 5   Nobody Comes

Sometimes a family or couple has been contacted and invited to attend a session, but has failed to show up. When this happens it is important to avoid taking precipitate action but rather to see things from the clients' point of view. Sometimes the invitation to the session may just not have been received, so a careful check needs to be made. Once we have an adequate understanding of what has actually happened then we need to get to work devising a solution.

Some therapists assume that if a family or couple do not turn up there is no point in pursuing the matter – the failure to show is attributed to 'lack of motivation', the referrer is written to and no further action is taken. Our approach is different and is based partly on our own experience and partly on the research work of Sager et al. (1968), Shapiro and Budman (1973), and Berg and Rosenblum (1977), all of whom have stressed the crucial role that *therapists* play in overcoming clients' reluctance to attend family therapy sessions. We believe that it is the task of the therapist to stimulate interest in therapy when this proves to be a barrier to convening.

Analysis

Teismann (1980) suggests some of the reasons why a family or couple might not attend:

1 Their 'position' on treatment is opposed to marital or family therapy; for example, they may believe that only a drug treatment administered to the presented client is suitable.
2 There is a lack of effort on their behalf to attend.
3 There is a lack of effort on the part of the therapist; for example, writing very unattractive, over-formal or even unintentionally hostile letters inviting the family to the first session, which imply that they are to blame for their problems.
4 There is denial of the problem by the family.

5 There is anxiety and fear about the outcome of attending sessions.

In addition we can suggest:

6 The family or some of its members have had previous bad experiences of therapy.
7 Financial and other difficulties (for example, transport) have cropped up and these have not been considered important by the therapist.
8 They have received contrary advice from neighbours or relatives (or in some cases other professionals) which discourages them from coming.
9 Other special difficulties (including illiteracy) have prevented family members receiving messages from the therapist in the first place.

Solutions

Obviously, specific custom-built solutions need to be devised if any of these factors are found. But drawing upon Teismann's work we can suggest the following solutions:

1 If the family or couple refuses an interview and asks for alternative treatment, then suggest that only one assessment interview should be undertaken. *
2 Offering to see the family or couple with a supportive professional worker (often the referrer) whom they know and trust.
3 Offering a more neutral meeting place such as a GP's surgery or a home visit so that the situation is less threatening. This offer is on a one-off basis unless there is a sound reason for not convening later sessions at the therapist's normal venue.
4 Offering a postponement giving the family or couple a chance to discuss and review whether they want to come. This works occasionally, but it is the final offer in the series and should be used reluctantly by the therapist.
5 In some cases it may be appropriate to force couples or families to attend by invoking the power of the courts. This may be because children are being abused or have been engaged in crime and the

---

* This approach often works because good joining techniques in the first session are sufficient to get the family or couple over their initial fears about what the therapy is going to do to them. The interview should be a genuine assessment interview with great stress on the options that can be offered.

courts are prepared to require the family's involvement in therapy. Alternatively, the *threat* of being taken to court by a social worker or probation officer may be used to make them come. Of course, once they have arrived it is up to the therapist to use her skills to show that she can understand the problem from their points of view and to make a contract to work together.

Problem 6   Agency Triangles: Who's the Customer?

Analysis

Occasionally when a couple or family fail to attend a session, careful exploration reveals that the reason for this is at least partially dependent on the role of the referrer or other agencies. This problem is very delicate because the therapist is caught up in a multi-faceted situation which is not of her making. Carl and Jurkovic (1983) have coined the term 'agency triangle' in order to draw attention to the three-sided nature of such phenomena, although in practice they may be far more complex.

Bowen (1978) has pointed out that a family under stress may inadvertently triangulate a spectrum of outside people and agencies as participants in the family problem – so much so that the original tensions within the family may, ironically, become defused and yet inter-agency tension may rise as agencies which have originally sided with different family members inadvertently continue the family dispute in another form.

Both Hoffman and Long (1969) and Carl and Jurkovic (1983) have identified the reverse side to this coin: families may triangulate agencies, but agencies may inadvertently triangulate families. Because of differences in agency function, philosophy, history and ways of working (plus personality clashes between staff) different agencies may not see eye to eye. So it is not unexpected that families can get caught up in complex inter-agency networks which, despite their best efforts, fail to solve the families' problems.

Carl and Jurkovic point out that such networks have a fairly typical natural history – inter-agency conflicts do not drop from the clouds, but normally result from conflict developing between an agency and its clients. Failure to resolve this conflict can lead to a third agency being pulled into the fray. Sometimes this is just a way of diverting conflict, sometimes it is an honest decision to get the conflict resolved;

but Carl and Jurkovic insist that it is such a common occurrence that they are prompted to coin the following axiom: 'The relationship between an agency and a family is unstable under stress and will tend to form a three-party system, often with another agency, to diffuse the stress.' They analyse a number of typical triangular situations which we have summarized in table 2.1.

Unfortunately, in our experience the picture is frequently even more complicated. Some boundaryless families have an uncanny knack of mobilizing several agencies, neighbours, and relatives on their behalf – thus creating not just a triangular situation but one of bewildering complexity. One of us recently supervised a case in which no fewer than eight agencies were involved. Clearly, in working with such complex systems, convening issues are of crucial importance. Some therapists feel that they can proceed to work just with the family or the couple, but our experience has taught us that it is more economical to adopt a networking approach, at least during the opening stages of therapy.

Solutions

Faced by the complexity of some of these situations in our everyday practice we have tended, at times, to feel that working with families is straightforward – it is other agencies that are the problem! This is an unfortunate stance to take up, but we are aware of the strange phenomenon whereby professional workers can mobilize endless patience when coping with families but become instantly peremptory and pejorative when working with other agencies. If we examine our own behaviour in these situations we realize that we are, in fact, operating a series of 'shoulds' – that is, other agencies *should* know how we work, *should* behave just like us and *should* accept that our position is the only justifiable one. This elitism is self-defeating and has to be confronted whenever it arises. However, we are optimists and believe that good working relationships can be built between different agencies as long as there is a modicum of motivation and good will on both sides of the fence. Specialist therapeutic agencies do tend to have elitist and isolationist tendencies, so it is not surprising that they find it difficult to relate to other agencies that are often much harder worked and less well resourced. In practice, good inter-agency working usually arises when workers from different agencies find themselves naturally working together because they have a vested interest in solving problems that cause difficulties to them both.

Table 2.1 Agency triangles (after Carland and Jurkovic, 1983)

Referring agency	Agency's position in relation to therapy	Family's position in relation to therapy	Therapist's position in relation to therapy	Summary of problem
Child care agency (e.g. NSPCC, Social Services Dept.)	Parents need to change otherwise children will have to go into care/will not be returned from care. 'Bad' parents must be changed into 'good'.	Since the prime motivation is the agency's, the parents' sole concern is to get the agency off their backs and to continue life as normal.	The referring agency tends to set a global goal, i.e. create better parents, but the parents basically want to be left alone.	The parents tend to lack motivation, the two agencies have difficulty in working together because of different viewpoints and methods of working. Family is caught in the middle.
Court	Therapy can be tried but the court will decide how and when the work will be undertaken. Both the family and the therapist are to be directed by the court as and when necessary.	Since the court wields the power the parents do not feel they control anything. Therapy may feel coercive because they have been directed to enter it by the court.	The therapist will have ideas about the necessary tasks of therapy and the likely timetable, but the court can disrupt such a timetable if it so wishes.	The court has control but little understanding of how therapeutic change can be achieved; the therapist has a wider perspective but no control. The family is caught in the middle.

School	Parents or child or both need to change because they are the problem, not the school.	Since the problem is at school and therefore not within the parents' direct experience the school can be blamed for the problem.	Since the therapist often does not directly experience the problem because it is rarely manifested in sessions the therapist can easily be confused about the location of the problem and the necessary steps to its solution.	The crux of the problem hinges around the *in loco parentis* issue. Who is responsible for what?
Mental hospital	Since the hospital's main role is medication, staff find it difficult to understand agencies that work in other ways. Referrals may be made to community-based agencies but these agencies are often criticized for not pulling their weight in relation to disturbed clients.	Families have complex attitudes to medication but may feel very exposed if therapy is proposed, especially in relation to a family member who is seen as the problem.	The therapist is often insecure because clients who have or are receiving medication create problems, e.g. who is really responsible for their care, the hospital or the community-based worker?	Since the family is caught between two very different agencies, double messages abound.

The first step in resolving these difficult triangular situations is to identify the exact nature of the problem. Following Kingston (1984) we can outline a number of possibilities:

1 *Where's the problem?*   The therapist may be invited by the referrer to define the family as the problem, and yet the therapist feels that the problem lies elsewhere. The common example is with schools – teachers may experience difficulties with a child at school and also with parents. They then assume that referral of the family for help will logically achieve a solution to the problem. Such a referral is highly seductive because it plays into the tendency of therapists to see themselves as omnipotent. A more mature (and difficult to achieve) response involves setting up a tripartite meeting between all the key figures involved. This has to be tactfully set up because it runs counter to the school's position on the problem. Some therapists chicken out when faced by this dilemma but the outcome is usually fertile because otherwise the family persists in framing the school as the problem while the school maintains its view that it is the child and/or the parents that are the problem.

2 *Passing the buck?*   Some referrers are in a situation where they cannot control the behaviour of a family (and yet their agency function calls upon them to do so); the solution is to make a referral to a therapist, but the real terms of the referral are not made explicit. This is yet another hot potato for the therapist because the family in question may be involved in behaviour which is causing widespread concern. The referrer is in the 'loser' position and yet cannot be open about it. The therapist has the unenviable task of meeting with the referrer (who may be of higher status) in order to clarify the situation and of meeting with the family to establish whether or not they are willing to accept a contract.

3 *Referral by proxy*   The referrer may be making the referral at the request of somebody else. This is potentially very complicated and confusing. Kingston cites an interesting example of a GP asking a health visitor to refer a family to a therapist. However, the difficulty experienced by the family may be their relationship with the GP. Clearly in this case the therapist has a difficult task in front of her. Eventually a meeting will have to be held with the GP in order delicately to confront the issues involved. Our colleague Brian Dimmock has pioneered some interesting ways of improving GP–therapist relationships including joint GP–therapist consultations with the family at the point of referral. It took some time to build up trust between the GPs and the therapists involved in the project reported by

Dimmock (1984), but eventually it became possible to 'close' the referrer–therapist–family triangle through having a tripartite meeting. Obviously such a meeting is not without its difficulties, but it does contribute to creating an honest appraisal of what the real problems are and how they can best be helped.

4 Who has the mandate?   The person making the referral may have only a limited mandate for doing so; for example a paediatric registrar making a referral (because she is keen on family therapy) but her consultant is less enthusiastic. In the event of some sort of crisis occurring, the family may well be called back by the consultant who responds to their difficulties in a well-intentioned way which nevertheless conflicts with the way in which the therapist has been working.

5 Statutory work   If a therapist has a statutory involvement with a family then it is unlikely that the motivation for change emanates from the family. It is the therapist who is motivated initially – if she is uncomfortable about her statutory responsibilities then they will merely become a covert aspect of the work and will certainly cause feelings of mistrust. As Kingston points out, our colleague Marjorie Ainley has demonstrated how a probation officer working with juvenile offenders can overcome these in-built features of the role. Initially when working with a family she clarifies the nature of the statutory sanction but she attempts to do this at the *pre-court* stage so that the family does not feel so coerced and can see that the crisis they are caught up in has a positive side to it if changes in the family and the offender can be achieved. Above all else, she defines her work as enabling the parents to maintain (or reclaim) their role as *parents* in relation to their adolescent. Her own role is to support and not undermine.

Kingston also draws attention to the grey area of statutory work which causes workers so much pain and distress. This area, which he calls 'informal social control', involves the statutory agency monitoring the family (and not instituting statutory proceedings) because the evidence is not conclusive enough or because the parents are either *apparently* willing or unwilling to co-operate. Such a situation is fraught with ambiguity. One solution is derived from our Bristol colleagues Brian Dimmock and Dave Dungworth who have summarized their approach as follows (Dimmock and Dungworth, 1983, p. 58):

Once the responsibility for monitoring the family circumstances is located in the social services department it is vital that this function is made explicit to the family and other agencies involved and that exactly what has to be done to comply is spelt out. The social worker can then seek from the agency and the case conference precisely what is required to remove suspicion.

The clarity gained from this intervention opens the way for the therapist to negotiate a contract with the family; through achieving agreed goals the family can then ensure that the monitoring is abandoned by the agency.

Conclusion

It is important at the end of this chapter on convening to make clear our policy when our attempts at full convening have failed. We have stressed the importance of trying to get either the family or both partners to attend sessions, but it is in no way contradictory to insist also that the show needs to go on if convening fails. We have already pointed out that individual marital therapy is perfectly viable (cf., Bennun, 1985) although our preference is usually for conjoint therapy. It is also important to draw attention to the work of Szapocznik and his colleagues who have developed a form of structural family therapy which is called One Person Family Therapy (OPFT).

Szapocznik et al. (1982) have argued that one person family therapy can actually be the 'treatment of choice' in relation to a number of presenting problems. Included in their list are the following examples:

1 A family identifies an adolescent as the problem but refuses to attend.
2 A single parent is the presented client so a certain degree of privacy is required if he or she is not to be exposed to the put-down of having his or her problem reviewed in front of the children.
3 A family is too volatile and too fragmented to attend as a family.
4 A very young child is the presented client.
5 An adolescent placed in a residential institution far away from home is the presented client. (It is often not feasible to convene the family except on a very occasional basis.)
6 An adolescent or child is referred but comes from a family with highly disturbed parents who are not approachable for therapy.

We are sympathetic to Szapocznik's position – its only difference from our own is one of emphasis. We would attempt wider convening first if our initial contact with the family indicated that it was worth pursuing such an approach. If our initial assessment was not positive then we would settle for Szapocznik's approach but periodically review with our client whether changes had occurred that would make wider convening a worthwhile possibility.

Further Reading

Specific approaches to convening families in different agencies are described in:

(USA) Berger, M., G.J. Jurkovic et al. (1984), *Practicing Family Therapy in Diverse Settings.*

(UK) Treacher, A. and J. Carpenter (eds) (1984), *Using Family Therapy*; and Campbell, D. and R. Draper (eds) (1985), *Applications of Systemic Family Therapy.*

Bennun, I. (1985), 'Unilateral marital therapy', in W. Dryden (ed.), *Marital Therapy in Britain*, vol. 2. Provides model and case example of working with one partner on marital issues.

Fisch, R. et al. (1982), *The Tactics of Change*. Chapters 2 and 3 provide an illuminating discussion of the negotiations between client and therapist which are necessary to form a contract.

Kingston, P. (1984), '"But they aren't motivated . . ." Issues concerned with encouraging motivation for change in families', *Journal of Family Therapy*, 6, 381–403. Considers the importance of referrers in assessing motivation and reviews aspects of the therapist–family relationship. Suggests some experiential exercises to assist in developing an understanding of motivation as a process.

Lewis, C. and M. O'Brian (eds) (1987), *Reassessing Fatherhood: New Observations on Fathers and the Modern Family*. See chapter 1 for a sociological review and chapter 12 on men in marriage counselling (Blackie and Clark).

3

Working Together

The Therapeutic Alliance

Since our model of therapy places such an emphasis on co-operation it is not surprising that we are very concerned with building and maintaining a strong working relationship with families and couples with whom we work. We have been influenced by the work of Minuchin and Fishman (1981), who have provided a succinct discussion of many aspects of this form of therapeutic alliance under the heading of 'joining' (1981, pp. 31–2):

> Joining a family is more an attitude than a technique, and it is the umbrella under which all therapeutic transactions occur. Joining is letting the family know that the therapist understands them and is working with and for them ... under her protection ... the family [can] have the security to explore alternatives, try the unusual, and change. Joining is the glue that holds the therapeutic system together.

The essential attitude that permeates successful joining is unconditional positive regard, although Minuchin and Fishman surprisingly do not make this link to Carl Rogers' seminal work. In order to work successfully with a family or couple a therapist needs to avoid being judgemental – to accept them warts and all. Ideally, the therapist should also have had similar life experiences and have experienced the stage of the family life-cycle that the family or couple are now encountering. If a therapist is required to work with situations that she has not experienced, then good joining hinges on her asking for help in understanding the complexities of the family's or couple's life given the stage they have reached.

This fundamental process of joining, referred to by Bordin (1979) as 'bonding', is but one component of the 'therapeutic alliance'. We agree with Dryden and Hunt (1985) that Bordin's work has helped clarify the theoretical and practical issues involved. They have summarized Bordin's position as follows (1985, p. 123):

> ... the therapeutic alliance is made up of three major components ... the *bonds* refer to the quality of the relationship between the participants, the *goals* are the ends of the therapeutic journey while the *tasks* are the means for achieving these ends. Disruption to the therapeutic journey might occur because the 'travellers' (a) do not get on or have a relationship which is not conducive to the goals or task of therapy (weak or inappropriate bonding); (b) disagree on journey's end (non-agreement about goals); and/or (c) prefer different ways of reaching the therapeutic destination (non-agreement about tasks).

Obviously, both therapist and client contribute to the development and maintenance of the therapeutic alliance. When it is working well, both client and therapist are able to bring up and discuss any issues that are disrupting the alliance. However, we believe that it is the therapist who needs to take prime responsibility for ensuring that the alliance does not fall into disarray. The therapist needs to monitor the relationship carefully and be sure to ask for feedback from her clients. Periodic feedback is essential because it enables the 'bridge' of the alliance to be repaired well in advance of any structural weakness being generated. Bordin (1983) has summarized a number of studies relevant to individual therapy. He reports that good therapeutic outcome was correlated with the ability of the therapist to pay attention to alliance-related problems and to intervene and repair effectively any damage to the relationship. Mere passive registering of these difficulties by expressing interest or concern is not sufficient to prevent disruption in the alliance.

These research findings make good sense to us. If we detect that a couple or family are slipping away from us in the session (a very tangible experience demonstrated, for example, by family members repeatedly looking at their watches, going silent or changing their body postures markedly) we immediately seek to remedy the situation. Usually we take a break in the session which enables us to begin to puzzle out why things are going wrong. On returning to the session we initiate a discussion of the difficulty with the family or couple rather than papering it over or hoping for the best. Our experience of doing this is very rewarding – the usual outcome is a deepening of the therapeutic alliance because the family or couple responds actively and positively to our attempts to correct our mistakes.

But we are jumping ahead of our argument. Before looking at some of the problems that inevitably dog the therapeutic alliance it is important to have a conceptual framework which enables us to grasp the complexities and subtleties of alliance building. Minuchin and Fishman (1981, p. 29) have summarized the most salient aspects of this task:

> So family and therapist form a partnership, with a common goal that is more or less formulated: to free the family symptom bearer of symptoms, to reduce conflict and stress for the whole family, and to learn new ways of coping. Two social systems have joined, for a specific purpose and for a certain time.

But they then question the functions that the participants in this therapeutic system need to adopt. They are certainly in the same boat, but the boat needs someone at the helm to guide it through the decidedly stormy waters ahead:

> In most cases the family will accept the therapist as leader of this partnership ... Like every leader, [s]he will have to accommodate, seduce, submit, support, direct, suggest, and follow in order to lead. But the therapist ... can feel comfortable in accepting the paradoxical job of leading a system of which [s]he is a member ... [S]he also has a body of knowledge and experience with families, systems and the processes of change. [S]he knows that by becoming a member of the therapeutic system [s]he will be subjected to its demands. [S]he will be channeled into traveling certain roads in certain ways at certain times. Sometimes [s]he will be aware of the channeling; other times [s]he will not even recognize it. [S]he must accept the fact that [s]he will be buffeted by the implicit demands that organize the family members' behavior ... [Her] job as a leader requires [her] to be able to join the family in this way. But [s]he must also have the skills to disjoin, then rejoin in a differentiated way – and there's the rub. (Minuchin and Fishman, 1981, pp. 29–30)

This is an eloquent piece of writing which explores many features of the therapeutic alliance; but it does not, in our opinion, see the alliance in a sufficiently two-sided way. There is too much of the (originally macho) hero-innovator for our taste. If the therapeutic alliance is built upon good joining skills but also involves skilful contract making then clients feel much more engaged and hence have a vested interest, for example, in helping the helmswoman when the fog comes up or in negotiating a turn on the helm when they feel empowered by the contributions that they have already made (as crew) to running the boat.

In fairness to Minuchin and Fishman the next part of their discussion, which explores another facet of therapy, comes much closer to our position (1981, p. 30):

> Early theories of therapy portrayed the therapist as an objective data gatherer, but this myth has largely been discredited. Even in psychoanalysis, the understanding of the analyst's use of self in the process of countertransference has sparked great changes in psychoanalytic theory and practice. 'It is probably true,' Donald Meltzer writes, 'that any analysis which really taps the passions of the patient does the same for the analyst and promotes a development which can further his own self analysis'. The necessary state for inspired interpretation is 'that type of internal companionship which promulgates an atmosphere of adventure in which comradeship develops between the adult part of the patient's personality and the analyst as creative scientist . . .' implying therapeutic possibilities for both parties to the adventure.

As Minuchin and Fishman argue, joining is not necessarily a reasoned or deliberate process. At its best it occurs effortlessly as therapist and family share anecdotes, information and ideas about each other. An ability to be chameleon-like is an advantage, or as Minuchin and Fishman argue (1981, p. 33),

> . . . the therapist's own style may be compatible with some families, with whom she will find she can be very much herself. But in other families she may find herself acting more boisterous than usual or more proper. With some families she will find herself being more verbal. With others she will talk less. Her rhythm of speech will change. With some families she will find

herself talking more to the mother. In others she will talk to all family members. She should observe changes in herself as responses to family's implicit transactional patterns and should use these external signals as another level of information about the family.

In more general terms, the therapist can join couples and families in different ways. Minuchin and Fishman distinguish three positions – close, median and disengaged – but in reality families are strung out along a continuum, so often they do not fit neatly into these categories.

1 *Close position*   The therapist works in close proximity to the couple or family, affiliating with its members even to the point of entering into coalition with some. The therapist is directly confirming of all, and continually emphasizes positive ways of looking at their functioning. In practice such an approach leads to the therapist running the risk of being too heavily inducted into the process. Intensity can be achieved but the therapist, as a participant, is caught in the rules of family participation. Manoeuvrability needs to be maintained and the therapist must find ways of disengaging when the need arises.

2 *Median position*   The therapist joins as an active but neutral listener. The main skill mobilized is tracking: the therapist prompts responses from the couple or family but keeps herself at a distance from them, avoiding the direct 'confirming' tactics of the close position.

3 *Disengaged position*   The therapist adopts the stance of an expert containing the couple or family and yet at the same time creating scenarios which enables them to have a sense of competence or hope for change. As an expert, the therapist is primarily concerned with monitoring their world view, establishing how family members frame their experience and exploring their communication patterns. When adopting this position, the therapist can also ask them to demonstrate their difficulties in the session (enactments) and so establish how different dyads and triads operate within the family. The therapist is therefore mostly very distinctive in her stance and maintains a position of leadership within the therapeutic system.

In our experience, it is the third position which is the most hazardous. To achieve valid and productive enactments with a family or couple that have been joined using a disengaged mode is extremely difficult unless you have the prestige and experience of Minuchin.

When we use the disengaged position we begin by negotiating a 'puzzle' contract with the family or couple. This puzzle contract is designed to provide a framework for therapy which enables us to be more exploratory and more probing and questioning than is customary. We use such a contract particularly with families with adult 'psychiatric' members. Such families are usually very fearful of change, so that the intensity that can be induced by close joining is inappropriate. A puzzle contract enables the family slowly to build up a trusting relationship with the therapist – once trust is established then issues to do with change can be placed on the agenda in a positive and productive way.

Minuchin and Fishman's work is valuable, but despite their very detailed discussion of joining they do not discuss contract making. Minuchin exploits his charisma in order to move families and couples in directions they would (at the moment) sooner not travel, but the ethics of doing this are troubling. As discussed in chapter 1, we prefer to use a contract making approach rather than using power plays as Minuchin does. We think that our approach is not only more respectful of families and couples but also much safer: it does not result in defections from therapy because it attends to all aspects of the therapeutic alliance (see Bordin, 1983, above).

We favour a social phase in the first interview because it enables us to introduce ourselves to the couple or family and to get them to introduce themselves to us. This means that we set up a message which says 'we are interested in you as a family that has a life away from the problem', rather than 'we are interested in you solely because you have a problem'. A well-executed social phase in the first interview can open up important vistas for therapy as well as enhancing the joining process. Goal setting is equally important and also has profound joining implications because the family is able to get feedback about whether the therapist has heard what they think their problems are and whether she is sensitive to discussing possible ways of solving the problem that are acceptable to the family. Obviously, this approach is very much in step with the work of Bordin (1979) which we have already cited. Attention to joining, defining the problem, and goal setting (manifested in the contracting phase) ensure that the building of the therapeutic alliance is central to the work of the first interview. But it is important to avoid making mechanical assumptions about the process. The therapist may well have appropriately gone through the motions and yet the therapeutic alliance may still be shaky. The essential safety check on this state of affairs consists of directly asking the couple or family to give feedback about the session.

Asking clients to review the session can be a powerful experience – beginning therapists, who usually have an idealized view of how they themselves should have performed during the session, find it very difficult to ask for feedback. And yet it can be one of the most liberating things to do in therapy. A family that answers frankly enables the therapist to come to terms with any mistakes she has committed and build on the successes. This means that the bridge (the therapeutic alliance) is repaired (and prepared) ready for the heavier traffic that it must take as therapy enters its deeper phases.

Problem 1   Dealing with Differences

Analysis

There are innumerable ways in which joining can be disrupted. A marked age-difference between a couple and their therapist (especially if younger) can be really difficult to handle. A family's style of interacting may be very different from the style of the therapist. A young single therapist of either sex may find it extremely difficult working with families who have young children. The list is potentially endless. In practice if the agency offering family or marital therapy has a group of therapists of either sex who also differ widely in age then there can be some attempt to match clients and therapists right from the start of therapy. Where this is not possible, other solutions must be sought.

Solutions

Sometimes the therapist and family seem manifestly incompatible, at least at first contact. Sometimes clients seem quite unpleasant and objectionable; but as Minuchin and Fishman say (1981, p. 40), 'The therapist should then remind herself that it is simply impossible for this family to be absolutely devoid of qualities that [s]he shares. It may be difficult to find them but they have to be there. The problem is just that the therapist is not sufficiently motivated to look for them.'

When confronted with clients who differ greatly from us it is perhaps natural to think the worst of the situation and assume that no bridges can be built. In practice, however, if we set ourselves the task of exploring the client's position in detail we will inevitably find points of genuine contact. We therefore need to be anthropologists who combine a very rich sense of the complexity of human life with an ability to detect points of agreement even when we arrive at a given position from different starting points.

Needless to say, if no commonality can be found then therapy will flounder. It is rare, however, for a family or couple to be totally in agreement so there remains the possibility that the therapist can, in practice, puzzle over contradictions in her clients' positions rather than emphasizing contradictions between her own position and that of her clients. The following example illustrates this.

□ One of us was able to work at least partially successfully with a couple who were bringing up their children in accordance with the family bed philosophy, in which all members slept together. The woman in the family was a passionate advocate of this approach and had influenced her reluctant husband to join in. But this was precisely the problem because his heart was not in it. After initially (and naively) being sucked into a dispute over the merits of such an approach, the male therapist retreated from the scene while at the same time encouraging the husband to stop colluding with a way of life that *he* actually found unlivable. Sadly, while this tactic worked, the therapist was not able to support the wife as she was confronted by her husband. With the benefit of hindsight he should have been more honest about *his* inability to sympathize with her approach and should have sought the help of a woman co-therapist who could have joined the woman around her concerns about rearing children who were loving and non-competitive. □

Problem 2 Working with Clients who do not have the Same Class Background as the Therapist

Analysis

Obviously, this problem potentially overlaps with the previous problem; we have chosen to deal with it separately because it is a neglected topic within the marital and family therapy literature. The difficulty as we see it centres around the issue of working-class expectations of help.

Rees and Wallace (1982), in their valuable book evaluating social-work practice, provide an interesting summary of what clients expect from their social workers. It is worth looking at their findings before considering working-class clients' attitudes to family and marital therapy. Rees and Wallace (1982, p. 44) report that clients seek a concerned, friendly approach because they equate listening with caring. They also distinguish between social workers as 'persons' and as 'professionals'. However, concerned, caring practitioners are only considered helpful up to a point, since promises or even expressions of interest must be coupled with action. A model of family therapy which stresses joining and yet is also actively problem-solving can be expected to be well received by clients with these sorts of expectations.

Rees and Wallace also explore clients' perceptions of competence. A practitioner is seen as competent if she is similar to the client by virtue of age, sex, or the way she refers to her own experiences, and either has some specialized knowledge of the problem at hand, or conveys that she knows how to obtain such information. More subtly, clients also distinguish between the apparent possession of competence and the way it is exercised. People with some experience of solving problems and handling officials (such as parents of handicapped children) seek a relationship of some equality. Other people who feel both ashamed and powerless appreciate workers who demonstrate competence by taking action on their behalf.

Solutions

If family and marital therapists (who are predominantly middle class) are to work satisfactorily with clients from working-class backgrounds then they need to develop a sensitivity to their clients' view of therapy itself. Hence the importance of using a contract-making approach such as that described in chapter 1 – an approach which asks for the clients' understanding of the problems and how they should be tackled.

There is also another side to the coin. Lorion (1978) has demonstrated that clients can be 'prepared' for therapy through the medium of initial orientating interviews which carefully explain the whys and wherefores of the therapy the client is about to enter. In a way the process is concerned with creating informed consent to begin therapy: instead of throwing clients in at the deep end they are helped to explore what the process of therapy will feel like and what its likely goals will be. The project carried out by Pam Pimpernell (which was briefly discussed in chapter 2) is an example of this type of approach.

Problem 3   The Therapist and the Clients are from Different Ethnic Backgrounds

Analysis

Family therapy and marital therapy in Britain is largely practised by white middle-class people, so it is not surprising to find that there is a dearth of literature concerning ethnicity. In the USA the situation is substantially different – for example McGoldrick and colleagues (1982) have contributed to a major textbook which reviews work with clients from a very wide range of ethnic backgrounds. Fortunately, Lau (1984) has contributed a preliminary article which offers some useful guidelines for work with ethnic minorities in Britain.

Lau suggests that there are four major 'transcultural interfaces' (to use her term) between therapists and families:

1   Congruence between basic cultural positions of the therapist and family, where both belong to the same cultural group. This type will not detain us here, although it is important to add that people from the same cultural background may not have shared assumptions if there are marked religious, political or class differences between them.

2   Dissonance between basic cultural positions of therapist and family; for example, the family is non-Western European or from extended family traditions. A typical clash here would be between the apparently egalitarian orientation of such occidental middle-class culture and autocratically-orientated cultures, such as Latin or Chinese. A therapist with the former type of background may stress differentiation and independence while the families she works with stress mutual dependence and loyalty. Such cultural clashes are particularly hazardous when the therapist has statutory responsibilities for the children in an ethnic minority family. As Liverpool (1986) observes: 'Many black parents are dismayed by the tendency of [white] social workers to treat the child as a separate entity with a capacity to think and act independently. This gives rise to the suspicion that the worker manipulates or colludes with the child and also accusations that ideas and words are being put into the

child's head.' Similarly, the fact that children are traditionally brought up to show great respect for adults can mislead the therapist into a concern that they are unduly passive. Again, the common expectation that older children should look after their younger brothers and sisters is sometimes interpreted as a lack of concern and interest on the part of their parents. It is, however, in relation to physical methods of discipline that most conflicts between white therapists and black parents occur. We discuss a case example of such a conflict in chapter 6.

3   Dissonance between basic cultural positions of the therapist and family when the therapist is from a non-Western European tradition or an extended family tradition. This combination is relatively rare but most commonly occurs in psychiatry: immigrant psychiatrists, especially from the Indian sub-continent, find it difficult to adjust to a society with a different set of cultural values. Not unexpectedly, they tend to hold on to the certainties of the crude organic model popular in British psychiatry (see Littlewood and Lipsedge, 1982, pp. 23–4). This model is used to explain away as 'illnesses' phenomena which require sophisticated sociological and psychological interpretation.

4   Dissonance within the presenting family. This category includes (a) families with first generation English-born children (b) cross-cultural marriages. In both cases there is a clash of values within the family itself, so the therapist's task in maintaining any form of therapeutic alliance is especially difficult. The situation can, of course, be exacerbated if, for example, the therapist shares the values and ethnic background of one section of the family (the children or one of the spouses).

Lau's classification is valuable in drawing attention to the possible mismatches between clients and therapists; but there is also a bewilderingly complex fifth category that could be postulated – that is, dissonance within the family *and* dissonance between the family and the therapist.

Solutions

Despite the complexities of such situations, Lau does offer five practical guidelines for working with ethnically diverse families:

1   The therapist needs to familiarize herself with the family's cultural and religious background in sufficient detail in order to assess the content of the clinical aspects of the problem presented

to the therapist. (This may require collaboration with an interpreter when there are language problems.)

2   The therapist must be aware of cultural rules to do with authority structures, differentiation and boundaries so that she can avoid communicating with the family incongruously.

3   The therapist should be aware of existing cultural defences and the natural support system within which the family functions.

4   Communication problems between the therapist and the family need to be clarified and resolved – often this is a difficult task since interpreters are likely to have their own view of what should be going on and do not adopt a neutral role (cf., Shackman, 1985).

5   In joining the family the therapist needs to confirm the parents' authority with respect to the children. The family's sense of power and competence needs to be mobilized and used effectively for solving problems. Wherever possible the presented client's behaviour needs to be normalized and re-framed positively. Cultural metaphors can be used when formulating the problem and feedback to the family.

Surprisingly, Lau makes no real mention of the difficulties that therapists can have in accepting the value system of a different culture. How, for instance, is a white feminist therapist to accept what she sees as the monolithic chauvinism of some non-Western cultures? Ballard (1979, p. 151) identifies the problems caused when a therapist lacks cultural sensitivity:

Whites often believe South Asian family life to be too constricting. If a . . . woman is in conflict with her parents or husband, an outsider may assume that the subordinate role which South Asian women are expected to play towards their fathers and husbands, or the institution of the arranged marriage, is at the root of the problem. Such an interpretation may be partially correct, but the woman would be unlikely to be seeking to alter her situation fundamentally. To do so would be to reject a major part of the cultural values of her own ethnic group. It is important that solutions should be sought within the particular cultural context, that is the values in terms of which people organise their own lives. Solutions which, unintentionally or not, have the effect of ignoring or condemning those values are likely to be unacceptable to the recipients.

An example of marital therapy for spouse abuse is discussed in terms of its cultural context in chapter 6.

At a practical level, ethnic minority clients can be successfully worked with by white therapists if two conditions are met: first, if staff have had special training in order to heighten their sensitivity to their clients; secondly, if they have acknowledged and examined their own underlying racist assumptions and beliefs. As Liverpool (1986) argues, in a discussion of training, 'merely providing cultural information by itself would not sensitise the worker to the strengths of black families and their culture. Likewise, racism awareness training without some way of integrating this with cultural knowledge, and developing cross-cultural skills, could be ineffective.'

Ahmed (1986, pp. 142, 147ff) has identified 'cultural racism' in social workers (and, presumably, other professional workers) in which simplistic cultural explanations, always of a disparaging nature, are applied to ethnic minority families as a substitute for a thorough assessment of their difficulties. For example, she quotes the case of a baby girl of Sikh parents who was admitted to hospital with a fractured skull. At a subsequent case conference, there was a marked tendency amongst the professionals to assume that, because of a traditional preference for male children in South Asian culture, the female child must have been unwanted and therefore abused.

Similarly, conflict between South Asian parents and female adolescents may be explained in terms of 'culture conflict', the clash between traditional Asian and modern Western values. (Note the disparaging comparison between 'traditional' and 'modern'.) Indeed, such is the popularity of this 'explanation', Ahmed (1986, p. 148) suggests, that young Asians often present problems to white professionals in a way which they have learnt will gain a sympathetic response. Thus, complaints of ill-treatment by parents and unwillingness to make an arranged marriage are now '. . . known ways to capture attention'. The white therapist may be tempted, therefore, not only to 'take sides' with the adolescent (in a way which she would instantly recognize as inappropriate if working with a white family), but also to act as if 'culture conflict' were the sole possible explanation rather than just the presenting problem. Again, to make the contrast, few therapists would rest with a culture-conflict explanation of a dispute between a white adolescent and her parents even if the disagreement concerned the girl's total rejection of her parents' 'middle-class' values.

☐ A seventeen-year-old Hindu girl was referred to a psychiatric unit by a physician who had been investigating her for abdominal pain, for which he could find no medical explanation. He had concluded that the pains were emotional in origin, and this hypothesis had been confirmed in his mind when the girl had become very distressed when talking with a nurse about her proposed arranged marriage. His referral letter expressed the view that her problem was a cultural clash between her and her orthodox parents.

The girl was very reluctant to be seen with her parents, saying 'My father will kill me!' She did come to a family meeting, but refused to speak. Her father acknowledged that she seemed upset at the prospect of marriage but was more concerned about her pains. Her mother could not understand her daughter's behaviour because she had seemed to like the boy in question. Eventually, the girl blurted out 'It's not that!' but declined to say any more. The (male) therapist suggested to the father that they should leave the room, leaving the mother and daughter to talk. When they returned, the two women were holding hands and were crying. The mother explained that her daughter had been sexually interfered with by a cousin, thought (wrongly) that she had lost her virginity and feared marriage only because her shame would be exposed. ☐

This example illustrates the danger of relying on simplistic cultural explanations which then obscure the therapist's assessment of family relationships. On the other hand, some 'cultural' factors which reflect badly on Western society are all too easily ignored. Here we refer to overt racism, including racial abuse at school and attacks on members of ethnic minority groups in the neighbourhood. Rather than engage in invidious comparisons between cultures, the therapist should remember that her primary task is to understand, as far as she is able, the world from her clients' points of view. This is a task which requires an open mind and a willingness to ask for advice and information.

Unfortunately, the enthnocentrism of most white practitioners has created a tradition in Britain of approaching clients from ethnic-minority backgrounds as though they were unsuitable for therapy. However, Bavington and Majid (1986) were able to report some innovative projects which provide some working examples of what can be done. For example, they draw attention to the work of the psychiatrist Dr Aggrey Burke at St George's Hospital, London, who has introduced a regular staff-sensitivity group for combating racism. In Bradford, the Transcultural Psychiatric Unit at Lynfield Mount Hospital has taken this approach a stage further by attempting to provide a psychiatric service that is directly relevant to its clients. The service functions through a weekly clinic staffed by a multidisciplinary team who speak a wide range of relevant languages. Most of the clients come from the hospital's catchment area, but increasingly the unit has become a resource centre for professionals seeking advice about how best to work with their clients. Weekly meetings of the unit, to which visitors can be invited, have created a useful forum for wider discussion of the issues involved, so that there is a continual process of mutual education from which everybody can benefit. Once a month the meeting is replaced by a much larger open meeting attended by people from various local services (Rack, 1982).

Obviously, any area of the country which has concentrations of clients from ethnic minorities needs to develop similar units. Lau's recommendations are essentially utopian unless such a development takes place. Isolated practitioners working without the support of such units can scarcely be expected to devise custom-built therapy for their clients. Language barriers alone are usually sufficient to defeat any solo efforts, but as Bavington and Majid (1986) point out, there is the underlying issue of trust. Clients will not come for therapy unless the agency they attend has credibility in their eyes. This will not occur unless the agency has street credibility. In practice this means that it needs to be staffed with practitioners from ethnic-minority backgrounds; it also needs an outreach policy and an ability to run a wide range of activities (advocacy clinics, support groups, play groups) which are specially designed to respond to the needs of the clients it must attract. Family therapy will therefore be but a small part of a wider package on offer.

Finally, we conclude this section with a list of recommendations that seem particularly relevant to the practice of family therapy with black families. The reader is advised to consult the references and the suggestions for further reading for information and ideas which we do not have the space to record.

1 Recognize that the therapist's own agency as well as her own
   roles and duties are important elements in assessing the problem

system. A black family's experiences and expectations of statutory agencies are often different from those of white families, and are inevitably tainted by 'institutional racism' (Triseliotis, 1986, p. 209).

2 Always focus on the extended (and not just the nuclear) family (Farrar and Sicar, 1986).

3 Always use an interpreter if you are not fluent in a language, and never permit children to act in this capacity – it is humiliating for their parents and breaches generational boundaries (Shackman, 1985).

4 Be informed of differences in family structure and organization, particularly with regard to authority (Lau, 1986, p. 241).

5 A 'close' joining position is usually essential for work with South Asian families. Because difficulties are expected to be kept within the family, the therapist has to become almost part of the family before being trusted with its problems (Farrar and Sicar, 1986).

6 An active, mediating, bargaining and conciliatory approach to internal conflicts is more familiar to South Asian and Afro-Caribbean families than one based in discussing feelings. As Triseliotis (1986, p. 213) suggests, it is appropriate within this model for the therapist to see the 'executive' members of the family separately, even if briefly, to pave the way towards an agreement. This avoids the danger of 'shaming' and demonstrates respect for the family roles.

Problem 4   The Wrong Sex?

Analysis

The sex of the therapist may be a problem for the couple or family in therapy. For example, male heads of South Asian families may have difficulty in relating to female social workers (but less difficulty with female doctors because of their higher social status). This problem also emerges sharply when working with single-parent families. For example, a male therapist working with a single-parent family headed by a woman who has recently divorced may well run into difficulties either because he is idealized (a caring man very different from the ex-husband) or because the woman has had enough of men, at least for the time being.

Unfortunately, we are not aware of any sound research in marital and family therapy which examines whether the sex of the therapist is of any importance. However, Parloff, Waskow and Wolfe (1978) suggest in their review that 'as in the areas of race and social class, it may well be the attitudes and values of the therapist that are of primary importance rather than his or her sex per se.' (1978, p. 264) They cite a number of commentators who urge greater sensitivity on the part of therapists concerning sex-role issues, and who stress the need for all therapists to acquire more knowledge about the psychology of women and the role of social and environmental factors in influencing women's problems.

It is equally true, however, that men's issues have been ignored by family and marital therapists working within the systems framework. They tend to forget the fact that they are dealing with *men* and *women* (and not equipotential sub-systems, to use still-current jargon). Men are usually discussed only in a negative sense (particularly when they are violent or missing from sessions), but there is a real dearth of a sympathetic literature which seeks to understand their particular difficulties. There has been some discussion of fathers'/husbands' work roles and how these impinge on families (for example, L'Abate, 1975), but much more research is needed.

Faced with working with a single parent household headed by a man, the dilemma remains. Would a man or a woman be more helpful? Judging from our experience it seems to be generally true that a man is more useful because the joining process is more easily achieved, but we would once again echo Parloff, Waskow and Wolfe (1978) that it is really a question of the therapist's values and attitudes.

Solutions

Since the research is so tentative we are guided by the sole thought that the matching of attitudes and values rather than of sex may be the most productive way of approaching this issue. However, when working with single parents it is usually very helpful to include a group experience in the package of therapy undertaken. This policy helps to dilute the intensity of the therapist–client relationship and at the same time overcome the isolation normally experienced by single parents. As the example below shows, sometimes the therapist is clearly the wrong sex, and it is probably best to accept this rather than to attempt the impossible task of talking oneself out of a near-impossible situation.

□ One of us (A. T.) got off to a very bad start with a woman who came to the clinic a few minutes after having a very bitter row with her husband and father-in-law. Less than ten minutes into our interview it became clear that my sex was an insurmountable barrier to progress. Fortunately, the client had been welcomed to the clinic by a woman colleague of mine, who had sensed her distress, so I was able to suggest that this colleague – who was very flexible and supportive – should take over the interview immediately. She did so, and was able to negotiate a successful contract. □

Problem 5   Rejecting Parents

Analysis

Some parents are adamant that it is one child and one child only who is the problem. It is, of course, pointless simply to contradict. The therapist, albeit reluctantly, is usually able to 'join' the parents on this issue by uncritically accepting that their felt experience is precisely that the child *is* a real monster. Such a child will often behave impeccably in sessions, hence confusing the therapist further. Careful tracking can reveal a number of patterns of behaviour: the therapist may be convinced that this is definitive proof that the child is exceptionally difficult; but on the other hand, she may discover that it is the parents' unrealistic expectations of their children's behaviour which are problematic.

Solutions

Scapegoating is very stressful for most therapists because the task that confronts the therapist is, as Bentovim (1981, p. 140) has argued, to join the rejecting parent:

> The single most important act is for the therapist to join with the *rejecting* parent in the first instance. Rejecting parents need sympathy for finding themselves saying such bitter, angry, painful and hateful things towards members of their own family, their own flesh and blood, part of themselves that they helped to bring into the world, have parental care of and yet who are the cause of so much pain, anger, shame and

humiliation. It is also important to sympathize with the parents having to come to a professional and say such bitter, cruel and hard things about their own children. This major statement of joining is an absolute prerequisite for any sort of therapeutic move, particularly before joining with the rest of the family, the other parents who have to experience their partner in such pain, the children who experience it, and the other children who have to be party to the pain.

Needless to say, the child, who may be at risk of physical or emotional abuse, cannot be neglected by the therapist. For social workers and other professionals the child, not the parents, will be the 'client' and will have the right to protection. Family therapy will not always be enough (cf., Bentovim et al., 1987). But the therapist must also recognize that the child is quite capable of stimulating chaos should the therapist fail to see that the child is caught in a contradiction – on the one hand she is loyal to her family, but on the other she is enraged because the family exploits her. Above all else, direct criticism of the family must be avoided, since this can produce quite explosive responses from the presenting client.

However, even if the joining is successful there are major difficulties ahead because at some point the therapist needs to succeed in reversing the perennial pattern of rejection that lies at the centre of family life.

☐ Mrs. B's rejection of her son, Danny (aged fourteen), was emphatic. In reply to the qustion 'What do you most dislike about your son?', she answered 'His presence'. Every time she saw him she would become very angry and try to hit him. Fortunately her husband had a different view – he wanted Danny to remain at home and got along with him pretty well, whereas Mrs B had got to the point where she wanted him taken into care. The therapist was able to empathize with Mrs B's rejection, but at the same time insisted that whether they liked it or not they could not forsake their responsibilities to their son – they still needed to be parents to him. Equally, they would experience an enormous sense of failure as parents if they sent him into care and this would inevitably leave them with a sense of despair. A six-session contract was negotiated with the parents in order to explore their expectations of parenting and to sort out how they could discharge their duty to Danny. In the end a compromise solution was devised – Danny became a weekly boarder at a local agricultural school, returning home at weekends and during school hoidays. This solution enabled enough steam to be taken out of the situation for life at home to be tolerable, if far from ideal.

A follow-up six months later revealed that the situation had not changed very much, but Danny was not being struck any more. Significantly, Danny was able to report that the meetings had been helpful because he realized that he was not all bad and the sole cause of the problem. □

Problem 6   Working with Disorganized Families

Analysis

With some families, often those most in need of help, it seems impossible to work effectively. They are typically the clients of public-service and child-protection agencies in the USA and social services and probation departments in Britain. They are characterized by disorganization and appear to live in continual upheaval; it is difficult for an outsider to understand how they manage to survive from one day to the next because the high degree of internal conflict and low level of parenting and problem-solving skills are inevitably accompanied by poverty, poor housing conditions and debt. The parents have few personal resources: they were often abused themselves as children, have lived for many years in children's homes or a succession of foster homes and suffered a number of unresolved losses during their lives. In addition, if fortunate enough to be employed, they are in the lowest paid and most physically draining jobs which offer little self-respect or status, and consequently they have little if any enthusiasm or energy to devote to family life. Personal initiative is rare, therapy or counselling an alien concept; and if they do contact a therapist, they will inevitably have been sent rather than have come of their own accord.

Solutions

Given the gross deprivation and social and emotional handicaps suffered by such families, it is easy for therapists to feel hopeless, to conclude that therapy is impossible or irrelevant and, with a sense of relief, to write back to the referrer saying that the family failed to turn up to their appointment and that no further action will be taken! But it is undeniable that these families need help, and in our opinion one of the most encouraging developments in marital and family therapy over the last few years has been the efforts made to adapt the approach to reach them (for example, Clark et al., 1982; Mattinson and Sinclair, 1979). In offering some guidelines we will draw on a useful article by Weitzman (1985) which describes how conventional family therapy methods have to be modified in the interests of effective working relationships.

We have grouped the guidelines advocated by Weitzman under a number of headings:

1 *Secure a therapeutic alliance*   Joining in a positive, supportive way with families that are permeated by blame and negativism is vital. What is needed is a special sensitivity to the family's initial self-presentation – its rules, its structure, and its values and beliefs. Such families are heavily invested in their own stabilization and often resort to old dysfunctional patterns when threatened by imminent breakdown. But this does not mean that the therapist should allow the family to control the therapy. She must establish certin essential conditions – for example, controlling all forms of violence. At the same time she must avoid attempts to change the family before making an adequate assessment of both its capabilities and its desired goals and its darker side – its hidden agendas and contradictory motivations. In practice, in order to achieve any progress the therapist usually needs to be working with the family within some form of statutory framework, since the temptation for the family to flee from facing its problems is understandably strong.

2 *Reduce intensity*   Since such families typically present with very difficult symptoms (including incest, violence, alcoholism, delinquency and suicide), encouraging family members to interact around such issues can unleash destructive and emotional behaviour that is difficult to control. This means that it is imperative to avoid open warfare in the session, since there is already more than enough conflict in the system.

Weitzman advises therapists to avoid using either paradoxical injunctions or experiential techniques since both contain the seeds of confrontation between therapist and family. Instead, such families need support and empathy for their difficult and often perilous circumstances. Neither too much optimism nor too much pessimism should be displayed by the therapist. Care is needed in re-framing behaviour, since this can often anger parents who are struggling with the crushing realities of having to deal with a severely troublesome child. As we argued in the last section, it is the parents who must feel most joined.

Parents who abuse, reject and inhibit their own children have usually had the same experience as children themselves. The therapist is faced with having to take a strong positive-parenting role. At least initially, she may have to act as adviser, limit setter, mediator, benevolent authority figure. As therapy develops and the parents become more skilful in adopting sound parenting techniques it is possible to resolve some of the unresolved intergenerational conflicts, but this work usually need to be done by working with the parents by themselves.

3 Structuring the interviews   Since such families feel (and are) out of control, it is essential for the therapist to model control by setting limits and establishing rules of conduct during the family sessions. Violence and other extreme behaviour is unacceptable, and if necessary the therapist should restrain acting out, for example, by holding a younger child or excluding a member from the room. It is important to stress that limits help the family members organize themselves and create a working atmosphere. Rather than feeling bound to work with all the family all the time, the therapist might exclude members from some of the sessions.

Ainley (1984), like Weitzman, points out that parents should not be expected to exercise control over an aggressive child when they have not been able to do so for many years. Such control of a child's behaviour is a long-term goal, and the therapist should expect to take charge at first, especially if the parents are likely to resort to hostility and violence directed at the child, or one another. The use of statutory power is often essential here.

4 Anticipate the impact of interventions   Since such families live day by day and typically go from one crisis to another they have difficulty in thinking ahead. The therapist therefore needs to help them understand the implications of the changes they are attempting to achieve. Her ability to predict what will happen next is important in establishing her credibility. Weitzman particularly advocates the use of restraining techniques (cf., Fisch, Weakland and Segal, 1982) to help the family to decide whether they do indeed want any significant changes in the way they live. The therapist should not assume that families want to remain together – both children and parents often want physical separation from one another. So significant interventions should be discussed with the family before being implemented, lest the family be enlisted into causes they do not believe in. For example, having a structural map of a disengaged father and daughter is in no way decisive in determining the course of therapy. Encouraging father and daughter to get closer is likely to be a mistake unless both of them are carefully included in the decision and the ramifications of such an intervention are fully explored. A structural map is useful, but it cannot dictate the pace of intervention which is crucial to joining successfully with the family and which necessarily occurs over many weeks or months.

Again, we like what Weitzman says here; it has become fashionable to assume that brief therapy is the only justifiable form of therapy, and in some circles to demonstrate how good a therapist you are by boasting about how few sessions it took you to 'fix' a family. It is also fashionable to write of only the magical 'cures' that took a few sessions. This creates a totally distorted impression of the realities of therapy; it also avoids a real discussion of families' *needs*. Therapists may for personal reasons need to feel that they are brilliant, but the most oppressed families in society need a quality of care to match their needs.

5 *Devise realistic goals*   Agreed goals must be within the family members' capability and motivation; they should be concrete and behavioural, rather than vague and idealistic, such as 'improved parenting' or 'fewer interpersonal conflicts.' Parents should not be asked to nurture when they cannot nurture. Rather, they should be encouraged to consider carefully their position toward one another, their capabilities and expectations. Families should not be directed to resolve massive conflicts of interest if they have not acquired the skills for managing disagreements. Parents should not be pushed to discuss marital problems if this risks aggression and violence. Such problems can only be tackled at later stages in therapy and will require clients to join well-structured programmes.

It is important to emphasize that family therapy will be quite inadequate if it takes place in isolation from a wide-ranging approach which also deals with the financial and housing problems that such families usually experience. We believe that well financed and staffed family centres which offer a wide range of services can meet their needs best. Family therapy may well form a part of the package offered by such centres, but other aspects of the work are equally important. Fortunately, there is a rapidly growing family-centre movement in Britain which is creating innovative ways of dealing with disadvantaged families (National Council of Voluntary Child Care Organisations, 1987). Pioneering work has also been undertaken by Dale and his colleagues from the Rochdale NSPCC, and their book *Dangerous Families* (Dale et al., 1986) is a milestone in the assessment of the treatment of child abuse.

Problem 7   Holding the Balance in Marital Therapy

Analysis

It is not easy to maintain a therapeutic relationship with both partners in marital therapy. We have chosen to deal with this problem separately (abandoning our usual policy of discussing marital and family issues jointly) because it requires special discussion.

Joining both partners is the crucial task facing the therapist during the initial stages of therapy. This requires her to listen well, show respect for the clients and avoid being judgemental. But at the same time each client must feel equally accepted and supported by the therapist. This balance is often difficult to achieve when one or both partners enter therapy insisting that they are right and the other wrong.

As Broderick (1983) describes, some couples come prepared to argue their case as eloquently as possible. They are skilled at making their own sins seem small and insignificant while presenting those of their partners as manifestations of unforgivable insensitivity, selfishness, and even cruelty. Often such couples are well matched in their ability to put forward their own cases and to discredit their partners'; but in some couples one partner is a master or mistress of vituperation, sarcasm or virtuous recitation, and the other inarticulate, introverted, or stubbornly silent. A third possibility involves one partner having done something violent, treacherous, disgraceful or crazy while the spouse has been trying to cope with the resultant mess. We will consider each of these cases in turn because they require different responses from the therapist.

Solutions

Arguing

The symmetrical couple who argue interminably, each stubbornly upholding their point of view, require an intervention from the therapist which brings home to them the fact that therapy cannot proceed if they continue their endless sparring match. Indeed, not only is protracted arguing frustrating, but, as O'Connor (1974) has shown, the therapist's inability to deal with it at the first session is predictive of the outcome of therapy. One approach is to point out that they cannot both be right. This is often best achieved indirectly by telling them a story such as that attributed to the Mullah Nasrudin:

> The Mullah was acting as a magistrate. A man came to see him to complain about his wife's behaviour. The Mullah listened carefully and, at the end of the long list, pronounced, 'You must be right!' The clerk of the court begged him to restrain himself because the wife had not yet been heard. He sent for the wife and heard her similarly long list of the husband's faults before asserting, 'You must be right!' At this point the clerk intervened to say, 'But, your Excellency, they can't *both* be right.' To which the Mullah replied, 'You must be right!' (Adapted from Shah, 1975, p. 67)

Most partners will see the point of this story – they both insist they are right, but they cannot *both* be right. Their own perception is right for them but will not be right for their partner, who inevitably perceives things differently. The therapist's task is not to decide who is right and who is wrong, but rather to help each of them understand and appreciate that the other can be right in her/his own terms.

If the arguing persists the therapist might try looking sad, shrugging her shoulders and, once assured of each partner's attention, making a remark along the lines suggested by Broderick (1983, pp. 40–41):

> 'I feel so sad listening to the two of you attack and hurt each other. You have both suffered long enough. You need love

and support from your partner *and* you have love and support to give . . . but somehow it just never quite happens. Instead you get bogged down in this awful, destructive arguing, but at the same time you are both desperate for what each other has to offer. You came to me for help out of this trap and I haven't succeeded in finding a way to help you. I feel really terrible about it. So much love, so much to give . . . and yet so much pain and unhappiness.'

Alternatively, we have found that videotaping a small section of a session and then playing it back to the couple can have a powerful effect. The couple can also be invited to reverse roles – to play each other and then feed back their experiences. If this is too threatening, co-therapists can role-play the couple so that they can get an observer's view of what they look like arguing so destructively and unproductively.

The ill-matched couple

In the cases where the couple are ill-matched, the therapist needs to perform the difficult task of facilitating the silent or beleaguered partner while avoiding the trap of alienating the more active partner. A combination of methods is required; Broderick even suggests the possibility of individual sessions with the silent partner but we only use this *in extremis* when nothing else has worked. The hazard of having a session with one partner is that the other sulks or feels paranoid about what is happening. Individual sessions with each partner are therefore preferable. If working with a co-therapist, the partners can be assigned a therapist each and there can then be a report-back session to compare notes. This method can work well and often enhances the silent partner's ability to contribute to future sessions.

   In conjoint sessions we use touch to restrain the dominant partner who insists on interrupting. Touching the over-eager partner lightly shows them that they are not forgotten and that the therapist wishes to remain in contact. However, in very difficult cases the therapist needs to touch the client with one hand and hold the other in the air using a traffic control gesture.

The wronged partner

The most difficult case is when one of the partners has unjustly
wronged the other. Broderick suggests that such a situation can be
genuinely helped by identifying the fact that while there can be no
balance of guilt there may well be a balance of pain.

□ A woman in her early sixties was referred for depression.
Although invited to attend the first session, her husband did
not come. The reason for this soon became apparent to the
therapist when the wife explained that the reason for her
distress was her discovery, some months previously, that her
husband had spent all the redundancy payment he had received
on taking early retirement. Having expected a comfortable
retirement, she was instead faced with having to resume work
herself in order to try and pay off the considerable debts he
had now acquired. She was understandably very angry and
hurt, and revealed that she no longer spoke to her husband
for fear she would physically attack him. Being concerned to
present herself as the wronged woman, she did not know what
her husband thought about the matter.

With the wife's consent, the therapist wrote to the husband
offering him an individual interview and an opportunity to
'discuss the situation from his point of view'. When he came,
he readily admitted that he had tricked and cheated his wife,
frittering the money away on extravagant gestures designed to
impress the affluent members of the social circles to which he
aspired. As his money had disappeared, he had turned to credit
cards. Now that, to use his own words, 'the game was up',
he was consumed with guilt and fear of exposure. The therapist
stressed that while he could not condone his behaviour, he did
feel great sympathy for the man's position and offered to try
and help him resolve the crisis in his marriage.

At the subsequent conjoint session the therapist began by
expressing his sympathy for the wife, emphasizing that her
anger and distress were entirely legitimate and pointing out
the very real damage that had been done to her life and her
hopes as well as to the trust which was the basis for their
marriage. Turning to the husband, the therapist remarked that
he too must be feeling awful. Not only did he have to face

the justified feelings of his wife, knowing that he was to blame, but he would be reminded of his wrong-doing every time they went to spend money and were unable to do so. He had to face the disgust of his children and relatives and the knowledge that his 'friends' were probably laughing at him behind his back. Everyone could see that it was his fault and had all turned against him; he could have no self-respect.

This intervention enabled both partners to acknowledge to the other the deep feelings that they did have. Further, as each responded with tears of distress, they could begin to appreciate the pain of the other, which the wife had been too preoccupied to see in her husband, and which the husband had been too frightened to see in his wife. On the basis of these shared feelings, the reconstruction of their relationship could begin. □

In considering this example it is important to stress that we are not taking the position that the wife was equally to blame. As we state in chapters 1 and 6, we do not subscribe to the doctrine that victims must always be guilty co-conspirators in their own betrayal or victimization; but there are always two sides to every question, and in most cases there is room for both partners to change and grow.

Problem 8 The 'Technology' of Family Therapy Gets in the Way

Analysis

There are many reasons why families find it difficult to engage in family therapy. One that should not be overlooked concerns the 'technology' of family therapy. To be interviewed in a special room with a video-camera and a one-way screen can be a very daunting prospect, so it is important to check that families actually find it comfortable and acceptable to work in this way. Some families make clear at the outset what they can tolerate. Some find the one-way screen (and team back-up) acceptable but fight shy of being videoed. Some find both unacceptable. Our policy is to accept and respect the clients' position rather than assuming that there is a plot afoot to disrupt therapy. However, our policy also involves asking the clients whether we can review the position at a later session. Some clients are very nervous at first interview, but if the joining process succeeds they then relax and can be more accepting of our position – that is, that the one-way screen and the video are helpful in achieving therapeutic results.

If neither the screen nor the video is acceptable then the therapist can be in difficulties, but it is usually possible to negotiate a compromise which allows the therapist to retain her manoeuvrability. Most clients will accept the presence of a live consultant in the room (Smith and Kingston, 1980), so in the face of resistance to her usual structure the therapist might try negotiating an arrangement of this kind.

One other scenario should also be carefully considered. Some clients do in fact find the screen and/or the video inhibiting but are too reticent to let therapists know (and some therapists are effective at not allowing their clients to tell them). It is therefore very important to check periodically how they feel – if they are uncomfortable then it is essential to make whatever changes are necessary in order to create the right mood for therapy to continue. Some clients benefit from a 'closed' session involving no video and only the therapist (and possibly a consultant), but are then perfectly happy to revert to the full show when they are feeling more robust and ready to move on.

It must be stressed that the justification for using technology is the belief that it will help the therapist help her clients. We do not know of any research which substantiates this belief so the advantages and disadvantages must be judged in each case.

Problem 9 'You're Not Much of a Therapist'

Occasionally one member of a couple is impelled to challenge the therapist directly, putting her on the defensive and effectively beginning to control the session. (This type of challenge can also occur in family therapy, but since our method of handling it is essentially similar in both situations we will not explore a family example.)

Solutions

Like Broderick (1983), we suggest that the therapist respond to a challenge straightforwardly, saying something like: 'That's a very valid question. I wish more people had the wisdom to evaluate their therapist's competence before committing themselves to therapy. I was trained ... (and so on). Have you any other questions? Good. Now what brings you ...'.

If the challenge persists, the therapist can respond: 'Mr Smith, I'm sorry that we've got off to such a bad start, but I feel I must let you know that I am already finding the session hard going. You seem to be questioning my credentials; this is well and good, but what sort of answer would satisfy you?' If the client could not map ahead of time what sort of answer he required, the therapist might then say something along the lines of 'I'm puzzled by your reply – I don't mean to be impertinent, but could it be that you're unhappy about being here in the first place? I would find it difficult to go to a therapist if my marriage was under stress. Perhaps we need to talk about how it feels to be here. Do you feel criticized and coerced?'

If the situation is even more tenuous than this, we use a version of the 'devil's pact' devised by the Palo Alto group. Faced by an enraged, angry or unsettled client the therapist can say, 'Mr Smith, I'm sorry to interrupt the flow of the session but I'm getting increasingly unhappy about how things are going. I badly need to say something to you but I'm not sure how you will respond. Could you possibly agree ahead of time that you will not leave the session but stay and have the issue out with me?'

This intervention is a real show-stopper: the client is nonplussed and usually agrees to allow the therapist to proceed. Given this agreement the therapist can then say, 'Mr Smith, I have to be frank with you. Your persistent criticism of me is very punishing and I feel very hurt. I'm willing and able to help you and your partner but we must have some rules to work by. The first one has to be that you give me a chance to show how I can help. I do have the credentials, but the proof of the pudding is in the eating. Why don't we set aside my credentials, work hard in the remainder of the session and then review whether you still want to work with me before we decide on the next appointment'.

It seems to us that this approach is safer than confronting or re-framing. We are able to model good negotiating skills and at the same time give the client the benefit of the doubt. If such a client does not find the session useful then we should be prepared to negotiate a transfer to another therapist. Of course, the reality of the situation may be more complex than this. The client's partner may well think that we are suitable therapists; if so, we can then encourage them to negotiate what they both want to do rather than letting the unsettled partner dominate the proceedings.

Problem 10   Dropping Out

There is perhaps nothing more frustrating and even punishing for a therapist than when a family or couple drop out of therapy. Some therapists harden themselves against such experiences by using such formulas as 'They obviously weren't motivated' or 'Clearly change was too threatening for them' or 'Obviously there wasn't a customer'. Our approach does not allow us to be so cavalier. If a couple or family has dropped out then we assume that either the therapeutic alliance must have been seriously weakened by factors which we need to discover, or some major change in family circumstances has taken place. (In some cases, of course, both may have been true.)

Some families or couples may well be experiencing a major financial or housing crisis, so that therapy becomes an irrelevance to them. On the other hand, major personal or family crises may have occurred – the main breadwinner may have been sacked, a couple's relationship may have dissolved by one partner leaving home, or a family member may have become seriously ill. It is still difficult for the therapist to view the situation with equanimity because the first question that occurs to us is, 'Okay, it turns out that there was good reason why the family dropped out, but why on earth couldn't they put us out of our misery by phoning or dropping us a letter?' Obviously, this is a somewhat precious attitude which overlooks first the very real pressures and problems that families and couples experience, and secondly, the fact that some clients do regard professional agencies with considerable reserve and suspicion. This is especially true of some ethnic-minority groups, who may have experienced discrimination at the hands of such agencies.

Analysis

The literature on drop-out is valuable in helping therapists orientate themselves when faced with a family or couple that have failed to turn up. It is clear from this research that men are the most problematic clients as far as marital and family therapy is concerned. Shapiro and Budman (1973) interviewed drop-out families and found that it was the father who was perceived as being least committed to continuing therapy, a finding substantiated by Le Fave (1980) and Berg and Rosenblum (1977). These observations tend to cast the father in the role of the baddy, but interestingly Berg and Rosenblum (1977) report that lateness of appointment hours is a key factor in maintaining engagement. This suggests that men are often inappropriately designated the 'problem' when they find it difficult to attend on account of work and financial pressures.

However, although work and financial pressures are important, they are by no means sufficient to explain the extent of men's poor attendance. L'Abate (1975) has attempted to explain this phenomenon in terms of 'pathogenic' role rigidity. He argues that a great deal of dysfunction in the family, whether in the marriage or in the children, is determined by the father's inability to shift from his occupational role to his role within the family. There is also the related problem that men tend also to be lost in instrumental roles inside the family. A rigid division of labour between an expressive wife/mother and an instrumental husband/father is likely to create difficulties, since both partners find it difficult to undertake negotiations in areas which are the preserve of their partner rather than themselves.

L'Abate's argument effectively turns on its head the position taken by the sociologist Talcott Parsons: rather than seeing the instrumental/expressive division of labour as functional, L'Abate (in common with many other commentators) sees it as a source of dysfunction. In fact, L'Abate argues that there is even in some cases a direct link between the occupational role of the father in a family and the form of presenting problem. The importance of L'Abate's work is that it draws attention to the crucial necessity of understanding how the father's work can impinge on family life. In practice, careful tracking of such information during the early stages of therapy can enhance joining and prevent the therapist from construing any rigidities in the father's/husband's behaviour as simply a function of his personality.

Other research sheds further light on the drop-out phenomenon. For example, Slipp, Ellis and Kressel (1974) found that drop-out rates are higher when: (1) only one parent (usually the mother) initiates the request for therapy (as compared with situations where both sought therapy); (2) there is a high level of authoritarianism in the parents; (3) the family has a low socio-economic background. This last finding is generally in step with the findings of most psychotherapy surveys, but it is important to stress that these are 'passive' findings which do not really understand drop-out as a dynamic process. As Lorion (1978) has confirmed in his review of psychotherapy for disadvantaged people, the therapist's attitude to such clients is crucial. Again, Shapiro and Budman (1973) found that the majority of both individual clients and families who dropped out felt that their therapist had been too inactive or lacked interest in them. (The reverse was true of clients and families who stayed in therapy.) A more detailed study by Anderson et al. (1985) has reported similar results, with the activity level of the therapist again emerging as a very important variable.

We believe it is the therapist's task, as a reflective practitioner, to continue to refine her joining skills as she gains more experience, so that the amount of drop-outs becomes insignificant. Obviously, we are not utopian about this. As Gaines (1978) has pointed out, there are also 'actuarial' variables that can influence drop-out, such as referral source, the distance clients must travel for the appointment, and the waiting time before experiencing the first interview. But as we suggested in chapter 2, it is possible to develop effective policies in relation to these factors. For example, referrers can be better informed about how to make more effective referrals, voluntary drivers can be found to bring families to sessions from outlying districts and waiting times can be reduced by changing intake policies. It is much better to confront these issues and seek change rather than allowing a 'natural' attrition rate to decide how the work pans out.

Solutions

Obviously, the first task of the therapist who experiences a drop-out is to try and gain some accurate information in order to clarify what is going on. Ideally, direct contact with the family or couple should be made by telephone (if this is possible). The best time to do this is during the period set aside for the session. We have also found it very productive (if time allows) to undertake snap home visits. This policy entirely contradicts the normally contractual approach that we adopt, but we believe that we do have the right at times quite straightforwardly to *react* to clients' behaviour rather than always being proactive.

The purpose of the visit or telephone call is to discover (a) what's happened, and (b) whether we did anything wrong which stopped the couple or family from attending. Our first approach is to express our disappointment that they did not feel able to attend the session, and ask whether it would be possible to spend ten minutes or so discussing what went wrong. We have never been refused entry at this point because the client has felt respected through our having bothered to come out of our way to see them. (Obviously if home visiting has been the main means for delivering the therapy then the response will be different.) Usually we have then been able to undertake a brief interview and have gained important information which either allows us to finish the case or negotiate a new contract.

There may well be contra-indications for using our approach. If drop-out has occurred in the context, for example, of a stormy session with threats of violence to the therapist, then it is advisable either to undertake the home visit with a colleague to give support, or to ask the original referrer to follow up the clients. In less threatening circumstances it is possible to use a 'consumer advice' framework: that is, a colleague contacts the family or couple saying that she wishes to interview them because the agency is very concerned to improve its service to its clients, and would very much benefit from knowing what went wrong when they were working with therapist X. There is no question of this approach being a deception – we do need this type of feedback with drop-out cases and we need to be able to collect the relevant data. However, one possible outcome is that the clients are prepared either to recommence work with their therapist, albeit on a new basis, or to consider a transfer to another therapist. Sometimes the therapist thinks that further work is necessary but the clients do not want to re-engage; we consider this problem in chapter 9.

Problem 11   The Absent Member

Analysis

Different schools of therapy adopt differing stances in relation to absent members. An extreme position is adopted by Palazzoli who assumes that absence is always a manoeuvre which '. . . although carried out by only one member of the family, and apparently on his own initiative, is in reality a total family manoeuvre, in which the rest of the family collaborates' (Palazzoli et al., 1978, p. 117). It is not clear whether Palazzoli is talking solely of families in 'schizophrenic transaction' when she makes this statement, but in practice there may be innumerable reasons why clients absent themselves from sessions. As always, it is more productive to gain accurate information about the absence before trying to understand its theoretical and practical significance. Sometimes there *is* evidence of collusion between the attending family members (or the attending partner) and the non-attending family member (or the non-attending partner). For example, nobody made any attempt to remind a family member to come, although everybody knew that he or she was going to be exceptionally busy on the day of the session. However, on many occasions there seems to have been genuine forgetfulness on the part of the absent member, who was duly contrite when they next attended.

Some absences are the result of the partner or family member not feeling involved in what has been taking place. Often this is the adolescent brother or sister of a younger child who has been presenting problems. The therapist should then not only review what efforts she made to include the adolescent, but also re-assess the reasons for his or her involvement in the sessions. As we suggested in the previous chapter, if the adolescent is in the process of leaving home, it may be more appropriate that they are *not* present. On the other hand, if the member absent from a family session is the father, the therapeutic alliance is in severe danger.

Solutions

Obviously, therapists need to be able to respond flexibly to the wide range of possibilities that they will uncover on assessing the reasons for absence. As we have already mentioned in chapter 2, it is useful to place a chair in the session to symbolize the absent member. If the absent member is a parent or a partner then we usually plan to finish the session early (rather than carrying on as normal) because we want to give the message that the absence is important and that we cannot really get much done without the absentee being present. Our preferred approach to the problem is to try and phone the absent member from the session. This can be very effective because it really brings home to everybody that we mean business when we say that everybody needs to be present. If this proves impossible then we use the energy of the convened members to devise a letter which is then sent off immediately by post. If the convened members advise us that a telephone call or a letter will not work then we agree other approaches, for example making a home visit.

Even if none of these tactics work, possible solutions still remain. For example, if the family or couple was referred by a GP who has a good working relationship with the clients then it may be possible to get the GP to convene a meeting to which everybody will come. Teismann's general advice on convening is, of course, applicable to such situations, but we have the added advantage of being able to use convened family members to evaluate which approaches are likely to work.

☐ Much to the therapist's surprise, a husband failed to turn up for a marital therapy session. Careful discussion with his wife revealed that the therapist had insensitively touched on some personal issues to do with the husband's family of origin in the previous session. He felt that the therapist was threatening to explore this further and had decided that it would be too painful to attend the next session. The therapist showed despair at committing this error and asked the wife to return home immediately to apologize on his behalf. She also agreed to warn her husband that the therapist would make a visit to the house some fifteeen minutes after she had returned. On turning up for the home visit the therapist was able to complete the session, first apologizing for his insensitivity and then carefully negotiating a contract which agreed to put the husband's personal issues on the back burner. Several sessions later the husband spontaneously returned to these topics and agreed to undertake some limited problem solving in this painful area. ☐

As this example demonstrates, when an important member drops out of therapy the therapist must be prepared to apologize and then go back to the initial task of building the therapeutic alliance. In order to do this, she would begin by asking about her clients' experience of the therapy sessions so far, listening carefully and resisting any temptation to defend her approach. It is only if clients feel that criticisms have been heard that they are prepared to give the therapist another chance.

In some cases, a member's absence may represent a real change.

□ Mrs R, a widow in her sixties, who described herself as having been depressed for many years, came to a family therapy session with her divorced only daughter and her granddaughter. The therapist patiently explored the enmeshed relationships between these three in great detail and negotiated a further assessment interview three weeks later.

Three days before the next meeting was due to take place, the therapist received a letter from the older woman saying that she would not be coming because her daughter had said 'I'm never going to that place again'. The therapist telephoned in reply, said he was sorry that he had apparently upset the daughter, and asked for more information about what had gone wrong. Mrs R responded by saying that the meeting had been a disaster because it had been followed by a tremendous row with her daughter who had made great efforts to avoid her ever since. She was now even more worried about her granddaughter than usual because she knew that her daughter couldn't cope without her help.

On asking for more information about the row, the therapist learnt that the daughter had roundly criticized her mother's 'interfering' attitude and said that she hadn't realized quite how much her mother treated her like a child. She had no intention of going to another session to be humiliated in this way. The therapist commented that he could see that Mrs R wanted very much to be a good mother and that she must have been very hurt by her daughter expressing herself so forcefully. However, he could also appreciate that her daughter wanted to change the relationship. He persuaded Mrs R to come to another appointment and also wrote to the daughter who replied politely, but firmly declining the invitation.

Two weeks later an angry and determined Mrs R arrived by herself and announced that she had been 'doing some thinking'. She had concluded that she was fed up with being 'taken for granted' and had decided to set about making a life of her own. In striking contrast to the depressed woman of the previous month, she was energetic and resolute. The therapist encouraged this independent attitude but also suggested to her that she would want to repair the breach with her daughter, if only to resume contact with her granddaughter. Mrs R declined any further sessions but agreed to a review meeting six months later.

At the review meeting, Mrs R reported great progress in reconstructing her own life and also that she had negotiated an arrangement with her daughter to see her granddaughter. Their relationship was strained, but improving. □

As this example illustrates, it is essential to recognize and evaluate what took place during and after the previous session. In this case it was crucial to recognize that changes had taken place – the daughter's absence was not an attempt to sabotage the therapy.

Conclusion

Throughout this chapter we have stressed the importance of the therapeutic alliance, of the therapist and her clients working together co-operatively. We have discussed the therapist's joining skills and argued that it is her responsibility to ensure that the alliance does not fall into disarray. The therapist must monitor the relationship carefully, asking for feedback from her clients, and take steps to resolve problems as they arise, rather than pressing on in the hope that they will disappear. Our consistent experience is that when we approach our clients positively, in the expectation that they want to change, a good working relationship can be established. This is certainly the case in what is, for many therapists, a problem area – working with young children. This is the subject of our next chapter.

Further Reading

The Therapeutic Alliance

Dryden, W. and P. Hunt (1985), 'Therapeutic alliances in marital therapy', in W. Dryden (ed.), *Marital Therapy in Britain* vol. 1, chapters 6 and 7.

Broderick, C. (1983), *The Therapeutic Triangle: A Source Book on Marital Therapy.*

Ethnicity

Barot, R. (1988), 'Social anthropology, ethnicity and family therapy', *Journal of Family Therapy*, 10, 271–282.
Rapoport, R. et al. (eds) (1982) *Families in Britain.*

Social Work Perspectives

Ahmed, S. (1986), 'Cultural racism in work with Asian women and girls', in S. Ahmed et al. (eds), *Social Work with Black Children and Families.*
Ely, P. and D. Denny (1987), *Social Work in a Multi-Racial Society.* Useful chapters on perspectives in social work practice and practical 'face-to-face' issues.

Psychiatric Perspectives

Cox, J. (ed.) (1986), *Transcultural Psychiatry.*
McGoldrick, M. et al. (1982), *Ethnicity and Family Therapy.*
Rack, P. (1982), *Race, Culture and Mental Disorder.*

'Disorganized' Families and Couples

Clark, T. et al. (1982), *Outreach Family Therapy.*
Mattinson, J. and I. Sinclair (1979) *Mate and Stalemate: Working with Marital Problems in a Social Services Department.*

4

Young Children in Therapy

Young children frequently present problems in therapy sessions. This is hardly surprising, since the kind of activity in which therapists and parents typically engage – sitting and talking – is quite alien to most children: therapy is part of the adult world. Involving young children in family therapy is, therefore, a difficult task for the therapist, and their very presence can create problems for the parents too who can feel uncertain about how to behave. In this chapter we will analyse some of the problems and then make some suggestions about how to work effectively, but first we should consider why and when we should involve children in family therapy.

Why Involve Children?

It will be evident in what we have written so far that our theoretical orientation to work with couples and families is based on systems theory. Systems theory asserts that it is impossible to isolate the behaviour of one part of a system from the behaviour of the other parts of that system. So, as we have discussed in chapter 2, we try to involve all members of the system in an effort to resolve the problems experienced by its members. This makes obvious sense when a young child is presented as the problem, for example to a child guidance clinic, when it would appear very odd if the child were to be excluded. (See Carpenter, 1984a; Street, 1985 for discussions of therapy in such settings.) More problematic is the situation in agencies focused on marital problems, such as Marriage Guidance, and on adult psychiatric illness. The question usually asked by the parents, and sometimes by the agency, is: What does it have to do with the children? The answer, from a systems perspective, is that all children, even babies, are affected by the troubles or distress of their parents – a point borne out by research studies on marital discord and psychiatric illness (Rutter and Madge, 1976). Conversely, children can contribute to parents' difficulties. As Lerner and Spanier and their colleagues (1978) have documented, there is considerable empirical support for the influence of children on marital and family interaction.

A familiar example of the relationship between children's difficulties and marital problems is disturbed sleeping (Street, 1985). Such difficulties are very common and may be caused by minor neurological immaturities, noisy neighbours and physical illness as well as emotional worries. Unfortunately, in some cases the parents' attempted solutions to their child's sleeplessness may exacerbate the problem, particularly when they disagree. The child may then become a focus for marital conflict – an example of what family therapists call triangulation. Further, one of the parents may leave the marital bed so that the child can sleep with the other and in this way the child can become a regulator of the intimacy or distance between the partners (Byng-Hall, 1980). Other examples of triangulation are discussed by Street (1985).

Haley (1976) maintains that couples' problems invariably involve a third party and, as we have discussed, this is frequently a child. However, the other corner of the triangle may well be a parent, a lover and even, in more complicated cases, a therapist. As we have stressed in chapter 1, the essential task is to assess who is involved and how, and this includes the identification of such triangles. Obviously, this is an important argument for including young children in the *assessment* of family problems: by seeing them with their parents it becomes possible to assess the nature and extent of their involvement in their parents' problems. Nevertheless, we would draw a distinction between assessment and therapy. If the therapist decides that the major problem lies in another part of the problem system – for example, in the relationship between parents and grandparents – and that the focus of therapy should be there, then the children need not be present. To put it another way, children should only be invited to therapy sessions if their contributions are to be heard and used. As we go on to describe, involving children effectively requires skill and thought from the therapist; without these therapy is an imposition.

What then are the functions of young children in family therapy sessions? We like to identify three: (1) as signallers or 'co-therapists'; (2) as participants in direct work on child–parent relations; (3) to help expand the focus of therapy.

Most of us will have had experience of the refreshingly direct, not to say uncomfortable way in which young children can talk and question. Remarks such as 'I don't want my Daddy to go away' and questions like 'Why are you crying', come straight to the point in a way which can cut through parents' and therapists' tentative or long-winded discussions. But only a part of what children have to communicate is spoken, and the most revealing information, because it is the less conscious, comes through their movement and play. Thus children are particularly sensitive to the tension felt by their parents and will signal this by creating a noisy diversion, becoming quiet and looking sad, asking to go to the lavatory and so on. They may point directly to another family member, directing the therapist's attention to them, or use drawing, puppets or doll figures to act out family conflicts. To an alert therapist, young children are often invaluable allies.

Direct work on the relationships between parents and children in the session is a feature of Minuchin's structural family therapy (Minuchin and Fishman, 1981). As we will elaborate later, the children's presence and their enactment of family problems provide a great opportunity for the therapist to intervene directly to help create alternative solutions.

Finally, children can help the process of therapy by expanding its focus, particularly by lifting the pressure from the family member identified as the problem. It is often easier to discuss a theme or issue such as the giving and receiving of love and affection or the extent of a parent's control of children, in relation to a younger child than to an older one or an adult. Family rules can be explored more straightforwardly and generational boundaries established more easily by referring to the children as a sub-system of the family.

We are recommending, therefore, that young children should be included at least in the assessment of family problems and, if the therapist is ready to elicit and make use of their potential as allies in therapy, they should be included in subsequent sessions too.

Problems

Children are easily left out of family therapy sessions, and thus feel unable to contribute in an adult environment. This can lead to anxiety and distress, frustration and boredom, and misbehaviour. At the same time their parents, who are likely to be aware of a sense of failure or hopelessness in their own relationship and/or their parenting, may be concerned about the therapist's attitude to them, especially if they fear it will be critical. They may not know how they are expected to behave as parents in the session, and become anxious, embarrassed or angry. It is easy to see that in the absence of effective communication and clear guidelines for all, a therapy session with young children can degenerate into chaos or sullen unco-operation on both sides.

However, a lack of skill in relating to young children is not the only reason why therapists are reluctant to include them in therapy. Two others are their own attitudes to and experiences of children and parenting, and their lack of knowledge of children's needs.

Analysis

Therapists' attitudes

O'Brien and Loudon (1985) suggest that therapists, like most adults have an ambivalent attitude to children which oscillates between enjoying their company and wanting to dismiss them. We usually want to communicate with children only on our terms and tend to treat them as unimportant. These attitudes are rooted in Western culture, which – while it has given more attention to the needs of children over the last one hundred years – has increasingly separated them from the rest of society, patronising and undervaluing them. Child-rearing practices have also changed, and a wide range are now used, varying on a continuum from restrictive, Victorian to *laissez-faire* philosophies. Furthermore, different cultural groups have different attitudes to children and child rearing (see Rapoport et al. (eds), 1982), and a therapist from another culture may be entirely ignorant of these. Clearly, one of the main problems in therapy with parents occurs when there is disagreement with the therapist about how the children should be treated, particularly when this disagreement is covert.

Such disagreements about philosophies of child-rearing will result in competition between therapist and parents over who can be the better parent; it may also be related to unresolved issues in the therapist's own life – for example, when she is seduced by the task of 'saving the child' as she perhaps wished that she had been saved from her own parents. As O'Brien and Loudon (1985) observe, we all have painful childhood memories, including fear of the dark, of being lost or left and the frustration and resentment at being thwarted by powerful adults; and these memories can be re-awakened by seeing a child suffer. Again, the therapist's current as well as past experience will subtly influence her behaviour; for example, as a parent herself she may over-identify with the parents' predicament at the expense of understanding the child's.

The difficulty of relating to the needs of both children and adults is sometimes resolved by excluding the children altogether, even when the presenting problem is a child's. Thus, some therapists rationalize that the problem is basically a marital problem expressed through the children; and that since it is the parents who have the power in the family, it is through them that effective interventions will be made (Carpenter and Treacher, 1982). As we have argued above, this position is tenable only if the children have been included in family assessment and the major difficulty located elsewhere; if the presenting problem is the child's then the child must be dealt with as a necessary, integral part of its resolution (Montalvo and Haley, 1973).

Alternatively, the therapist, and also the parents, may exclude children out of a fear that they will be damaged by painful, rejecting or hurtful feelings or revelations. Certainly, as we will argue in relation to secrets, it is wise to respect the parents' opinions concerning their children and to discuss with them the reality of their fears. Nevertheless, as Dare and Lindsey (1979) have pointed out, children are almost always exposed to experiences at home which are more difficult and painful than the structured family meeting with an outsider, the therapist. In our experience, children feel reassured by the therapist's concern for all those present, especially for the support that they themselves receive, and by the hope that the difficulties or worries are being tackled.

Therapists' knowledge

A second set of problems for therapists arises from their ignorance of children's development; disturbingly, this can mirror the ignorance of the parents themselves. Skinner and Castle (1969) reported that abusing parents tend to perceive the vulnerable child as being older and more capable than is developmentally possible. Therapists who demonstrate unrealistic expectations could exacerbate this factor. An important part of therapy for families with young children is helping parents learn how to parent their children. As Gorell Barnes (1984, pp. 73–6) proposes in discussing therapy for child abuse, some education about normal child development can help parents know what to expect of their children and how to help them. Needless to say, we think that such knowledge is essential for family therapists, too (Stratton, 1988).

Therapists' skill

McDermott and Char (1974), in an influential critique, castigated family therapists who treated children simply as miniature adults, expecting them to sit still for an hour or more and to answer complicated questions; the skills of making contact with children and providing them with opportunities to express their own needs were not being developed. As Dare and Lindsey (1979) suggest, family therapy could easily deteriorate into marital therapy in the presence of the children – the result of the therapist being most comfortable when in verbal communication with adults. There is no doubt that communicating with children is a skill in itself, but even therapists who have acquired such skills in previous training may find that these are difficult to exercise when they are simultaneously required to communicate with adults. They may feel that the parents are intruding and hampering the formation of their relationship with the child and may experience them as 'insensitive' or 'rejecting'. Alternatively, they might worry that their ability to relate to and 'understand' the child might make the parents feel inadequate. Finally, their attempts to interpret the child to the parents may be disqualified; the parents too have seen what has been happening in the session and will have their own interpretation of its meaning.

The therapist's lack of skill may, on the other hand, be a matter of dealing with difficult or disruptive children, and there is no denying that some children are more than a handful! We have had experience of children attempting to destroy electrical equipment, climbing out of a first-floor window, chanting the words of a pop song and refusing to speak at all. There is nothing quite so undermining of a therapist's self-confidence as a group of children out of control.

There are a number of possible reasons for children's disruptive behaviour: it may be a protest, an expression of boredom, a way of centring attention on themselves and diverting it from elsewhere;

on the other hand, it may simply be their usual behaviour. As we have already stated, an adult therapy session is an unnatural environment for a child and, unless the therapist makes it clear that she is interested in the child's contribution, the result will be an ordeal for all concerned. At the same time, it must be emphasized that the disruptive behaviour is part of a child's contribution to the session and merits consideration in its own right. The following example illustrates this.

□ A mother sat helplessly while her four children, all under eight years old, marched around the therapy room chanting the words of a pop song. They had succeeded in interrupting her attempts to explain her difficulty in managing without the help of her absent husband. The words of the song, delivered in a robotic voice, were: 'I am your automatic lover, automatic lover'. The children's message was either a protest at the lack of affection they were receiving or, possibly, a comment on their mother's resort to occasional prostitution as a method of supplementing her income. □

Similarly, when the child's difficult behaviour has been the reason for referral, the demonstration of an aspect of that behaviour should be seen as a most helpful contribution to therapy, since it offers a direct opportunity to initiate change. It gives the therapist the chance to observe the family patterns and to help the parents work out new solutions, as we will discuss later. It is most important to understand the child's behaviour in relation to what else has been taking place; in other words, to identify the sequences of behaviour involving other family members. Frequently, the child's behaviour will have been triggered by signs of anxiety or tension on the part of one or both of the parents which then disappear after the distraction. Such sequences can be noticed with very young children and even babies.

□ A four-month-old boy repeatedly disrupted a family session involving his mother, her five older children, his maternal grandmother and his mother's boyfriend. He would sit contentedly for a while on the lap of his mother, his eldest sister and his grandmother; but then, quite suddenly, he would wail inconsolably and struggle to be free. The noise, which was dramatic, could not be put down to hunger or pain and was disconcerting for everyone present. Eventually the baby would be calmed by his mother and would remain with her, usually to the end of the session. This happened in three successive family meetings, but its significance was not appreciated until an analysis of the videotape recording was made in a supervision session. The analysis revealed the following sequence: grandmother criticized her daughter as an 'inadequate' mother; boyfriend intervened to attack grandmother and an argument ensued between these two; baby whimpered and struggled in whoever's lap he was sitting; grandmother reached forward towards him, or if she was holding him, clutched on to him more tightly; mother or sister held baby more tightly; baby cried and struggled more forcefully. This sequence was obscured by the escalating argument between grandmother and mother's boyfriend which became the focus of attention until the baby began to wail loudly as described above. Once recognized as part of the family pattern, the baby's behaviour could easily be understood as an aspect of the struggle over who was to parent him – mother or grandmother – and over the boyfriend's place in family. (He was not, incidentally, the baby's father.) □

We suggest, therefore, that rather than viewing children's behaviour as disruptive and a nuisance, we recognize it as their unique contribution to the therapy, a contribution that is all the more useful because it is not filtered through the more sophisticated intellectual processes of adults. How then can we ensure that children's contributions can be encouraged and heard?

Solutions

Involving children in therapy

The first point, which we wish to stress, is that therapists should ask parents to bring their children to therapy sessions only if they, the therapists, are clear why they are making the request. What is the purpose of involving the children in any given interview? The answer may be, for example, in order to assess family relationships or, at a later stage, to undertake direct work on teaching communication or managing difficult behaviour. If there is no such answer, or if the goals of the interview could more easily be achieved without them, then it is foolish to invite them.

The reasons for including the children should be given to the parents, since it is their responsibility to decide whether to trust their children to the therapist. If the parents are reluctant, then rather than label them resistant, the therapist should consider them conscientious and examine the reasons she has offered for the children's involvement. The therapist's first move should therefore be to join with them and to understand their views on the problem and the help that has been offered. Such an approach is especially important in engaging families whose members are subject to statutory orders or who are listed in registers of actual or potential child abusers. Parents of such families are justifiably suspicious of outside intervention, since they face the real risk of losing all their parental functions and responsibilities. As we indicated in chapter 2, there is no golden rule which stipulates that the first interview should always be with 'all the family', and in many cases the first session or sessions will appropriately take place without the children.

□ A man was referred with his wife to a marital therapy service by a psychiatrist because of his violent temper. During the course of the first three meetings it emerged that one of the most sensitive triggers of his temper was his five-year-old daughter's 'disobedience'. He described himself as becoming almost incapacitated by rage and by resentment of his wife's attempts to mollify these incidents. Through discussion, the couple began to see his temper in terms of a pattern of family interaction rather than as a product of his psychiatric illness. Only at this point did the therapist propose including the daughter on the grounds that she needed to understand what made her father angry and he to understand her 'disobedience'. □

At their first meeting with the therapist the children may be quite in the dark as to what is going on. Bloch (1976) cites an example where the children had been told that they were going to see the therapist in order to 'wish him a happy holiday'! One of us had sessions in a building which included a dental clinic, and it was not uncommon for children to think that they were coming to see the dentist. Similarly, children visited at home by a social worker or probation officer may have been informed that they are going to be 'taken away'.

It is, therefore, very useful to ask the children whether their parents explained the purpose of the visit to them. If they have not been told, or have been given an inaccurate reason, then the therapist can immediately begin an exploration of family relationships by suggesting to the children that they should ask their parents, or alternatively, asking the parents to explain to their children. The temptation, of course, is for the therapist to cast herself in the role of expert and explain to the children why they need to be there. This trap should be avoided as it implicitly places the parents in a subordinate position.

From the first moment she meets the children, the therapist can begin to formulate ideas about the family. Not only is it important to notice *where* they sit (this will give some preliminary ideas about family structure) but also *how* they sit: stiffly, hunched up, relaxed or, indeed, whether they sit at all. Do they greet the therapist or hide behind one of their parents, or a chair, or run out of the room? Minuchin (1974), arguing within the structural framework, insists that the first task is to accommodate to the family: 'To join a family system, the therapist must accept the family's organisation and style and blend with them'. If one of the parents puts him or herself forward strongly as the leader of the family then the therapist should respect that position and make her initial contact with the children through that parent. Alternatively, the parents may hold back as one of their children approaches the therapist, as if waiting to see how the child will be dealt with before committing themselves. In general it is worth stating that beyond the making of an initial contact with each member, usually to discover names and perhaps to touch, there is no rule as to how one should proceed. It is, however, generally useful to seek the parents' 'permission' first before carrying out any probe. Thus, although formats for the initial interview have been suggested (for example, Haley, 1976), they may not be appropriate for all families: asking each member of the family in turn what they think are the problems may in some cases be quite unhelpful and even disastrous. The following is a good example of this point.

☐ A family consisting of two daughters (aged seven and nine), their father and their stepmother attended a family counselling service. The presenting problem was the refusal of the two children to communicate with their stepmother, who felt very angry at their rejection of her. (Their own mother had committed suicide during a period of depression following the birth of the second child.) This family had previously been in treatment with a child guidance team which had unfortunately got into a fight with the stepmother over the issue of whether the children's behaviour was normal or not, given the context of the sudden loss of their own mother. At the first interview the stepmother was extremely angry and demanded that the therapist's supervisor should enter the room from behind the one-way screen and that videotaping should not occur. Normal joining techniques involving the whole family were clearly impossible in this situation – instead the therapists accepted the stepmother's position unconditionally by saying that they clearly understood that she had not been helped previously, and asked her to guide them so that they could be sure not to make the same mistakes. This approach, combined with a simple labelling of the children's behaviour as understandable but disrespectful, enabled the stepmother to relax and contribute very positively to the session. The therapists maintained their therapeutic alliance with the stepmother throughout the session, and only attempted to join the children towards the end of the session when the stepmother and father jointly gave permission for the therapists to show them how the one-way screen worked. The success of the tactic was confirmed at the end of the session when one of the girls spontaneously began to talk to her stepmother about an event which occurred at school the previous day. □

One of the frequent problems which faces beginning family therapists concerns their being quickly drawn into the family's pattern of organization. Typically, what happens is that the parents give a description of their child's 'strange' or 'wicked' behaviour and then they and the therapist turn to the child to ask for an explanation. Although the therapist may at a theoretical level consider the problems from an interactional perspective, she can reinforce the child's behaviour by agreeing that the child is responsible for providing an 'explanation'. Usually the child responds with an answer which confirms his madness or badness, or alternatively refuses to speak or provide any explanation.

The other reason why children do not respond to a therapist's questions may well be that they simply do not understand them. Developmental psychologists and teachers have long been aware that cognitive and linguistic abilities develop throughout childhood and adolescence. Children are unlikely, therefore, to make much sense of the kind of abstract questions and interpretations used by adult-orientated therapists. It will be more fruitful to concentrate on short, concrete questions that are easy to answer. It may be useful to pose a question which suggests alternative answers, but not to fall into the trap of continuing in this vein so that questioning becomes a guessing game. It is best to make more demands by gradually increasing the complexity of the information required, or to ask 'open' questions which require more lengthy answers. As with adults, if you ask children long-winded questions, the answers will be very short. Fortunately, children are adept at answering the kind of questions in which an interactional therapist is interested. The 'What happens when . . . ?' questions, through which the therapist can build up a picture of the sequences of family interaction, are particularly productive. It is here that children can often be much more helpful than their parents.

The task that confronts the therapist at this point is joining and forming the 'therapeutic system' in which she has a position of leadership or co-leadership. The therapist is perhaps best described as a 'guide', who leads with the consent or permission of the family. It is important to remember that the rules of the therapeutic system will be unfamiliar to the family. This may be highlighted by considering therapy in the family's home. In this case the therapist may have to seek the family's permission in breaking the normal rules of social intercourse: declining a cup of tea until after the session; asking for the television to be switched off and the chairs to be moved so that they can see each other; requesting that they should all stay in the room for the duration of the session.

In the clinic or office, on the other hand, the family may also be uncertain about how to behave. From the parents' point of view, bringing their children to therapy may feel like bringing themselves as parents as well. If the children behave badly they may be unsure whether they or the therapist should discipline them. Perhaps the therapist wants to see, or they want the therapist to see, just how difficult the children can be. (It is not unusual at the end of a session for the parents to remark that their children are much worse at home – rather like taking a car to the mechanic and finding that the squeaking or vibration disappears as soon as you drive it into the garage.) On the other hand, the parents may be embarrassed or annoyed by the children's poor behaviour or silence and unfriendliness, and reprimand them. However, it is crucial to remember that the parents are not simply controlling the children, but also showing the therapist how they control the children. If parents seem uncertain about dealing with their children the therapist should say, 'What do you usually do at home when this happens?' and invite the parents to deal with the interaction. The resulting sequences of behaviour will enable the therapist to see how the family members deal with the management of the children.

Dealing with disruptive behaviour

We have argued that the children's disruptive behaviour should be recognized as their unique contribution to therapy rather than simply as a nuisance; as such it should be used therapeutically. However, one of the most important principles of good therapy is to choose the right focus at the right time. If, therefore, the therapist has become engaged with the parents in a discussion about whether their marriage should continue, then to change focus in order to deal with the children will almost certainly be ill-advised. Their problems in managing their offspring are secondary to their marriage. In this instance it would be better to exclude children, taking them to play elsewhere and arranging that they do not attend the next session.

On the other hand, if the presenting problem is one of controlling the children then their behaviour provides an ideal opportunity for direct in-session work on this problem. The therapist's task becomes that of coaching the parents in managing the children's behaviour, a task that depends on conveying support and encouragement as well as resisting any temptation to take over and show how it is done.

□ A young mother and her common-law husband had been referred to a social services department following the physical abuse of the woman's four-year-old daughter. The social worker saw all three at home with the intention of undertaking therapeutic work with the family. She found it difficult to get started talking to the adults because the little girl kept shouting at the mother, demanding that she take notice. The mother retorted, telling her to 'shut up', but with no apparent effect on the noise. Soon she was having to shout to make herself heard by the therapist, stopping only to yell at her daughter from time to time. Suddenly her husband, who until this point had been sitting with his head between his hands, leapt out of his chair and said between clenched teeth, 'If you don't stop that bloody kid . . .'. His voice trailed off and he sat down.

This sequence clearly illustrated the dynamics of the child's abuse. The temptation would be to rescue her by giving her attention and perhaps something to do whilst the adults could continue talking. Instead, the incident was used as an opportunity to empower rather than to undermine the mother any further. The therapist said, 'Yes, it is a little difficult to talk above the noise, and what you've been telling me is very important, so do you think you could help her find something to do.' Quietening her child was not easy but, with encouragment, the mother achieved it – not by shouting but by sitting her on her lap and talking gently to her. A little later the girl spontaneously moved over to the man and showed him a toy. □

Play and enactment

The importance of play in solving the problem of finding effective ways of communicating with children in the session cannot be overstressed. It has long been recognized that children communicate extensively through play, which can therefore provide a rich source of information and an opportunity for therapeutic interventions. The provision of even a few toys will quickly reveal patterns of conflict and co-operation among chidren. Do they share the toys or fight over them? Perhaps two will play together, excluding a third. Is there any stable pattern, or do they keep changing? How quickly do their parents become involved in the play?

Conflict between the children may be followed by an intervention from one or both parents, who may take the side of one child against the other(s). This intervention may have been solicited by a child, or it may be an inappropriate interference in sibling affairs. The most important question concerns the context in which it has taken place: the therapist must continue to be aware of the sequence of the family's behaviour. Thus, the therapist may observe two children playing quietly together with a doll's house, when the father suddenly interrupts to chide his son for being 'cissy'. This action might remain puzzling if the therapist has failed to note that it followed the beginning of a marital dispute.

In other words, whatever the *content* of the child's play, the therapist's first concern should be for its interactional *context*. This is not to deny that the content may be very interesting in itself, but the information will be greatly enhanced if one is aware of what else is going on in the room. Children will often illustrate what their parents have to say either pictorially or by having dolls or animals act out the behaviour described. (Jenkins and Donnelly, 1983, and Zilbach, 1986, provide detailed accounts of understanding the drawings produced by young children in family sessions.)

From the therapist's standpoint play can provide an excellent and enjoyable means of joining children, and as such achieves one of the therapist's initial objectives. However, it is only a means to an end, for the eventual goal of therapy is not that the children should establish a good friendly relationship with the therapist but rather that they should establish or re-establish a better relationship with their *parents*. Thus, while it may be 'meaningful' for the therapist to play with the children, it is usually much more effective for the therapist to concentrate on facilitating the parents and children playing together. This task is one that many therapists seem to avoid. It may represent the therapist's, or indeed the parents' opinion, that play is not 'serious' and that therapy must concentrate on the content of verbal communication. Alternatively, it may be that the therapist, accurately or otherwise, senses a difficulty that a family has in playing together and is wary of exposing this problem.

Inviting members of a family to play together should come naturally out of the context of the session, in exactly the same way as they might be asked to talk together. Similarly, the therapist must be prepared to set the stage: ensuring that the materials are available, adjusting the seating positions, encouraging a parent to get down on the floor, blocking the interference of another family member and intervening in the action to facilitate, punctuate, re-frame, and help create the new experience of a relationship. Once again, it is the process of play more than the content which provides the most interesting information. Play involving two people requires sensitivity to space, intensity and timing. To be successful it requires co-operation and, on the adult's part, a reasonable assessment of the child's capabilities and appropriate help, encouragement and praise.

☐ During one session the therapist had asked the parents to discuss the father's absence from home on long-distance lorry trips, and what happened when he came home. The six-year-old son had been playing with Lego bricks and approached his mother for help in making a roof for a house. She remarked that she was 'no good at Lego' and then ignored him. The boy then approached the therapist, who suggested that he ask his father. The therapist gestured to the father that he should help, at which the father remarked that his son hardly ever asked him for help when he was at home. The father then picked up the bricks and quickly and efficiently built an elaborate roof and tower. In order to do this he had to demolish one wall and rebuild it. Throughout he made no reference to his son who, when the building was finished, grabbed it and broke off the tower, stamping his foot on the floor. At this point the father turned to the therapist with an exasperated look, as the mother intervened to criticize the child's ungrateful behaviour.

The therapist ignored the mother and addressed the boy, saying that his father was obviously a good builder but he did not know that you do not put towers on a garage. Perhaps they could start again, but this time he should explain to Daddy what he was trying to build so that they could then plan and build it *together*.

Advising the mother that she had 'earned a rest', the therapist then encouraged the boy and his father to discuss the different types of house they might build. He complimented the father on his son's imagination, suggesting that this was a quality they shared, and then asked him to find out how practical he could be. Predictably, as the therapist praised the father, so he in turn began to praise his son's achievements, indicating that the therapist's structural manoeuvre had, for the moment, succeeded in creating a new pattern of behaviour within the family. ☐

Play is not, then, an end in itself, but instead may be a part of the overall therapeutic plan to re-structure the family. Its value lies in its general acceptability to children and its richness as a metaphor for many aspects of family life. As O'Brien and Loudon (1985) describe, it is an effective means for the therapist to communicate to the children. Visual aids may be used such as mobiles (to illustrate interdependence), balancing scales (to illustrate complementary roles or perceptions) and families of dolls (for sculpting relationships). Similarly, games can be effective both as 'warm-ups' and for learning such things as mutual trust (for example, 'blind' walks), how to manage success and failure (snakes and ladders) and allowing every family member to have his or her say (only the one with the cushion may talk).

Conclusion

We believe that young children should be included in the assessment of family problems and should be brought into marital therapy if it appears that they are an important part of a couple's difficulties. However, they must be involved purposively so that effective work can and does take place, and this requires the therapist to have basic skills in including the children in the therapy session.

Further Reading

Combrinck-Graham, L. (ed.) (1986), *Treating Young Children in Family Therapy*. Short papers, with case examples, including children with chronic illness and disability, elective mutism and those in foster homes.

Dare, C. and C. Lindsey (1979), 'Children in family therapy', *Journal of Family Therapy*, 1, 253–69. Using interpretations of children's behaviour in sessions.

O'Brien, A. and P. Loudon (1985), 'Redressing the balance – involving children in family therapy', *Journal of Family Therapy*, 7, 81–98. Describes the use of visual aids, including mobiles and scales.

Stratton, P. (1988), 'Circles and spirals: the contribution of developmental psychology to family therapy', *Journal of Family Therapy*, 10, 207–31. A comprehensive review with an abundance of references.

Zilbach, J. (1986), *Young Children in Family Therapy*. A psycho-dynamic approach with useful ideas about drawings.

5

Secrets

Secrets are both intriguing and alarming: intriguing when they seem to offer the therapist the key to understanding the family puzzle; alarming when the price is being drawn into a conspiracy of silence with the consequent loss of therapeutic control. Secrets have the fascination and the fear of a spider's web, but – knowing the danger of becoming trapped – we tend to steer clear.

Revelation and Concealment of Secrets

Problems

The main problems concerning secrets are:

1 How to handle a secret revealed in the referral information or at the initial contact with one member of the couple or family.
2 How to deal with the offer of a secret revelation.

In our experience both these situations are common, and the following are examples of how they can arise:

□ The referring agent writes: 'Mr and Mrs X are very concerned about their daughter Y. . . . During the course of their consultation with me, they explained that Y was not actually Mr X's child, having been born as a result of her mother's previous liaison with another man. They emphasized that Y did not know this and they asked for my undertaking not to reveal this information to her.' □
□ Mr S, meeting the therapist for the first time in an individual interview, reveals that the cause of his anxiety and depression is that he has been having an extra-marital affair, about which he now feels guilty and fearful, particularly as his lover is also

promiscuous and he worries that she might have AIDS. He tells the therapist that his wife has no knowledge of the affair and that he intends to keep it secret because 'it would destroy our marriage'. □

Similarly, during the course of therapy, one member of the couple or family might ask to have a 'private word' with the therapist on the telephone or before or after a session.

□ A parent telephones after a first family meeting and speaks to the therapist: 'I couldn't say this in front of my daughter, but . . .'. □

□ A husband hangs around in the room at the end of a marital therapy session and asks for 'a couple of minutes' with the therapist. □

What is common to all these examples is that the therapist is told, or is offered, a secret on the more or less explicit understanding that the secret will not be revealed. In accepting the secret the therapist, wittingly or unwittingly, becomes involved in a deception – she is expected to feign ignorance of the secret information in the presence of those who do not know and in so doing becomes secretly allied to her informant. Furthermore, as Palazzoli and Prata (1982) point out, such secret or denied coalitions are established *against* someone or some people. Far from being neutral or impartial, the therapist now becomes a partisan actor in the family conflict.

Once party to the secret, the therapist can feel 'trapped' by her informant: if she refuses to honour the injunction to keep the secret, she risks alienating a powerful member of the system; if she accepts her place in the denied coalition, she not only loses the opportunity to use the information to therapeutic advantage, but also becomes beholden to her informant and risks the accidental or deliberate uncovering of the conspiracy. The fear that her 'deception' of the unaware members of the family will be revealed can become a powerful weapon in the hands of her informant, who can at any time expose her untrustworthiness to the others. The threat of such exposure can become a form of blackmail.

Alternatively, the therapist, rightly or wrongly, can come to believe in the consequences of the revelation anticipated by her informant – be they the destruction of a marriage, insanity or suicide. Unfortunately, this fear is compounded by a sense of powerlessness: how can the problem be resolved if the secret is not made known? But if the secret is made known, the consequences will be disastrous.

Analysis

For Palazzoli and Prata (1982) the offer of secret revelations is one of the snares of family therapy: to accept such a revelation is a 'great error, since it means accepting a denied co-alition'. In their paper they describe the tactics they have devised to 'foil' this kind of snare with reference to a case example from their Centre.

□ The offer to reveal a secret came in the form of a letter delivered in person, from the successful, professional aunt of a family invited for therapy. The therapist, Dr Selvini-Palazzoli, invited the aunt into the session, thanked her for coming and remarked that she (the aunt) would '. . . certainly be able to supply a great deal of information', telling all she could in front of the family. If there were things she could not say, she would be 'well advised not to say them, not even to Dr Selvini'. She comments, 'This communication is given in a hearty and neutral tone, as if imparting a routine instruction'. At the end of this family session, the therapists invited only the nuclear family to the next meeting, 'dismissing' the aunt, to the evident satisfaction of her sister-in-law, the mother in the family. The description of the case continues with other successful foilings of the aunt's 'manipulations', including a telephone call from her which is cut short with the following interruption by the therapist: '. . . before you continue, I must inform you about something. Everything you tell me on the phone I shall have to relate in full during the next session with your brother's family. You must know this, because this is the routine procedure we have adopted at our Centre. Knowing this, you may act accordingly.' □

In commenting on the above case, Palazzoli and Prata emphasize the importance of avoiding, on the verbal and especially the non-verbal level, attitudes or tones of voice implying 'moralistic' messages to the potential informer. They observe that it risks making a powerful enemy not only of the informer, but also in this case of the family member with whom the therapists assume she is covertly aligned. Nevertheless, it is difficult to square these comments with the distinctly negative connotation ascribed to the aunt's behaviour by the authors in their description. As we noted in the introductory chapter to this book, the language is drawn from the battlefield: the encounters with the aunt are described as 'skirmishes' and the therapist's task as being to 'foil her manipulations'. Furthermore, the thrust of the therapist's interventions was, in structural terms, to define a boundary between nuclear and extended family: the aunt was 'dismissed'.

However, in spite of the above reservations about their case study, Palazzoli and Prata do highlight the crucial relationship aspects of secrets: 'The important information is the fact that there is somebody offering us a co-alition ... In the light of such information ... even the content of the alleged revelation becomes of secondary importance.' But, are all secrets 'snares' and all attempts to share them with therapists intended maliciously? Is the therapist's only solution to foil their expression, and, if so, where does that leave the therapist who has inadvertently stumbled into them? In order to answer these questions, we will first of all examine the nature of secrets more closely, drawing on a very useful article by Karpel (1980).

Secrets, privacy and boundaries

Karpel offers a simple typology of secrets in terms of the boundaries created in the system of relationships: individual, internal and shared family secrets. Individual secrets are kept by one member from the rest of the family: an extra-marital affair is a good example. Internal secrets are those kept by at least two members from at least one other: for example, the secret about a child's parentage described above. Shared secrets are known by all the family but kept from the outside world – secrets such as alcoholism, illegitimacy or homosexuality. We would add that very often such secrets, although known by all, are never discussed and family members pretend that they do not know, not only to outsiders but also to each other. It is for this reason that it is sometimes asserted that there is no such thing as a secret in a family – they all know. As Karpel's classification indicates, this is sometimes, but not always, the case, and it is a mistake for the therapist to assume that they 'really' know. Finally, we should remember, following Pincus and Dare (1978, p. 9), that secrets are not necessarily factual events: they may arise as fantasies from strong emotional feelings which have had to be kept secret.

From a structural perspective, secrets are important in that they create or strengthen boundaries within families, and between families and outsiders. For example, a secret incestuous relationship between father and daughter creates a boundary between daughter and mother (as well as father and mother) that distances them both at a time when the daughter needs her mother's protection. These boundaries, as Karpel notes, depend not only on who knows the secret but on knowing who knows. Thus, two members of the family who have separately been sworn to secrecy by a third will not know that the other knows, and the boundary between them will be just as real as if one had known and the other had not.

Of course some secrets are quite benign – the 'secret' of Father Christmas, for example – and much other information is 'private' rather than secret. Cultural and moral values and assumptions enter here, and these will be different for different families and individuals and at different stages of the life cycle. For some, the free sharing of information will be a strong obligation; for others, considerable privacy will be emphasized. So what makes a secret? We would suggest that a secret violates a particular family's rules about sharing information and that such violation provokes at least a measure of guilt at the deception.

Thus, if a couple has agreed to practise an 'open' marriage, whereby each partner is free to engage in extra-marital affairs, then they might also agree that the details of these affairs are 'private'. On the other hand, if the assumption is one of marital fidelity, then the concealment of an affair is a matter of secrecy rather than privacy. We would agree with Karpel that the distinction hinges also on the *relevance* of the secret information for those who do not know it. In the second case, the affair is extremely relevant in that it threatens the very basis of the marriage, and the perpetrator, knowing this, feels guilt. Similarly, it might be argued that partners' sexual affairs before meeting and marrying one another are private if they have no implications for the marriage. But if one partner discovers that a previous partner has developed AIDS, or if that earlier relationship had been psychologically damaging and was affecting the current marriage, then to withhold that relevant information would be being secretive.

Judgements concerning whether or not the family rule about sharing information has been violated and about the relevance of the information for the other parties, are not easy to make; and they do, of course, have to be made by the holders of the secret. This difficulty is compounded by the usually expressed wish to protect either the other parties or the relationship itself, although naturally this wish will include self-protection.

What we trust is emerging from this discussion of secrets is that the example quoted by Palazzoli and Prata is very much a special case. There are at least three main types of secret, and these in turn pose different kinds of problems for their holders. The attempt to share secrets with a therapist is not necessarily a snare laid with malicious intent; it is far more likely to be an effort to express guilt and confusion. The wish to protect oneself and others from the feared consequences of revealing a secret is only too human – for the therapist to view it as a devious manipulation which must be foiled is to take up a very cynical position, one which denies the opportunity to help in a troubling matter. This is not to deny that becoming involved in the discussion of a secret, whether of the secret itself or simply of its existence, carries the risk of becoming trapped in a coalition. Nevertheless, it is our belief and experience that a therapist can maintain a sympathetic, supportive and yet impartial position, and that this carries the best hope for a resolution of the problem.

Solutions

As we have stated above, our position is to assume that when someone reveals, or offers to reveal, a secret it is because they are genuinely troubled. They are troubled by guilt and/or fear of the consequences for themselves and others of revealing the information. With this assumption, we can see that the therapist's task is to help the holder(s) of the secret to manage the secret either by revealing it appropriately and considerately or, in certain cases, by deciding in good faith that it should remain concealed. What is required is that the therapist help the holder of the secret to examine the implications of both its existence and nature for the other involved people. This implies helping the holder to see it from the others' point of view and distinguishing that from his or her own: to establish who is really being protected and from what. Finally, the therapist should help with the decision about when and what to reveal. We will quote two case examples to illustrate this process. The first concerns a secret which is revealed during the course of family therapy, the second is known to the therapist in advance.

An extra-marital affair

□ A depressed woman had been referred for family therapy and attended with her husband and two children, who were in the process of leaving home. Following the second session, the husband telephoned the therapist, asking to see him privately. He stated that there was something he wanted to tell, but that he could not do so in front of his wife and children. Without inquiring what the secret was about, the therapist asked the husband to consider who he was trying to protect by concealing it. The latter said that it was his wife, but with further prompting he acknowledged,
—And me too.
—Does your wife have a right to know?
—Yes, I suppose so, but . . .
—You're worried about how to do it and what the consequences will be?
—Yes, I think it will be the last straw for her.
—Well, I'd be prepared to help you consider the likely consequences and to help you plan how to tell her. I'll see you separately, but only with her knowledge, and I'll also give her the opportunity to see me separately too.
    In the individual sessions, the husband revealed that he had been having an affair with his wife's 'best friend'. He contended that it had no great emotional significance for him – it was 'just for sex', albeit homosexual sex. It was but one of a number of secret homosexual affairs he had had over the last few years since discovering his sexual interest in other men. He emphasized that he remained committed to his wife and family, and that he was consumed with guilt and the fear that he would be found out and the disastrous consequences that this revelation would have for his wife's mental health and on his relationship with his children. The therapist's task here was difficult but straightforward. He helped the husband to consider what had happened from his wife's and children's perspectives, to anticipate the consequences of his revelation and to plan the circumstances in which he would tell them.

The wife, in her individual sessions, expressed a great deal of anxiety about what her husband might have to say, and the therapist supported her in anticipating the worst possible information and its consequences. She concluded that, no matter how angry she might be with him, she didn't want to lose him. When he did tell her, privately, at home, she was indeed almost beside herself with anger, which her husband did not try to suppress. However, over time the anger did subside and was replaced by a real effort on the part of each to re-negotiate and re-vitalize their relationship, with continuing help from the therapist. □

In reviewing this example, what we want to emphasize is that, far from being a snare, dealing with the secret was the essence of this marital therapy. It would have been unhelpful and inappropriate to resist the husband's overture as a manipulation or to insist that the revelation be made promptly in a conjoint session. Of course, not all marriages will survive the revelation of extra-marital affairs. Pestrak et al. (1985), in a review of the (American) literature, noted that when divorce does occur it is usually because the extra-marital sex was designed to break up the marriage in instances when one partner could not openly or directly leave his mate. Sprenkle and Weis (1978) even assert that the revelation of past affairs to an unknowing spouse is usually 'counterproductive'. However, given our discussion of the relevance of such secret information to the ignorant party, such a position can be defensible on moral grounds only if the affairs pre-date the existing marital relationship, in which case they can appropriately be considered as private rather than secret. If they have occurred during the relationship then they are probably in breach of the rules about sharing information, and their concealment inevitably creates a boundary in the relationship, the result of 'living a lie'. On the other hand, as Humphrey (1981) states, it is not the prerogative of therapists to decide when, or if, affairs should be 'confessed'. The task of the therapist, as distinct from that of a moral or religious counsellor, is, in our view at least, to help the client weigh up the advantages and disadvantages of a particular action – in this case the immediate rupture of the relationship, with a hope of reconciliation, as against living a lie in a relationship that depends on trust. This is not to say that the therapist is obliged to go along with what her client decides. If she cannot accept a man's decision to continue deceiving his wife whilst

at the same time protesting his fidelity, then she should state that
she can no longer continue to work therapeutically with him.

A question of parentage

Here we would like to consider an instance when the referring
agent, a GP, conveyed the secret of a child's true parentage in the
referral letter, from which we quoted at the beginning of this
section. This is a clear example of an internal secret, kept by two
members of a family, the parents, from at least one other – the
daughter. The secret had then been shared with someone outside
the family system, the GP, but it was not clear from the letter
whether or not the parents had given their permission for the
information to be imparted to the therapist. In our experience this
should always be checked; and, if it is not the case, the referrer
should be asked to see the client(s) again in order to obtain such
permission and to explain the reasons for so doing. If secrecy is an
issue in a family, then particular care should be taken with
confidentiality if the therapist is going to gain their trust.

In line with what we emphasized above, the therapist's first
concern was with the relevance to the daughter of the information
that her father was not her biological father. In this particular case,
the relevance was not immediate in the direct sense of involving
the daughter's right to know – she was only seven years old. It
seemed reasonable to argue, as had the parents, that it was justifiable
to protect her from the information: to be told that her Daddy was
not her 'real' Daddy, that her real father had left when she was six
months old and that he had not seen her since, would have been
unsettling to say the least. A child of seven could not be expected
to handle such information; but, of course, if she had been ten
years older, it would have been a very different story.

Why then had the parents imparted the information to the GP?
What was the relevance for them? On the basis of our assumption
that if someone reveals a secret they are troubled, the therapist
guessed that the mother felt guilty about having kept the secret and
feared having to tell her daughter in due course; perhaps she wanted
reassurance and help? Secondly, it seemed probable that the parents
had offered the information to the doctor in the hope that it would
shed light on their daughter's troubling behaviour: perhaps her
mother feared it was 'bad blood', or that the girl would turn out
like her despised father? Perhaps the husband was (or his wife felt

he was) withdrawing from his part in caring for the girl on the 'unconscious' grounds that she was not 'his' child? It was with these speculations in mind that the therapist decided to offer an initial meeting with the parents on their own, in order to learn about and discuss their fears and to plan the therapy accordingly. In this particular case, the major issue was the extent to which the wife felt unsupported by her husband in managing not just the daughter but also the other demands of family life, at a time when he had become increasingly preoccupied with his own business concerns. The question of parentage was essentially a functional rather than a biological one.

In both these examples, of an individual and an internal family secret, the therapist held sessions with sub-systems of the family; there was no demand for 'openness', for revealing all in a family meeting. As we argued previously, it is a mistake to equate family therapy with conjoint family interviews, always seeing all the family together. As we have demonstrated, this is particularly true in work with families who have secrets. This is true even when the secret is shared, when they all know but feel constrained to keep the secret from the outside world. Cases of incest provide a particularly difficult example of secrets which are shared but then denied, as the following case illustrates.

A *shared secret of incest*

☐ An eight-year-old girl hinted to her teacher through pictures drawn in class that she was being molested by her father, but clammed up when questioned. Nevertheless, the teacher was sufficiently convinced to speak to the visiting schools social worker and they asked the child's mother into school for a joint interview. The mother was visibly shaken, and said little beyond that she would speak to her daughter.

The following morning mother and father came to the school and demanded to see the class teacher and the headmaster. The father verbally attacked the teachers for 'meddling' in his family's affairs, accusing them of having 'dirty minds' and vehemently denying any implication of sexual abuse on his part. He insisted on seeing his daughter's pictures and proceeded to denounce her as a 'dirty little slut'. At this point his wife left the room, returning a few moments later with the girl,

instructing her to 'tell the truth'. Not surprisingly, the frightened
child denied that the pictures were anything to do with her
father, saying, unconvincingly, that they were something she
had 'seen on TV'. □

It should be emphasized that a pattern of disclosure followed by
denial is common and can be seen as two of the characteristic
stages of a child's adaptation to incest (Summit, 1983). Secrecy,
helplessness, entrapment, and accommodation to the abuse are
followed eventually by unconvincing and often conflicting disclosure
and then retraction. In this case it was not possible to say whether
or not the mother knew the secret before the girl's disclosure via
the teacher; however, it seems highly probable that if she did not,
she would certainly have gone away from the first meeting to think
out what evidence there was to support or deny the suggestion of
incest. It is likely that at this point the secret became shared – they
all knew – although this is not to say, of course, that she and her
husband acknowledged its truth: they probably did not, because
the consequences would have been too great. As the Kempes have
written (Kempe and Kempe, 1978, p. 62),

> It is understandable that the family resists disrupting the
> existing relationships: disclosure will result in public retribution,
> with the firm expectation of total family disruption, unemploy-
> ment and economic disaster, loss of family and friends for the
> victim, and probably incarceration for the perpetrator at least
> until bail is stood. For each person involved there is also a
> public sense of failure in his or her role as father, mother and
> child, with further loss of self-esteem by all.

It is also important to note that whilst in this case the girl's
disclosure was accepted by the professionals involved, this does not
always happen: the recognition of sexual abuse in a child is entirely
dependent on the individual worker's inherent willingness to
entertain the possibility that such abuse does happen (cf., Sgroi,
1975; CIBA, 1984, p. 81). If the abuse is denied by the professionals
then the secrecy is compounded.

□ To continue with the case, the social worker concluded that
in spite, and to some extent because of, the father's vehement
denial, there was sufficient concern for the child's protection

to apply for a Place of Safety Order from a magistrate. The child and then the parents were interviewed by the police and the father was eventually successfully prosecuted. The family was, however, assessed in a psychiatric report as being a possible case for rehabilitation, in that the parents were no longer denying the abuse and seemed to accept some responsibility for what had happened; they also agreed to attend a child guidance clinic for treatment (see Bentovim et al., 1987, on guidelines for prognosis of rehabilitation after abuse). Nevertheless, as is usual in such cases, there was still the problem of secrecy to overcome: although the family members had been separately interviewed for the investigation and for the court reports, they had not talked about it together. □

In tackling cases of sexual abuse within a family, immediate conjoint family therapy has been found to be inappropriate (Giarretto, 1982). Roberts (1984) reminds us of the extent to which secrecy has often become a dominant feature of a family's life together, and this is especially so in 'conflict-avoiding' families (Furniss, 1985). Roberts argues that it is unrealistic to expect family members in a conjoint meeting suddenly to begin revealing crucial information about the family's intimate functioning. His strategy is, rather, in line with that which we have been recommending, to work initially with individual members in order to earn their trust and learn their fears. The therapist thereby creates a new, therapeutic system, effectively re-structuring the family in the process by breaking up the coalitions that created the conspiracy of silence. Therapy can then proceed, as in the pioneering Santa Clara (USA) Programme (Giarretto, 1982), with work on the neglected relationships in the family between mother and daughter and husband and wife, and thence to conjoint family therapy. Alternatively, and more directly, an earlier conjoint meeting can be held in order to set the foundations for therapy. Thus, the Great Ormond Street team in the UK (CIBA, 1984, p. 86; Furniss, 1985) aim to conduct at least one meeting with the following aims: (1) to establish the facts of the sexual abuse for all to hear; (2) to help the father accept sole responsibility for the abuse; (3) to help both parents come to an agreement about their joint responsibility for the care of their children; (4) to talk openly about separations in the family; and (5) to set up a therapeutic contract. Whichever method is used, uncovering the secrecy which so damaged the family members is the essential first step.

Conclusion

We have observed that therapists tend to be both intrigued and alarmed by secrets. However, clients' attempts to share secrets with their therapist should not be seen as snares, but rather as efforts to express guilt and confusion, and to seek help. There are three main types of secret which are important to distinguish, and the therapist's task can be seen as helping the holder or holders to 'manage' the secret. We believe that if the therapist can maintain a sympathetic and supportive *and* impartial position the problems can be resolved.

Further Reading

CIBA Foundation (1984), *Child Sexual Abuse within the Family*. Especially chapter 3 on family patterns, and part 3 on detailed management of disclosure.

Pincus, L. and C. Dare (1978), *Secrets in the Family*. A psychoanalytical approach to secrets, myths and fantasies in marriages and families.

6

Violence

Violence and the threat of violence present difficult problems to marital and family therapists. Violence can arouse strong feelings of repugnance and fear, leading to blame and censure and the loss of a therapeutic role. Conversely, the therapist's attempts to hang on to such a role can produce a denial of the existence of threats or actual violence; and the attempts to understand it systemically can become a form of blaming the victim. In cases of violence involving children, the therapist will often be charged with the statutory role of managing or supervising the abuse: is it possible to combine the roles of therapy and control?

Problems

The Fear of Violence

The fear of violence can lead to a most dangerous snare. The denial of the threat or actual incidence of violence, whether between parents and children, husbands and wives or workers and clients, carries potentially fatal consequences – as has been demonstrated in a succession of tragic cases. In many instances, workers apparently adopt what Dingwall et al. (1983) term 'the rule of optimism'; in an unrealistic, unfounded hope that family circumstances will improve, they ignore or tolerate abuse until it is too late. Dale and his colleagues from the NSPCC Special Unit in Rochdale refer to such workers as 'dangerous professionals': their attempts to form caring and supportive but naive relationships with their clients can actually increase the risk of violence (Dale et al., 1986, pp. 33ff). What dangerous professionals (and they can be of any discipline) have in common is a reluctance to deal with the violence itself. This is as true of social workers or health visitors who are tentative in investigating or monitoring abuse, preferring to discuss less contentious topics or to help with practical and financial problems, as it is of therapists who prefer to explore family history or neutral areas.

Why do therapists avoid the discussion of violence in marital or family sessions? There are two main reasons: the fear that violence may erupt in the session or afterwards; and the fear of losing the perpetrator from therapy. The fear of violence in the session itself is, of course, something which is likely to be shared with the spouse or family as well. They will have had painful experience of the dangers of provoking the abuser and, following the pattern established at home, will tend to avoid stirring him up. Indeed, as we mention below, with abused wives there is a tendency during the 'repentance' phase of the battering cycle, for the victim to believe so firmly in the good intentions of her partner that she does not want to entertain the idea that he might repeat his actions. This can be complementary to the therapist's 'rule of optimism' described above. Since the abuser himself is likely to fear being blamed by both spouse and therapist, he is understandably reluctant to raise the subject of his violence, so the elements for denial are complete. A variation on this pattern is that the participants engage in a limited, and therefore safe, discussion of violent incidents in a way that minimizes their seriousness. Such discussions may even be initiated by the perpetrator, demonstrating a serious, or apparently serious, intent to sort out the problem. However, a real or imagined threat prevents the discussion being taken much further.

The actual occurrence of interpersonal violence in formal therapy sessions at an office or clinic is probably extremely rare. It is much more likely in a family's own home, and as a response to the exercise of a statutory power such as the compulsory removal of an adult to psychiatric hospital or a child into care (Brown et al., 1985). What is more common is the actual or implied threat of retribution *after* the session. For this reason, the victims of abuse may remain silent or even divert the course of the discussion to safer topics.

Blaming or Rescuing the Victim

Serious cases of spouse- or child-abuse present a significant challenge to therapists using a systems approach. There are two possible snares: blaming the victim; and abandoning therapeutic neutrality to rescue the victim, thereby losing the perpetrator. We will consider these snares in relation to spouse-abuse because the elements are somewhat more complicated.

Marital and family therapists are most likely to encounter those couples who stay together in spite of continuing violence in their relationship. Although the abused spouse may leave after particularly severe incidents, she usually returns home, often to the dismay of those friends and professionals who helped her move out. There are, of course, a number of important economic and social reasons why women do not break off relationships with abusive partners, including lack of money and accommodation, doubts about their own ability to survive independently, and fear of social stigma. Another important factor, though, is a belief that their spouse will reform (Gelles and Cornell, 1985, pp. 76–9). This last reason can be seen as part of the cycle of violence first described by Walker (1979) and elaborated by Deschner (1984, pp. 12–20) in seven stages: mutual dependency; the noxious event; coercions exchanged; the 'last straw' decision; primitive rage; reinforcement for battering; and the repentance phase.

☐ A twenty-three-year-old woman from a Pakistani family who had been brought up in England had married a man from a small town in the Punjab. She had left him and taken their two children to stay in a refuge following an episode in which he had beaten her severely with a broom-handle. He had since managed to find the refuge and had taken to hanging around in the street outside, occasionally on his knees and crying. He arranged for bunches of flowers to be delivered, attached to which was always a letter imploring his wife to return, swearing on oath that he would never touch her again and maintaining that he could not live without her. His brothers too had visited, begging her to return for the family's sake.

This extravagant repentance on the part of the abuser can be recognized as one stage in an escalating cycle of violence. The couple's relationship was characterized by the husband's strong dependency, as a newcomer to a strange land, on his wife, and by her passionate attachment to him as a sexual partner. However, he was intensely suspicious of her 'Western ways', especially the free and easy way in which she talked to men. This feeling had developed into an extreme jealousy which, although sometimes used to add spice to their relationship, frequently fuelled the violent response to some trivial incident. Thus, the most recent injuries had followed an argument about a visiting delivery man with whom the wife had been talking when her husband returned from work. He had accused her of being a whore, to which she had responded that he should go back to his village. As the argument developed, she cast doubt on his sexual prowess. This was the 'last straw' as far as he was concerned, and he seized the broomstick and beat her into submission. (Unfortunately, as Deschner observes, it is such life-saving submission which reinforces battering, since the victim ceases doing whatever it was that displeased the attacker.)

Until now, this pattern of argument and violence had been enacted on a number of occasions and the wife had always submitted. Indeed, she had usually followed it by making great efforts to appease her husband and to do her duty as a wife, thereby further rewarding his behaviour. On this occasion, however, the injuries were especially severe and she began to worry that he might also turn on the children. She therefore went to a local school teacher and thence to the refuge, where a few days later her husband appeared protesting his repentance. □

From the therapist's point of view, this last phase of repentance is most interesting. At least in the early history of a battering relationship, the abuser is shocked by his violence, and may try to disown it, but swears sincerely that it will never happen again. As Deschner (1984) describes, 'Since the repentance and resolve to reform are so genuine, the victims more or less overcome their shock and fear and decide it is safe to live with the contrite batterer.' In addition, if the repentance is accompanied by displays of gentleness and kindness, the woman is drawn into both unrealistic hope and a belief that his caring and loving are her husband's 'real' qualities.

In the terms of systems theory it is possible to describe such a cycle as part of a complementary relationship (Cook and Frantz-Cook, 1984), but this carries the snare of losing sight of the fact that there *is* a victim – the wife does get hurt. To say that the violence 'carries a function' for the relationship or that the relationship 'needs' violence for its homeostasis is akin to saying that women stay in such relationships because of their masochistic personalities. The danger here is not only as we described above that the physical harm is 'overlooked' or denied, but also that the therapist focuses on the wife's 'contribution' to the violence and begins to see it as her fault.

The woman's behaviour *can* usefully be understood as part of the cycle of violence, making the eruption of violence more likely; but it is essential to remember that rather than 'asking for it', she is trapped and does not know the way out. In fact, as Deschner demonstrates, her way of avoiding harm by submitting when her partner is in a rage, inadvertently reinforces his rages, since she has given in to his demands. It is a classic case of the attempted solution exacerbating the problem.

On the other hand, an emphasis on the abuser's responsibility for the violent act, combined perhaps with a sense of repugnance and an identification with the victim, can lead to the trap of a punitive, controlling response to the abuser and an attempt to rescue the victim. Certainly, control of the violence is necessary; but if, as Minuchin (1984, p. 138) suggests, most domestic violence is the product of a sense of powerlessness, then punishment and the deprivation of power will only make matters worse. Minuchin distinguishes between 'coercive violence' – the purposeful use of force to obtain a goal – and 'pleading violence', in which the perpetrator experiences himself as a helpless victim to the other's baiting. If, rather than trying to understand this sense of powerlessness, the therapist acts only in order to control, then this will increase the abuser's subjective experience as a victim, inviting him to drop out of therapy and making violence more likely.

Solutions

Managing therapy and control

Obviously, the most straightforward approach to managing violence in families is possible when abuse, or the suspicion of abuse, has been the reason for referral to the agency. Here the question of abuse can and, certainly in the case of children, must be addressed straight away (see, for example, Moore, 1985). Note that in these cases there is an important distinction between the investigative and the therapeutic roles and that the former has priority. Thus a conjoint family interview is *not* appropriate in the first instance: the victim must be given an opportunity to talk privately and the abuser should also be seen separately, giving the therapist an opportunity to convey her interest in hearing his point of view.

Cases in which violence emerges during the course of therapy are much more difficult to handle because of the tendency of all parties, including the therapist, to fear and deny its existence. We will consider this at two stages: recognition, acknowledgement and denial; and intervention.

Recognition

Whilst a large number of personal, demographic and economic factors have been shown by researchers to be associated with both spouse- and child-abuse, their presence (or absence) cannot be taken as a sign that abuse is occurring in any *particular* family (Gelles and Cornell, 1985, p. 59). Nevertheless, some relationship factors are of note, in particular the observation that abusive parents tend to have unrealistically high expectations of their children (Gelles and Cornell, 1985, p. 55), and that in marital violence there is often a status inequality in the woman's favour which is resented by the husband (Hornung et al., 1981). Therapists must, however, rely on their own assessments of such families, supported by the observations of other involved professionals, including the police, and by reviewing their case files.

The first, and most obvious, cause for suspicion is the *presence of an injury*, which is often associated with the cancelling or postponement of an appointment, a child being absent from a session, and an apparent worsening in the therapeutic relationship whereby the couple or family seem reserved, remote, anxious or defensive or, alternatively, where one member appears inappropriately friendly and cheerful and the others timid or frightened. In these circumstances, the therapist *must* enquire about the injured or missing member gently, but directly, for example:

'I can't help noticing that you have a nasty cut on your face, Mrs Jones. How did that happen?'
'I see that X isn't here today. Where is she?'

When violence has occurred, it is not likely that it will be admitted easily and openly, for fear of the consequences. It is more usual for there to be evasion or flat denial or, alternatively, a minimalizing of the incident. However, as is usual in therapy, it is the client's responses, verbal and non-verbal, that are the best indicator. The therapist's skill lies in continuing the exploration in as unthreatening and supportive a way as possible in the particular circumstances. For example:

'So you had a disagreement. Have you been having more of those recently? Are they getting serious?'
'I'm sure you'll understand that that's the sort of injury which (in view of what's happened before) tends to worry people. Can you tell me more about what happened?'
'As you know, it's part of my job to see that the children are well. Can we make an arrangement to see X, please?'

We should note that the therapist's most useful tool in the recognition of violence is her own internal response when working with the couple or family. If she feels uncomfortable, threatened and fearful, then it is very likely that at least some members of the family feel that way also. Similarly, Dale et al. (1986, p. 105) note that couples who deny any disagreement or tension within their relationship and relate to therapists in a 'passive–aggressive' way, invariable *relate to each other* in the same fashion. Rather than responding out of fear or frustration, the therapist can interpret such feelings as an indication that violence is present.

If the suspected abuser denies that anything has taken place and becomes angry with the therapist, his partner will usually signal her anxiety. If the therapist does not have a statutory responsibility to investigate, then the subject is usually best left at this stage and only returned to when the therapist has made efforts to re-join, demonstrating that she is anxious to understand his position. Nevertheless, in very many cases these tactics will remain unsuccessful and, probably from a combination of shame, guilt, fear and a genuine amnesia (Deschner, 1984, pp. 16–17), the abuser will resolutely deny what has happened or blame others. In the terms we have been using in this book, he is not a customer for therapy and he will not be one until he acknowledges he has a problem.

Unless and until the abuser admits to the problem, and in the absence of any forensic evidence, the only safe course is to remove the victim (if a child) or to counsel the partner to leave, providing help where necessary for her to do so. What most abusers have in common is the desire to have the victim back home: hence the repentance phase and the hoped-for return to a state of mutual dependency (see above). It is therefore at the point when the abuser and victim are apart that the abuser is a potential customer: he can then be faced with the demand that he engage in therapy to change his behaviour, otherwise it will be impossible to recommend that his child returns home. In the case of spouse-abuse, the victim will obviously have to be persuaded not to return until her spouse makes such an agreement.

☐ Returning to the example quoted above, the woman required a good deal of convincing that she should not return quietly to her husband. The therapist argued that, although if she felt it her duty to return to look after her husband, she also had a duty to her marriage and her family and that unless she required him to do his duty as a husband and to desist from violence, neither could work. (Note that this argument is expressed in terms of the cultural values of duties and responsibilities to the family. In an Anglo-Saxon family the values might more appropriately be those of the right to individual self-determination.)

In separate meetings, the husband was confronted with the seriousness of his violence and with the prospect of his wife never returning. He acknowledged that his anger had got out of control, but insisted that the cause was his wife's 'provocations'. The therapist, whilst agreeing that there were undoubtedly serious misunderstandings between the couple, which needed to be resolved, nevertheless demanded that the husband first undertake to control his violence. Only if the couple made an agreement to learn new ways of managing potentially explosive events would there by any chance of success. The husband accepted this and said that he would attend a meeting with his wife and the therapist to work out a contract for therapy *before* she considered returning home. ☐

Intervention – Protection before Therapy

Our view is that once violence has been identified, its management should become the primary focus for therapy. To deny or ignore violence will, at the very least, prevent the progress of therapy or slow its course. As Walker (1979) points out, standard marital therapy encourages the individual partners to subordinate their own needs to some extent, in order to make their relationship work; and, as we have seen, submission in the face of hostility tends to reinforce violence. In the worst cases, as Dale and his colleagues (1986) describe, a combination of denial on the part of the perpetrator and family, and the rule of optimism among the professionals, can be fatal.

The first step is to protect the victim from further abuse. We cannot emphasize too strongly the importance of taking this step *before* engaging in therapy. In cases involving children where the abuse is denied, it may be necessary to obtain a place of safety order authorizing their removal from the home. Here, effective therapeutic work might only begin once the children are in the care of the local authority. The parents may well remain unwilling 'clients' and actively resent the authorities; but they may, nevertheless, contract to work towards the goal of 'getting them off our backs'.

☐ The single-parent father of a badly beaten nine-year-old boy came from one of the smaller islands in the Caribbean. He was strongly aggrieved because one of his neighbours had reported him to the social services department and the child had subsequently been placed on the local 'at-risk' register. This action made him even more angry: he protested that it was his right to 'discipline' his child, whom he perceived as disobedient and lazy, and that the social workers had undermined his authority. The social workers, on the other hand, saw the child as anxious and vulnerable and the father as harsh and Victorian in his attitudes. Needless to say, the man refused the offer of 'social work support'. Following a second incident, the boy was placed in the care of the social services department and allowed home on supervision. ☐

An analysis of this case should begin with the different cultural assumptions about child-rearing held by 'client' and social worker. In the small Caribbean islands strict attitudes do prevail, as does a belief in the value of corporal punishment; the father was only using the methods of his own upbringing, and he resented the interference of the white authorities. However, it was also becoming clear to him that his methods were failing: the more he beat his

son, the more the boy became defiant ('disobedient') and un-
cooperative ('lazy'). Once again the attempted solution (beating)
had become the problem, which had escalated dangerously. Similarly,
the social workers' attempted solution (rescuing the child) had
served to undermine the man's authority, making it more likely
that he would reassert it by disciplining his son.

☐ The solution to this particular problem came when the social
worker was helped to see the father's point of view and
encouraged to join with him in his aspirations for the child –
that he should be obedient and work hard. Achieving this goal
was difficult for anyone, especially for a single parent in a
hostile environment. The social worker was then able to help
the man acknowledge not just that his methods of discipline
were getting him into trouble because they were unacceptable
in another country, but also that they were proving ineffective.
Whilst the social workers' role would necessarily involve
checking up, it could also involve helping him achieve his
hopes for his son. This help entailed joint meetings with school
staff about the boy's academic performance, as well as family
discussions in which the social worker helped them work out
a contractual approach with a focus on rewarding co-operative
behaviour. The social worker also made an agreement with
the father that he would recommend removal from the 'at risk'
register as soon as he felt able to provide convincing evidence
of an improvement in the father–son relationship and the use
of a non-violent approach to discipline. ☐

An agreement to manage future confrontations is itself the first
element in a contract to engage in therapy. In statutory cases of
child abuse, as Dale et al. (1986, pp. 83ff) describe, detailed
contracts, specifying the therapist's requirements of the family and
the service to be provided, should be drawn up. These have been
shown to be effective both in stopping abuse and as the foundation
for further work (Doctor and Singer, 1978). Similar contracts for
use in marital violence are described by Deschner (1984, chapter
6), the main difference being that in the absence of statutory powers
the therapist has to rely on the couple's commitment to change.
In marital relationships, stopping the abuse invariably means
making an agreement for managing the next confrontation – for
example, by an agreed routine beginning with taking a 'time-out'.

Deschner recommends the use of a non-verbal 'T'-sign made with both hands straight, one vertical and the other horizontal on top. This sign, which can be made by either partner, is a signal that an argument has got out of control and that at least one person is angry or afraid. By the terms of the agreement the other must acknowledge the T-sign, usually saying 'OK, time out'. The protagonists *both* agree to withdraw to another room or to leave the house in order to 'cool down'. This joint agreement is essential because walking out itself can otherwise be used as an aggressive act (see Deschner, 1984, pp. 100–4, 130–42). After they have cooled off, the family members involved in the conflict must agree to notify the therapist.

Finally, we should note that the programmes described by Dale et al. and Deschner use a combination of therapeutic methods, including group and individual therapy as well as marital and family therapy. Groups for the abusers seem to be especially effective in helping members overcome their denial with support from their peers. Nevertheless, we have found that the time-out procedure can be taught to individual couples and families, so long as it is agreed as part of a firm contract.

Conclusion

In this short chapter we have attempted to provide some guidelines for therapists in dealing with what is, for all of us, a highly charged and difficult area. Nevertheless, the therapist's own uncomfortable feelings, we suggest, can provide a most important key to the recognition of violence, and the threat of violence, within marriages and families. The denial of violence is, as Dale et al (1986) describe, dangerous in itself. Once again, in considering guidelines for therapeutic intervention, we have stressed the importance of the working alliance but also the essential task of ensuring protection first: protection before therapy.

Further Reading

Dale, P. et al. (1986), *Dangerous Families: Assessment and Treatment of Child Abuse*. Describes the use of a family systems approach by an NSPCC Child Protection Team in

140 *Violence*

Rochdale, England. Provides clear guidelines for engagement, assessment and rehabilitation using a contractual approach. Also indications for permanent separation.

Deschner, J. (1984), *The Hitting Habit: Anger Control for Battering Couples*. Presents a clear analysis of violence in terms of interpersonal, social, physiological and cognitive factors, together with a detailed description of her approach to teaching couples to manage anger and learn new ways of resolving conflict.

Gelles, R. and C. Cornell (1985), *Intimate Violence in Families*. Introductory text by a recognized authority in the field.

Minuchin, S. (1984), *Family Kaleidoscope*. Part 2, 'Patterns of Violence', is a very readable account of the interactional approach to violence. Discusses the influence of the problem system (for example, courts, social services and extended family).

7

'Oh no! Not the Smiths Again!'

In this and the following chapter we will explore 'stuckness' in therapy. As we argued in chapter 1, there is no point in blaming either the clients or the therapist and labelling them 'resistant' or 'unmotivated' if therapy is going round in circles and getting nowhere. It is crucial to remember that from a couple's or family's point of view, therapy is but one way of dealing with their problems. Furthermore, no matter how painful or peculiar their behaviour seems to the outsider, it represents the best 'solution' they have been able to find so far to the difficulties, real or imagined, that they face (Watzlawick et al., 1974). It is at least familiar and, as bad as they are, these known patterns of behaviour may be better than anything else the family can envisage (Greenberg et al., 1964).

Thus, the family's 'solution' demands the therapist's respect, and it is therefore best to assume that if a family proves incapable of change then there are fundamental reasons why this should be so. With this assumption, we are better placed to avoid the basic errors which flow from framing clients as 'resistant'. It is clearly quite appropriate for a family to exercise caution in following their therapist's advice and directions. Within this frame it becomes easier to understand stuckness in a multidimensional way – clients need to test out the skill and resourcefulness both of themselves and of the therapist. If this process results in stuckness, then we would argue that it becomes the therapist's responsibility to 'unstick' the therapeutic system. Whether this means freeing the therapeutic system and giving it fresh momentum or agreeing to terminate therapy matters less than preventing the continuation of a hopeless, ineffective and possibly damaging charade which often ends with the family being labelled as 'resistant' or 'untreatable'.

If, because of the legal or agency structure within which the therapy has been taking place, the therapist is required to continue her relationship with the family (for example, because they are on a child-abuse register, or one of their members is on a probation order or must remain under psychiatric supervision), then the relationship should be re-labelled. The task is no longer 'therapy', it is 'supervision', and it must be defined in such terms in order to make it clear that the worker is required to continue in a different role.

It is our contention that it is the therapist's responsibility first to recognize and then to determine where and how the therapy is stuck. It is only when stuckness has been adequately assessed that it becomes appropriate to try new tactics. The two most tempting errors are: (1) a failure to recognize stuckness and to persist in using the same approach when it is not working (what Watzlawick and his colleagues call a 'more of the same solution' (1974, ch. 3)); and (2) trying something new, usually the latest fashionable therapeutic gambit, on a 'suck it and see' basis, in the hope that some magical answer will emerge. Unfortunately, both these 'attempted solutions' quickly become the next problems that we have to tackle. Throughout this book we have emphasized the importance of a careful analysis of problems in marital and family therapy before reaching for solutions, and our discussion of stuckness is no exception. In this and the following chapter we put forward a series of questions which we have found useful to address in evaluating the nature and cause of stuckness. But first we need to say a little about recognizing the problem.

Recognizing Stuckness

We have called this chapter, like our original paper on the subject, 'Oh no! Not the Smiths again!'; we are confident that our readers will recognize the feelings of dread that precede meetings with certain couples or families! There are a number of possible reasons for this, including a sense of:

1 Frustration – the therapist has been working harder and harder, but not (in her terms) getting anywhere. The couple or family are defined as 'resistant'.
2 Fear – that she will be verbally, or even physically, attacked by one or more members for being incompetent or obstructive. This fear is often accompanied by anxiety that, against her better judgement, she will 'give in' to the clients' demands. Such clients

are deemed 'demanding' or 'manipulative'.

3 Disappointment – every time the therapist begins to feel that change is taking place something happens which (apparently) takes it back to 'square one'.

4 Inadequacy – the coming session will be just as useless as the last. The therapist feels that she simply doesn't have the skills or the resolve to stop her clients' self-destructive behaviour.

5 Hopelessness – a feeling that the couple or family can never change and that nobody will be able to help them: such clients are typically described as 'chronic', 'unmotivated' or 'untreatable'.

6 Aimlessness – when therapy degenerates into pleasantries, chat, or vague philosophical discussion but with the original problem just as bad, if not worse.

7 Anger – usually directed at one member of a couple or family, but sometimes at both parents and occasionally at the family as a whole. Typically, the therapist will describe such people as 'impossible', 'stubborn', 'arrogant', 'controlling' or 'manipulative'. In complementary fashion, the other partner in the relationship will be seen as the innocent victim of such a monster. The therapist will usually attempt to out-argue the 'unreasonable' client, who responds in like manner or with sullen aggression, driving the therapist to speechlessness or tears.

Of course, as therapists we do not often hear what our dissatisfied clients really think about *us*. We sometimes hear what they thought about their previous therapists, who are usually described as blaming, uncaring, unsympathetic, useless, rigid or arrogant. In other words, exactly the sort of remarks that dissatisfied therapists make about their difficult clients. We can safely assume therefore that when we are feeling bad about a particular couple or family, they will be feeling much the same about us. Such feelings are the clearest possible indicator that the therapeutic alliance is breaking down and that remedial steps must be taken. So, unfashionable though it may be to emphasize the therapist's feelings in a field which is increasingly dominated by technique, we contend that to monitor your own feelings is essential to good practice. If the signs of stuckness (feelings of anger, frustration, helplessness and hopelessness) are *not* recognized, then in our experience therapy will sooner or later break down in mutual recrimination. If these feelings are recognized and steps taken to analyse the source of the 'stuckness', then the alliance can be repaired and solutions found.

Stopping

Having recognized stuckness, the therapist's most difficult task is to *stop* – to stop doing whatever it is which is her contribution to the stuckness. As we have already noted, this is not easy because the imperative 'try harder' is so deeply ingrained in the personalities of all therapists. Translated into rationales for our actions this imperative may take many forms:

1 'Mr Smith doesn't understand how destructive his behaviour is to his wife's self-esteem. I'll confront him with it more forcefully.'
2 'The Smiths don't accept that they have a problem. I'll tell them once more.'
3 'Mr and Mrs Smith haven't done their task. I'll set it again.'
4 'Mrs Smith won't acknowledge that it's a family problem and that Johnny's behaviour is just a symptom. I'll re-frame it for her.'

Needless to say, such efforts rarely work, and certainly if something has been tried twice and still fails then it will never work. Hence our recommendation: *stop* – and think.

Analysing Stuckness – A Framework

In the rest of this chapter, and in the next, we will develop a framework within which stuckness can be systematically evaluated. We do this in the form of questions which we have found useful to address when considering our own practice and when giving consultation to colleagues in a variety of settings and agencies. Although we have categorized the questions under four major headings, the categories are not watertight – indeed, it is difficult to envisage any system which would fit the richness of the reality we are trying to encompass. Nevertheless, the headings are as follows:

1 *Context and Contract* Is the stuckness caused by the therapist's failure to understand the context in which therapy is taking place and to have made a clear contract with her clients? Under this heading we include a consideration of how the 'problem'

which brought the family to the agency has been defined and by whom. We also review the clients' own views on the advantages and disadvantages of change, and how it might be achieved.

2   *Method and Style of Therapy*   Is stuckness a result of technical features of the therapist's approach? In particular, are the therapist and her colleagues sufficiently skilled and able to offer a style of therapy which suits the couple or family?

3   *Sucked In or Locked Out? – The loss of manoeuvrability* If the therapist is not part of the solution then she has almost certainly become part of the problem. She may either have been 'sucked in' to the dynamics of her clients' conflicts or problems so that she no longer has any manoeuvrability, or 'locked out' from making any impact upon them. In systems language she has become a homeostatic part of the therapeutic system.

4   *Stuck supervision*   Supervision and consultation are safe-guards against stuckness and provide opportunities to find solutions to the problems of therapy. However, this system, the supervisory system, may itself become stuck, and under this fourth heading we examine some of the problems which can arise.

In this chapter we will examine a series of detailed questions relevant to the first two headings, leaving the exploration of the therapeutic system itself to the next chapter. We have found it useful both when analysing our own 'stuck' cases and when consulting to others to explore the answers to each of these questions. They have helped us identify the many causes of stuckness, and we provide a number of illustrations from our own experience. We also suggest some solutions. Once again, in the spirit of this book, they are not blueprints, but rather suggestions which have worked for us but which have to be evaluated in terms of the circumstances of each case. What will work for *some* clients with *some* therapists in *some* agencies will not necessarily work for others.

Context and Contract

What is the precise nature of the problem?

One of the obvious reasons for a therapist and her clients being stuck is a fundamental disagreement about whether or not there *is* a problem. Thus the therapist is keen to change the family, to rescue them from their 'pathology', but the family resist all her attempts. From her point of view this is a case of 'denial' – the family 'won't accept that they *really* need help'.

Many couples and families are able to make their position quite clear by opting out quickly, or even refusing to engage in therapy in the first place. Others come and continue doing so, even though they disagree with the therapist. In this type of case there are probably external sanctions (for example, the power of the agency, other agencies or systems including the wider family system) which determine their attendance. It should be assumed that they are going through the motions because, in spite of its being inconvenient or even painful, 'therapy' is preferable to the alternatives, at least as they perceive them. Thus, undergoing therapy may be less stigmatizing than being taken to court for your child's delinquent behaviour. It may also serve to reassure another member of the family that efforts are being made to solve the problem whilst ensuring that unsettling change does not take place. Similarly, as problems may 'protect' a family myth or secret (cf., Byng-Hall, 1978) so may unsuccessful therapy – the family's lack of co-operation hence ensures that the skeleton, which will so upset one of its members, remains in the cupboard. Alternatively, it may be that therapy is a solution to loneliness or lack of excitement in their lives (a problem, incidentally, which the therapist herself may share).

If the therapist is unable to describe the precise nature of the problem from the various points of view of the participants, the therapy is likely to flounder. Coleman and Gurman (1985), in an analysis of the cases described in their book *Failures in Family Therapy*, identified inadequate or inaccurate assessment of clients' problems as a major cause of therapeutic failure in nine of the twelve examples discussed by experienced family therapists. It is no coincidence therefore that the model of therapy we outlined in the first chapter lays such stress on defining the problem from the clients' point of view. However, if this has not been achieved and therapy becomes stuck we would recommend a direct approach. The therapist can make the following statement to the couple or family, either at the beginning of a new session or following a 'time out' for consultation with a colleague:

'I'm concerned that I don't seem to be helping you in any way. This could be because I have just not understood what it is each of you needs help with. On the other hand, the problem could be that you are attending these meetings only out of politeness or because somebody else thinks you should be here. Whatever it is, I'm confused and don't feel able to continue until I've got this straight. Can you help me?'

The client's response to such an approach usually reveals, as we have been suggesting, that there has been an inadequate analysis of the problem system (that is, the various systems which impinge on the couple or family and which are concerned with the problem (see chapter 1)).

☐ A woman who had been attending for marital therapy with her husband broke down in the session when the therapist commented as above on their lack of progress. She said, hesitantly, that it was really her relationship with her father that was the problem. She had had an incestuous relationship with him for over six years, and although she had let her husband into the secret neither of them had said anything to her father for fear that its revelation would literally endanger the life of her invalid mother. The experience of the incest together with the strain of keeping the secret had certainly created problems (including a disastrous sexual relationship) in the couple's marriage. However, their involvement in marital therapy could also be seen as a way of preserving the status quo and thus avoiding the perceived danger to the mother. For as long as they could attribute these problems to deficiencies in their own relationship rather than to the father's behaviour, the secret could be preserved: the father did not have to be faced and the mother's health could be safeguarded. In fact, the opening up of this secret in the marital session, followed by the close examination of the couple's fears along the lines suggested in chapter 5, led to a series of family meetings in which the earlier conflicts were eventually resolved. ☐

It is worth noting, however, that the couple's problems did not end with the wife resolving her feelings about, and relationship with, her father. The legacy of the incest had been carried into her marriage and distorted that relationship. Just as it was a mistake at first to assess the problem as a marital problem rather than a family problem, so it would later have been a mistake to assume that once the latter had been resolved so too would the marital problem disappear. The problem at this later stage was indeed with the marriage, for some of the difficulties had emerged as a consequence of the work undertaken in the family meetings. To make the point more generally: assessment is not 'once and for all'. As we described in chapter 1, assessment is part of the continuous process in which both therapist and client are engaged.

Other workers, notably Spark (1974) and Guerin and Guerin (1976), have drawn attention to the necessity of convening the extended family as a general procedure. But it has also been advocated by therapists of a different orientation as a tactic to use when 'stuck' (cf., Sluzki, 1978). Similarly, it is often important to establish whether neighbours, friends or lodgers play an important part within the system.

□ In the course of a family session the therapist asked an eight-year-old girl to draw her house. She promptly drew a house which was carefully labelled number 38. It was festooned with flowers and the door stood open invitingly. At the time the therapist did not realize that in fact the family lived at number 39. Subsequent questioning revealed that the house was that of a neighbour who provided the girl with a lot of surrogate mothering. □

By inviting children to draw their house or their family, valuable clues can be given about the wider social context in which they live. With adults, it is important to establish whose advice they have taken in dealing with their problems. Careful questioning in this area will often reveal someone who is apparently opposed to the idea of therapy, or perhaps a grandparent who is the main opinion-maker in the family and who believes that 'the problem' is something quite different. This opinion is, of course, one that the therapist would do well to consider. If she ignores it and insists on her own definition, she places her clients in a 'bind', requiring them to choose between two people, herself and the grandparent. Furthermore, the grandparent's assessment may very well be more accurate; after all, he or she will have known the family for a great deal longer than has the therapist!

Even if this influential person, be it a grandparent, friend, neighbour or priest, is unable or unwilling to come to a family meeting, the therapist can contact them by phone or visit them in order to hear their views. We have seen many examples of therapists who assumed that such 'significant others' were their rivals or opponents, only to discover, when they met them, a large measure of agreement and clear opportunities for a joint approach to help the clients. This is, however, dependent on how the meeting is handled.

The therapist should approach meetings with 'significant others' in exactly the same way as she would meetings with her clients. In other words, using the framework for 'contract building' described in chapter 1, she should first establish their views on the problem and how it should be tackled before trying to negotiate a joint approach. The following example makes this clear.

☐ Staff at a community mental health centre had been working hard to help a depressed and occasionally suicidal young mother. They had assessed the problem in terms of the woman's poor marital relationship, the lack of support from her husband in caring for their children and an intense and over-burdening relationship with her own divorced mother. The therapeutic contract involved marital therapy, individual counselling for the woman's mother to help her develop her own independent interests, and some medication to relieve the identified patient's symptoms. The staff sought a consultation when it emerged that the patient had also gone along to a nearby voluntary women's mental health project, a project which they characterized as having a strong feminist and anti-psychiatry ideology. They were dismayed that women's project workers would 'meddle' in 'their' case.

On the consultant's advice, the project worker was invited to the next session at the centre and her views were sought. As expected, she did define the problem in terms of oppression by both the husband and the psychiatric system, which she saw as trying to 'dose up' the woman and confine her to hospital.

Rather than trigger an argument, the centre staff were able to agree with the greater part of the project worker's position. They too could see that the woman was oppressed (although that was not the whole story), and could concur that medication and hospital were not the answer. They were able to outline their position on the woman's problem and stress that the approach they had offered was intended to increase her control over her own life and specifically to avoid hospital. At the same time, blaming the husband was not likely to be a fruitful approach, since it would simply drive him away from the therapy sessions. The project worker accepted this point and was able to convince the centre staff that by focusing on the marital relationship they had not paid sufficient attention to the woman's individual needs to develop her own identity.

Discussion with the client herself revealed that she had sought help from both agencies because they both had something to offer her; her difficulty was that they sometimes said different things and she didn't know which was correct. The stage was therefore set for an agreement between the three parties in which all could work together towards a common goal. □

Finally, in seeking to define the precise nature of the problem, we must re-emphasize that the problem is not necessarily 'in' the family or indeed in the relationship between the family and another system. Of course a problem in one system may well influence another system very strongly. For example, when a family member is experiencing problems at work they may come home and take it out on the other members, either aggressively or by retreating into their shell. Obviously, marital or family therapy *per se* can be directed only at the individual and family's response to such external stress – it cannot remove the source of the stress. The possible approaches to this type of problem are as follows:

1 Help the family work out ways to help support the member under pressure in another system. This includes discussing what helps and hinders when leaving and coming back home; for example, do they want to talk or not?
2 Together with the family, help the individual to plan changes in his/her behaviour designed to change the other system – the family's involvement in such discussions is a statement of their concern as well as a possible source of ideas.
3 Re-frame the stress or the system more benignly.
4 Evaluate the disadvantages and advantages for the individual and the family of staying as a member of the stressful system (for example, a highly paid but exhausting job). This involves attention to values and beliefs as well as practical matters.
5 Help the individual leave the stressful system without feeling blamed or inadequate and with the support of the rest of the family.

The following example illustrates how connecting two systems (home and school) can produce a rapid solution to a problem.

□ A school referred an adolescent boy to a child guidance clinic because they were concerned about his 'homosexual' behaviour. The therapist arranged an initial family interview at which the parents expressed shock and dismay and denied any problem at home. The therapist therefore arranged a meeting at the school with the parents and the school staff. It emerged that the 'homosexual advances' which the boy made towards other boys were an attempted solution to his fear of being bullied. Unfortunately, this 'solution' was flawed because although it was successful in making them keep their distance, he had to suffer their humiliating taunts not only at school but also in his home village. Working together, parents and teacher were able to help the boy develop new ways of coping more effectively with his peers in the village and at school. On follow-up he was found to have relinquished his 'homosexual' behaviour and to have made a number of stable friendships. □

To whom is 'the problem' a problem? How is it a problem? Is there a working agreement on 'the problem'?

As we discussed in chapter 1, 'the problem' will be different for the different members of the problem system because they will each experience the same situation from different points of view. Even when one person is labelled as 'the problem' and they themselves accept that definition, we need to examine *how* that behaviour is a problem both to themselves and to others. This applies both to the members of a family and to those who are trying to help, therapist included. It is for this reason that the contractual model we outlined earlier is so important: by hearing and clarifying the different views and then agreeing on the definition of the problem and how it should be tackled, many later problems can be avoided. Nevertheless, when therapy has become stuck, the basic question 'Is there an agreement on the problem?' should always be asked, since the circumstances may have changed and the working agreement may no longer hold. Alternatively, the therapist or family may have moved on to another set of problems without making an agreement to do so. The following example, presented by a psychiatrist for consultation, is described in his own words:

☐ Mrs M was referred to me on account of panic attacks. She had been taking lorazepam (Ativan) for these, but the GP had refused to go on prescribing them. This had precipitated the crisis: she had changed her GP to one who would go on prescribing, but he had insisted that she should go into psychiatric hospital so that her problems could be cured.

The present state of her problems is as follows:

1   Obsessional preoccupation with cleanliness and order in her home. Very troubled by an asymmetrical wall in the kitchen.
2   Long-standing sexual difficulties with her husband. She and her husband had agreed to have therapy for this, but she declines further help now.
3   Addiction to lorazepam.
4   Her only child, a girl of fourteen, who has a mild mental handicap, is frequently rude to her mother and is a source of distress to her.
5   She had an unhappy childhood, parents divorcing when she was ten. She now has poor relationships with her parents and in-laws.
6   Her mother, aunt and a sister have all spent time in psychiatric hospitals. She feels somehow she is blighted.

Our problem is what to do for her when she refuses to give up the drug to which she is addicted. Can we do anything effective in such a situation? Also, she declines all suggestions for help and shows no desire to make any changes, although she recognizes she has severe problems.☐

In considering this list of problems, it is important to remember that it is the psychiatrist's list and not the wife's or husband's. It is also clear that the therapeutic alliance has broken down – there is no agreement about the problem or how it should be tackled. In fact, it seems reasonable to assume that Mrs M's 'declining all suggestions for help' represents her attempt to re-negotiate the contract she was forced into making at the time of her admission. The original contract, at least as presented by the psychiatrist, was very one-sided: she could have further prescriptions of lorazepam if she went into hospital to be weaned off it. The only other 'treatment' mentioned was sex therapy – and we might suggest that she agreed to this only because she had been panicked by her husband's sexual advances. Once she was 'safe' in hospital she need no longer fear them.

In order to analyse the list more carefully we can ask of each problem, *'To whom is it a problem, and how?'* Our speculations about the answers are as shown in table 7.1.

If this analysis is correct, and it can of course be tested straightforwardly by questioning the parties involved, separately or together, it opens up new perspectives on re-building the contract. Thus, the main concerns for Mrs M are probably her daughter's rudeness, the state of the house and, possibly, her sexual relationship and problems with parents and in-laws. All these problems concern her husband, and she will need his help to change them: for example, they will almost certainly have to work together to control the daughter's rudeness (which probably reflects the father's unexpressed feelings towards his wife). He will also need to compromise over the tidiness of the house and give greater respect to her wishes.

Conversely, Mr M's main concerns – their poor sexual relationship, problems with parents and in-laws, conflicts about the home and the social embarrassment about his mentally ill wife – will need Mrs M's help if they are to be changed. In other words, both husband and wife can be re-engaged in therapy on the basis of a 'quid pro quo': if Mr M could agree to work on their daughter's rudeness etc., Mrs M could agree to work on the sexual relationship etc. Equally, the psychiatrist could agree to postpone work on the lorazepam addiction until these other problems were resolved. Helping the couple to solve these problems would in turn help him to overcome his problem of feeling that his assistance was of no value to the couple.

In this example (which is typical of many cases we have encountered), the problem which so concerned the therapist (lorazepam addiction) was not a problem for her clients. This often occurs in 'statutory' social work when the 'client' couple or family are in fact inappropriately described as 'clients', since they do not ask for the service. For example, a boy might be placed by a court on a supervision order for not attending school, although his parents consider that he can get all the education he needs at home. His refusal to go to school is a problem for the education department, the court and thence the supervising social worker. The parents and the child are likely to describe their problem as being the unwelcome

Table 7.1 Problem assessment

Problems (as listed by psychiatrist)	To whom?	How?
1 Cleanliness and order/ asymmetrical wall	Mrs M	If the home is not clean and orderly she feels she is not a good wife and mother.
	Mr M	Hates being 'nagged' about tidiness. The wall is not a problem – it won't fall down. Irritated by his wife's concern about it.
2 Sexual difficulties	Mrs M	Feels panicked by his sexual advances. (Not a problem now she is in hospital.)
	Mr M	Misses sexual relationship with his partner.
3 Addiction to lorazepam	GP Psychiatrist	Our responsibility to wean her off dangerous drug.
	Mrs M	Not a problem (but medics' interference is!)
	?Mr M	? [not known]
4 Daughter's rudeness to her mother	Mrs M	Feels distressed and inadequate.
	?Mr M	? [He may or may not be concerned about this.]
5 Poor relationships with parents and in-laws	Mrs M	? [This may not be a problem to her if, for example, they have been 'interfering' in the past]
	? Mr M	A possible conflict of loyalties to his parents and wife.
6 'Blighted with mental illness'	Mrs M	Feels stigmatized, helpless and devalued?
	Mr M Daughter	? Feel social embarrassment – daughter's rudeness could be a response to this.
7 Helplessness ('She declines all help')	Psychiatrist	Failing in job.

attentions of 'the authorities'. The social worker who defines the problem as 'not going to school' will never make a workable contract with the family. Rather, she should either accept the family's definition of the problem and agree to help them work out a compromise with the authorities ('to get them off your backs') or report back to the court that the use of statutory power – for example, to remove the child from home – would be the only way of enforcing the order; therapy would not be the solution.

In some cases, however, an agreed definition of the problem cannot be reached between the clients themselves. This is frequently the case in marital therapy. Usually it is possible to point out that what the two partners are complaining of are but two sides of the same coin. For example, when a husband states that the problem is his wife's meanness and she that it is her husband's wastefulness, the therapist can suggest they focus on their use of resources, both financial and emotional, as the problem. If such an agreement is still not possible then disagreement itself can be labelled the problem: if a couple disagree on what is the problem then they will certainly disagree on many other aspects of their lives. The focus for therapy can then be how to resolve disagreements, a task which will require both partners to appreciate that there are always two sides of the coin. As Anderson and Stewart (1983, p. 91) put it, families must learn to understand 'that being right is virtually useless in intimate relationships. No one can define anyone else's reality. What is important is how each person perceives the situation and how they feel about themselves, their family members and their relationships as a result. The therapist can help couples move from who is right or what are the facts, to an appreciation of and respect for one another's version of reality'.

We can add that the same goes for therapists too: it is pointless arguing with family members about whether they or the family are right about the problem, or how the therapy is going. The therapist must respect and accept their point of view and work to find grounds for agreement.

Why now?

In chapter 2 we advised that when assessing a new case the therapist should ask, 'Why now?' Similarly, when analysing stuckness, we recommend the same question. The answer will reveal that there has been a change in one or more of the three possible systems:

the therapeutic system – in other words a breakdown in the therapeutic alliance; the therapist's personal and/or agency system; and/or the family system. We will discuss the first two systems in the next chapter; here we will consider changes in the family system, since they usually concern the contract and specifically the family members' motivation to take part in therapy. The point we want to make is simple: when therapy breaks down following the making of a contract, consider the possibility that the family's lack of motivation is the result of a change in their circumstances. The following example will help make this clear.

☐ Mr and Mrs B were a couple who argued frequently and had trouble meeting their financial commitments. Every few months the arguments became so bad that Mrs B would leave and find a place to stay in a women's refuge. Mr B would approach the social services department for practical and financial help in looking after their children and this would be provided: debts would be paid off or more favourable repayments negotiated with the service industries on their behalf. Despite the cautions expressed by the refuge staff, Mrs B would always return home to the man she maintained she loved and a honeymoon period would ensue. (This is an example of the cycle described in chapter 6). During at least two revolutions of the cycle, the social worker attached to the case had sought to resolve the problems by arranging marital therapy for the couple, on one occasion with the local Marriage Guidance Council and on another with himself and a colleague as co-therapists.

The couple had attended only one session of marriage guidance, telling the counsellor that there was no need to continue because all their problems had by then been resolved. On the second occasion, the social worker had set up marital sessions as soon as the wife had returned home and had succeeded in negotiating a contract with them. However, after four meetings therapy had become bogged down; the couple denied having any real problems, maintained that they were getting on well and said that they did not need any help. The therapists on the other hand could not agree that any significant changes had taken place, and – in the hope of obtaining a defiance-based response – predicted a relapse, insisting that the relationship would break down again. It did. ☐

The answer to the question 'Why now?' is straightforward: at the time therapy broke down the couple did not consider that they had a problem – they were in the honeymoon phase of their relationship and, in addition, their financial problems were in abeyance. The crisis, the opportunity for change, had passed and the couple were no longer 'customers'.

□ In order to recover this case, the would-be therapists had to wait until the next crisis, when the wife had left home once more. This time the argument had been even more serious, involving physical abuse, and the wife was not as keen to return as quickly. The social worker established that they did, nevertheless, want to resume their relationship and negotiated a contract to begin work *before* she went back. This was to focus initially on what changes would have to be made if their marriage was to have any chance of success, and to agree how these would be achieved. Chastened by their experience, they undertook not to go back together until substantial agreement had been reached and changes implemented. For his part, the social worker said that his help with the financial problems would not be available until then – a position reinforced by his team manager who had become increasingly reluctant to 'bail them out'. In fact, over the course of the next few months significant changes were made and there were no further crises. □

Is there disagreement over the goals of therapy?

Even if the therapist has established agreement concerning the nature of the problems that require therapy, stuckness will occur if the goals have not been agreed. Disagreements over goals may be within the couple or family, between the family and the therapist and/or between other members of the problem system, especially the helping agencies.

Disagreements in the couple or family   Often different family members see the goals of therapy quite differently, but do not reveal this at the initial assessment stage of therapy. Sometimes this is because the therapist has allowed them to define their goals in very woolly terms such as 'better communication' and 'to get on together', or purely negative terms such as 'stopping fighting' or 'no longer being depressed'. Vague goals conceal potential disagreement. For example, 'better communication' may mean 'speaking my mind and getting conflicts out into the open' to one partner and 'being sympathetic and supportive' to the other. Similarly, negative goals beg the question 'What would you be doing instead?' One partner might want his depressed wife to 'get better' so that he didn't have to spend so much time looking after her. She, on the other hand, might want to spend more time in her husband's company, developing a more intimate relationship.

When therapy is stuck because the therapist is 'at sea' and unable to state her clients' goals, she should invite the clients to review progress and to define their respective goals more precisely. It is worth recalling that a clearly defined goal is always framed positively and specifies observable behaviour – for example, 'I want to have a closer relationship with my husband in which we will go out together at least once a week to enjoy ourselves', rather than, 'I want to stop feeling depressed'. This approach usually requires perseverance on the therapist's part, but it is highly effective in unsticking the therapy. Of course, in many cases it will reveal that the hidden agenda of at least one of the parties is separation.

Anderson and Stewart (1983, p. 93) remind us that many marital and family therapists engage in this work because they believe in relationships and want to help people make them work. We might therefore ignore or deny the fact that many clients come to therapy as a way of ending a relationship. This is frequently the case in marriage guidance counselling, where the partner who intends to leave comes in order to say to him- or herself, and the world, 'I'm not to blame. I tried everything and it didn't work'. The combination of a client with a hidden agenda for separation, and a therapist anxious not to recognize it, will certainly result in stuckness.

The solution to this form of stuckness is to help the clients place the hidden agenda on the table. This requires recognition, sensitivity and timing. The partner who intends to separate can usually be recognized as the one who makes very slight changes – if any – themselves, while dismissing or invalidating the much more substantial changes made by the other. At the same time, the therapist might also recognize, in her own feelings and behaviour, much greater sympathy for the partner who will be abandoned and a desire to work harder for their sake, to rescue the marriage. If the therapist realizes she is putting more effort into the marriage than one of the partners she should guess that that person wants to leave.

Once she has recognized the hidden agenda, the therapist should introduce the subject, remarking that separation is of course one of the possible choices facing couples who come to therapy. Such a statement almost always elicits a response from the partner who intends to leave. This response may occur in the session itself or through some contact being made outside the session. This secret way of handling the desire to separate needs to be brought back to the conjoint sessions, otherwise the therapist will be paralysed by the secret itself. As we have already noted, it is often the therapist's reluctance to acknowledge the possibility of separation that is the stumbling block. The same problem can arise when the potential separation is between an elderly person and his or her family.

☐ Mr P, an elderly man, had lived with his daughter and son-in-law for eighteen months following the death of his wife. At his daughter's request he was referred to a psychiatric clinic because of his bizarre behaviour. However, a thorough assessment failed to uncover any problems. A referral for family therapy was agreed to. The therapist thought Mr P unhappy, and supposed that he was having difficulty in coming to terms with his bereavement and in settling down to life with his daughter and her family. The daughter seemed excessively anxious to show the therapist that she was coping with insuperable problems but at the same time found reasons for not following any of his suggestions or making use of any practical help and support which were offered. This left the therapist quite exasperated.

The distress and anxiety increased to the point when Mr P's behaviour provoked a crisis in which his daughter and her husband united to say that they could and would no longer cope: Mr P was unceremoniously dumped in an elderly persons' home.

An analysis which focused on the supposed function of Mr P's behaviour for the family system would point to its unifying effect on his daughter's marital relationship and predict a succession of such crises, which would serve to maintain the marriage. In fact, shortly afterwards Mr P pronounced himself much happier in his new surroundings and remained so on long-term follow-up. His daughter was very pleased and admitted somewhat guiltily to the therapist that this was what she had wanted from the beginning. However, she had felt it her duty to look after him and had therefore been unable to say that she did not want him and to suggest that he would be better off elsewhere – she wanted first to show that she had tried. Regrettably, this could have been achieved much earlier, and at less emotional cost, if the therapist had recognized the signs which hinted at her hidden agenda and acted on them by opening up a discussion of separation as a possible solution. □

Disagreements between the couple/family and the therapist   As one of us has discussed elsewhere (Carpenter, 1987a) the goals of most marital or family therapists will usually be different from those of the individual family members, at least at the beginning of therapy. This is because therapists will be working 'for the good of the family' and will understand the problems or symptoms of an individual member in terms of family relationships; the family will have to change as its members change. However, therapists appreciate that this realization must grow, and that to challenge the family members too quickly on this point will provoke them to drop out.

Typically, the therapist leads her clients to an interactional view through discussions which seek to define the problems and set the preliminary goals of therapy. For example, a schizophrenic son's problem is defined in terms of his behaviour with other people: he is apathetic and withdrawn at home (that is, with his family), and when criticized lashes out (at his father). The goals are set in terms of action: for example, his parents will spend more time talking with him in the kitchen and will refrain from criticizing his behaviour. The therapist's goal of 're-structuring' the family and perhaps eventually the marital relationship needs to remain unspoken at this early stage of therapy.

Therapy can become stuck, therefore, when the therapist's premature attempts to re-structure relationships are resisted by her clients, who are still set on achieving more restricted goals. However, it can also become stuck because of inflexibility on the part of the therapist, who may be concentrating on issues which she sees as important while her clients value others more highly. Some families are compliant in presenting goals which they feel their therapist would like to work on; they will be reluctant to make their own goals explicit, and yet if these are not dealt with therapy cannot succeed.

Of course, in some cases therapy becomes stuck because the therapist may be intent on making changes within the family which are quite unacceptable to them. (A detailed example of failure caused by this error is presented by Myerstein and Dell, 1985.) This type of problem often arises when the therapist is working with a family from a different social class or ethnic background. It can be seen in sometimes rather crude efforts of therapists to convert the families they are working with to their own values concerning family life, the role of women, the place of children, responsibilities to ageing parents, the expression of feelings and so on. Clients are usually too polite to their therapist to express their disagreements as openly as the middle-aged woman who said to her (younger) female therapist, 'But I don't *want* to be like you. I don't want to go to work. I want to look after my children when they come back from school *and* prepare a meal for my husband. I want to respect him, to look up to him ... and I want him to treat me like a lady.'

This is not to say that a therapist should not challenge her clients' values and assumptions. To do so is an essential part of the therapeutic endeavour. Her challenge should therefore be open and honest, not an underhand effort to influence through covert means. She can, for example, point out that many aspects of women's behaviour, which are described by men as personal inadequacies, are in fact very heavily socially prescribed. Women can be helped to examine what they have been taught about being female and compare the results of this brainwashing with their actual abilities, interests and needs. Similarly, men can be assisted to explore what they have been taught to think both about women and about themselves.

In some extreme cases it becomes essential for the therapist to make her own value system explicit and state that she cannot continue to work on central issues with the family (Minuchin and Fishman, 1981, p. 40). Such cases might include criminal behaviour and the exploitation of weaker family members such as children, women, elderly people and people with disabilities. In some of these cases the therapist, as probation officer or social worker, might have statutory duties to inform or protect. In others, the therapist may decide to abandon her role as a therapist in order to act as

an advocate for the needs of the exploited individual concerned.
Disagreements in the problem system   As we have already discussed,
stuckness may occur when different members of the problem system
disagree about the nature of the problem. When they agree about
the problem but disagree about goals, the situation can be even
more tricky because it is less easy to recognize. Typically,
representatives of the professional agencies involved take on the
different goals of family members in conflict. Indeed, as Britton
(1981) describes, professionals may, in their own relationships with
each other, re-enact aspects of the family's own conflicts. These
conflicts are often about the goals of therapy.

> □ A social worker and a child psychiatrist were both involved
> with the same 'blended' family in which there was considerable
> conflict between a stepson and his stepfather. The professionals
> mirrored the covert conflict between husband and wife
> regarding the boy, with one insisting that he should go to a
> special treatment unit to help him leave home and the other
> that he should remain at home. □

Conflicts between professionals, of which the above is a straightforward example, are often attributed to the family. Thus, Reder
(1983) suggests that disorganized families often promote disorganization within the network of professionals working with them.
However, this is inevitably a two-way process and, as Will and
Baird (1984) have pointed out, there are significant differences
between professions and agencies which make some inter-professional relationships particularly prone to conflict. Some families
may promote conflict between professionals (for example, playing
one agency off against another), but it has to be recognized that
some professionals may also promote conflict in families (for
example, using the case to fight their battles for status and power).
In our experience, however, therapists who are stuck are all too
ready to blame the problems on the family rather than examining
the possibility that professional and agency conflicts are of primary
importance.
   In situations where a number of different agencies are involved,
the convening of a case conference which may or may not involve
the family is often essential. Sometimes therapists are reluctant to
use this approach, because they see it as less worthy of their time
and skills. At other times they fall prey to the illusion that the

therapist can take control of the problem system (Myerstein and Dell, 1985, p. 266). This illusion is common, and was unfortunately encouraged by Haley's assertion in his book *Leaving Home* that it was necessary for a family therapist to be in charge of all decisions regarding a person's treatment (Haley, 1980, pp. 59–60). As we illustrated many times in *Using Family Therapy* (Treacher and Carpenter, 1984), family therapy has to be, and can be, practised effectively in health and social service agencies without the therapist having such control. The problems arise when the therapist strives for the impossible and in so doing begins to see the various members of the problem system as people to be defeated, rather than as potential allies.

In our experience, a case conference can be liberating to the therapist who has become stuck in the role of 'expert', but this requires the therapist to make it clear that she is asking her colleagues for help. In a context in which their professional skills are acknowledged and valued, professional colleagues can and will help, initially by clarifying their roles and responsibilities and then by discussing their perceptions of the problem and their goals for the family. Finally, a joint approach to helping the clients can be agreed, with different professionals and agencies agreeing to make different but compatible contributions to the problem solving involved.

Some of our readers might think that the direct and open approach we are advocating is naive, since it appears first to ignore inter-professional and inter-agency conflicts and secondly to assume that the professional network is benign. In reply, we would assert that this approach is both pragmatic and principled – in practice it is those therapists who attempt to assert a one-up position (through adopting such tactics as 'prescribing the behaviour of the professional network') who are naive and disrespectful to their colleagues. Most conflicts between professionals which are based on misunderstandings about roles and responsibilities or a competition to be the most effective helper can be resolved quite easily if approached in the way we are recommending. If they cannot, then it is time to call in a consultant to organize the kind of network meeting described by Dimmock and Dungworth (1985), in their highly detailed and practical paper. This meeting is analogous to a family meeting with a therapist to resolve stuckness in the family system. In this case, the therapist is the 'client' who is asking for help with stuckness in the problem system – of which she is now a part.

Of course, a full case conference or network meeting will often not be necessary or appropriate. Frequently, all that is required is for the therapist to contact the relevant members of the problem system by phone or personal visit in order to establish their views and negotiate an agreed approach. Sometimes, however, the therapist will be unable to convene a meeting and may quite appropriately conclude that despite her best efforts a more powerful agency will determine the outcome of the case. This is most often true when such an agency has the power to remove a family member to prison, to hospital or into care. It is wise for the therapist to recognize that there are some arguments that she will just not win.

What solutions have been tried before?

Often therapy becomes stuck because the therapist has not paid sufficient attention to the solutions that her clients have tried previously. The more she insists on her solution, the more they will resist, on the understandable grounds that what failed before will not work this time. This is particularly frustrating for the therapist. She then tends to apply what she sees as the 'obvious' solution by labelling her clients' reluctance as 'resistance', rather than recognizing it as a lack of faith in the proposed solution. In many instances the solution *is* worth trying again, but the family will do this only if they can be convinced. Through a careful exploration of their previous efforts the therapist can learn what went wrong. Failure often occurs only because they did not persist long enough with a given solution. (A common example of this is parents' attempts to control their children's behaviour. The best solution, which they usually try, but for too short a time or too unconvincingly, is to be united, firm and consistent. When it does not work straight away, the parents typically try something else and become disunited and inconsistent.)

Our model of therapy (see chapter 1) emphasizes that the therapist should ask about 'attempted solutions' at the initial stage, and this is particularly important when the clients have been in therapy before. Coleman's analysis of the failed cases described in *Failures in Family Therapy* (1985, p. 335) revealed that seventy-five per cent had had previous therapy. We would not conclude that this failure was because they were 'resistant cases', but rather that the therapists were more likely to be pursuing solutions which had been tried before. Our suggestion, therefore, is that the therapist explore with her clients what the previous therapists had attempted – not from a position of arrogance ('They failed, so they must be fools') but from one of respect ('Although they were trying hard, it seems that what they were doing with you didn't work out. Please let me know what went wrong from your point of view so that I don't make the same mistakes').

What are the clients' understandings of what will be helpful and unhelpful in achieving change?

The client's views on how to achieve change (chapter 1) are often different from the therapist's, and this can be a fundamental cause of stuckness. Families with psychosomatic problems or problems that have received an organic label are particularly difficult to work with if they believe that a 'medical' approach is the only way to achieve a solution. But families with members who have been diagnosed as psychiatrically ill are equally problematic. If the therapist's re-framing of the problem in behavioural or psychological terms is unsuccessful, then therapy flounders. In such cases an adoption of an 'as if' technique can be valuable.

□ A husband and wife disagreed over whether their twenty-three-year-old daughter's childish behaviour was due to encephalitis, or (as the wife insisted) to psychological problems associated with her leaving home. Following consultation, the therapist took the husband's position very seriously and asked him to present his understanding of the case in great detail. He provided a blow-by-blow account of the ins and outs of the treatment of the daughter's encephalitis. This had involved two different hospitals, and eight different doctors, including two neurologists and two psychiatrists. His presentation took an hour and a half to record on a series of blackboards! The husband was clearly relieved that the therapist was interested in everything he had to say. He was able to accept the suggestion that, as all his medical advisers had said, it was not an organic problem and should best be treated, for a few months at least, as though it were a psychological one. The husband was able to accept this 'as if' contract without losing face – particularly as the therapist was respectful of the way in which he had left no stone unturned in his efforts to obtain the best possible medical care for his daughter. □

This 'as if' technique can also be used in reverse in order to gain manoeuvrability.

☐ In working with a man who thought he was manic depressive (although he had agreed to attend a marital therapy clinic), the therapist accepted his position categorically, saying that he respected the client's view but was puzzled as to why he had not sought help from a psychiatrist instead of coming to the clinic. The therapist then delivered a short 'lecture' on his understanding of the medical view of manic-depressive psychosis, stressing the use of lithium carbonate as the preferred form of treatment. Ironically, this had the effect of making a marital therapy approach to the presenting problem of 'moodiness' more acceptable. ☐

If the therapist and the client family cannot agree on a method of approaching the problem because the family or one of its members consider the 'cause' to be 'physical', it is advisable to offer to perform tests which will clarify whether or not there is a physical problem. It is essential to get the referrer's permission to do this, since they will often be the gatekeeper who determines whether such tests can be carried out. A joint consultation with the referrer in order to present the family with a united front concerning the issue of causation may also be helpful. To save time, a referrer can be telephoned during the session and the issue quickly cleared up.

There is often a danger of moving too rapidly to resolve this type of issue, so it may be advisable to prescribe that the most sceptical family member keep careful notes in order to keep the issue of medical causation alive. Careful monitoring of the note-taking from session to session will act as a barometer of the family member's attitude to therapy. If the therapist is successful with her work in the session or with a homework task, the medical view tends to die away, except in a minority of cases in which it returns with greater intensity. If this occurs, it is best to adopt a different approach which seeks to deal with the issue much more directly. For example, a genogram can be undertaken to establish whether the position is informed by a family script or myth. Often this proves to be the case, and direct homework tasks need to be set in order to deal with the issue involved. If the family still finds it difficult to accept an alternative view, the door to therapy can be kept open by inviting them in an open-handed way to try other methods and return to therapy only if they find other methods unsuccessful. If the referrer is on the side of the therapist then the family usually returns after an interval of trying out other approaches.

The advantages and disadvantages of change

Has the therapist paid sufficient attention to her clients' understandings of the advantages and disadvantages of change? In other words, what would happen if the goal of therapy were achieved? This question requires a many-sided answer. In some cases, clients seem to want to prove that their problem is impossible to resolve – and therefore that they are not so foolish to have it, and be unable to solve it.

This tendency can be encouraged by the therapist who adopts a superior attitude, implicitly assuming that the couple or family is ignorant or rigid. The issue is about who is in charge. A similar gambit can also be played by a referring agent who may not have come to terms emotionally with his own failure to solve the family's problem. Such a referrer may have reason to hope that his successor will also fail, apparently confirming that the family was impossible to help. Such a position is usually indicated by surreptitious interventions involving the family, which are not reported to the therapist. In order to gain manoeuvrability in such situations, the therapist needs to establish carefully the advantages and disadvantages of given changes, not just for the family but for the wider system.

□ Faced with the failure to get a small boy to return to school, the therapist took time to explore what would happen if he actually succeeded in doing so. The implications for both the school and the family were established, and this revealed that if he went to school not only would there be no one to keep his grandmother company during the day (cf. Pittman and Flomenhaft, 1970), but it would also weaken the case the head teacher was making to the education department for an additional part-time teacher to help with maladjusted pupils. □

Care should also be taken to establish the gains of not changing the system.

☐ For example, the analysis of one case suggested that if the wife's agoraphobia continued she would remain the centre of attention within her family, with her husband doing the shopping and generally protecting her from the outside world. The therapist's failure to understand the very tangible gains the wife derived from having the symptoms had led her to pressurize the wife to undertake behavioural tasks. Consequently, the therapy had floundered.

The hidden benefits of symptoms are well known in psychiatric circles and are usually discussed under the heading of 'secondary gain', although there is a tendency to concentrate on the gains for the patient only. A systems analysis, in this case, revealed that the 'well' spouse did not wish to go out with his 'ill' spouse because it might interfere with the extra-marital affair in which he was involved. The revelation of this secret ultimately led to separation and divorce, and eventually to the wife's re-discovery of how to lead a more fulfilling and less dependent life. ☐

Finally, to return to a theme in chapter 1, whilst all change has its disadvantages as well as its advantages, it is not necessary to subscribe to the doctrine that all symptoms have functions, and consequently to accept the position that clients do not want to change. If they do not change, it is usually because their vision is restricted and they can see no real alternative. In other words, they have not been persuaded that the advantages outweigh the disadvantages, and/or they feel they do not have sufficient energy to make the effort.

Method and Style of Therapy

Do the therapist and her support team have sufficient knowledge and skills?

It is a mark of wisdom to acknowledge your own limitations, and it takes courage to admit that you have exceeded them. It is not surprising, therefore, that many therapists end up in deep water: wisdom and courage are not always present! As we stressed repeatedly in *Using Family Therapy* (1984), inexperienced therapists should make every effort to build up their skills by working with the more straightforward cases referred to their agencies. Or, if more difficult cases have to be tackled, then the goals of the intervention should be strictly limited – for example, to an 'assessment' of the problem rather than marital or family therapy. The temptation to prove oneself or one's method of work to sceptical colleagues should be avoided at all costs.

However, even experienced therapists can find themselves out of their depth and lacking in the necessary knowledge and skills. Thus, it is often assumed that because theories of marital and family therapy are generic, therapists should be able to transfer their skills easily between age groups and presenting problems. This does not reflect our experience. For example, skills required to form relationships with young children are not the same as those needed for work with elderly people. Furthermore, the issues facing families at different stages of the life cycle are different, and so are the characteristics of the problem systems which are formed to help. A therapist trained to work in an adult psychiatric setting is not adequately equipped to enter the maze of child sexual-abuse work, and vice versa.

The obvious answer to a lack of skills and knowledge is to overcome our reluctance and ask for help from colleagues in our own or another agency. These colleagues need not necessarily be trained in marital and family therapy: the most useful knowledge often concerns the agencies which impinge on the family (the kind of knowledge usually held by an agency supervisor or line manager), and the most vital skills may be the expertise of a therapist trained to work individually with children or elderly people. Similarly, it is good practice to ask for advice from people with special knowledge about ethnic-minority families, step-families, the effects of physical illness and disability, the use of psychotropic medication, the availability of financial and material help, and so on. The illusion that marital and family therapists have all the answers and that marital and family therapy can provide the whole solution needs to be dispelled.

Finally, we should note that knowledgeable and skilled therapists can nevertheless have personal and theoretial blind-spots, a problem we examine in the next chapter.

Does the style of therapy suit the couple or family in therapy?

There is, as yet, little research evidence to guide marital and family therapists in choosing between the many competing 'schools' (Gurman et al., 1985, pp. 593–4). The most one can say is that the effectiveness of *some* methods have been demonstrated with *some* types of presenting problems – which is not to say that they are necessarily better than other methods whose effectiveness has not been tested. In any case, as one of us has discussed before (Treacher, 1983), there are a number of reasons why research on the effectiveness of psychotherapy has little impact on practice – the most important being simply that efficacy is unimportant. The average practitioner is influenced by other practitioners whose work appeals to her for emotional and intellectual reasons. Calam and Elliott (1987) have explored the reasons why practitioners undertake so little family therapy research. They stress that research has rewards that are remote and rarely seen – a sharp contrast with the rewards of therapy. (As they put it, 'The buzz that comes from family therapy is that of seeing an hypothesis confirmed, an intervention having some impact and of seeing people enabled to change through the therapist's assistance.') And the work that actually influences therapists is not formal accounts of treatment efficacy but descriptions of theory and practice written up in the form of clinical anecdote.

At a deeper level, Calam and Elliott point out that the main agencies employing family therapists (social services and the NHS) are themselves not interested in research, as it takes considerable fortitude for a worker to devote to research time that could be spent with clients. Calam and Elliott are therefore pessimistic about what can be achieved. They conclude that all that can be expected is for practitioners to provide detailed case reports that (a) are based on detailed accounts of the *process* of therapy and (b) include some measure of the identified client's symptoms and how they change through the course of therapy.

In principle, we would support Calam and Elliott's position; but it is, in fact, much more difficult to be clear about the process of therapy than they imply. Therapists may think they know what's happening in a therapy session, but it is important to remember that it is only their subjective construction of what is happening.

Returning to the issue of matching therapy to clients, an important paper by Hudson (1980), entitled 'Different strokes for different folks', has made the point that there is probably sufficient overlap between behavioural, structural and strategic methods of working to allow a therapist to custom-build her therapy to suit the style of the family. Again, in the field of marital therapy there is a move towards 'integrative' models which provide a framework for the practitioner who wants to use the theories and methods of different schools (for example, Crowe, 1985; Gurman, 1981; Treacher, 1988). Our own position, as outlined in chapter 1, assumes that there are a number of possible levels of intervention. Consequently, different techniques will be useful at different times with the same couple or family, and some methods will be more appropriate for some clients than for others. The basis for the therapist's choice of method should be not her own preconceived ideas about what is best for her clients, but rather her clients' understandings of their problems and the best way to resolve them. It is for this reason that we favour a problem- and goal-focused approach and stress the importance of the therapeutic contract.

A common cause of stuckness is the therapist's efforts to re-frame the presenting problem in terms of family interaction, a method which is stressed more strongly in some therapeutic schools than in others. We do not doubt that re-framing is a useful and often desirable technique (especially when a member of the couple or family is feeling to blame for all their problems), but it is a technique which must be used carefully. In particular, the therapist must listen to the family members' feedback and resist arguing with them that her interpretation is correct. Common family responses are: 'Yes, that's all very interesting, but what's it all got to do with X's problem? That's why we are here.'; or 'I don't see how all this talk about how we're getting on together is going to help my depression.' Alternatively, the presenting client might simply start complaining of symptoms or begin behaving in a problematic manner during the session.

If the clients express dissent in this way, it is essential that the therapist sees re-building the therapeutic alliance as her first priority. We consider that the clients' dissent should be taken at face value, rather than as evidence of resistance. The therapist should, therefore, explain the rationale for her approach and her interest in exploring marital or family interaction. For example: 'Learning about how you all get on together helps me to understand how you can help X and also the stresses and strains you are under'. Notice that this response accommodates to the family members' concern about the presenting client. We do not consider that this is 'harmful' or against the tenets of marital or family therapy. First, the effort to re-build the alliance makes it very much more likely that the clients will return for the next session; and secondly, it is supported by the available research evidence. Thus Gurman et al. (1985, p. 582) summarize a number of studies as suggesting that many adult (and perhaps child and adolescent) psychiatric disorders improve significantly in therapy that explicitly and systematically maintains a focus on the presenting client as 'the client', without attempting to re-frame the problem as a marital or family problem, but whilst remaining sensitive to the family members' contributions. Notable amongst these studies are those by Hafner et al. (1983) on agoraphobia, and Leff et al. (1982) and Falloon et al. (1984) on schizophrenia.

Other aspects of therapeutic style concern joining and pacing, which we will now consider.

Has the therapist adopted an appropriate joining position?

We discussed joining at length in chapter 3, drawing on the work of Minuchin and Fishman (1981) who have developed a useful way of understanding whether the joining technique adopted by the therapist has been appropriate. Writing very much within Hudson's frame of 'different strokes for different folks' (1980), they point out that different types of couples and families require different joining techniques. Or, to put it another way, during the process of accommodating to the family system, the therapist will find that she arrives at either a 'close', a 'median' or a 'disengaged' position. By allowing this to happen, rather than forcing the pace because of preconceived ideas about her clients, the therapist will gain important information about the style of therapy they may be able to tolerate during the initial phases.

All forms of therapy are based on good joining, but as Coleman (1985, p. 355) observes, the particular challenge of family (and marital) therapy is that unlike a group of strangers, family members have had years of experience of dealing with each other and with outsiders. The therapist joins the system in order to help it change, and if change is to happen then *each* member must feel safe with her in order to take the necessary risks. She must therefore connect with each member and convey that she wants to understand and respect their feelings and ideas.

In order to evaluate the therapeutic alliance, Kingston (1984, pp. 389–90) suggests the following questions for the therapist to ask herself (or be asked by a colleague/supervisor): 'How do you feel about this couple or family?'; 'How far does each member appear to feel understood by you?'; 'Are you identifying with one member against someone else?' Note that the emphasis on feelings is in line with the method for recognizing stuckness described at the beginning of this chapter; feelings are the clearest possible indicator that the therapeutic alliance is breaking down. As we stated earlier, we can safely assume that when we are feeling at odds with a particular couple or family or with one of their members, they will be feeling much the same about us.

The first step in repairing the alliance with a family member is to stop and think how that person feels about you as therapist, and more exactly, about what you are doing to them. Almost inevitably, this analysis will reveal that the client feels either uninvolved, misunderstood or blamed.

The most straightforward way of resolving this problem is to acknowledge it openly, as in the following examples.

'Mr X, you do not seem to feel involved in the discussion today. You must be puzzled as to why I asked you to come.' Or, 'Is there something which you think it more important to talk about?'

'Mrs Y, I suspect you don't feel that I really understand your point of view/how you feel, and you're probably right. Please could you help me to understand it. I'm sorry I'm being so unhelpful.'

'Mr P, I get the impression that you feel I'm blaming you for what has happened. If so, I'm very sorry. Let me tell you how I understand what's been going on . . .'

In our experience, a statement of this kind will usually retrieve the situation, and – provided that the therapist listens carefully to her clients' responses and acts on them – the therapeutic alliance can be restored. Sometimes, however, the therapist typically becomes stuck in a particular role within the couple or family system. This is a much broader topic which we will discuss in the next chapter.

Is the therapist working at a pace which suits the couple or family?

The issue of pacing is of crucial importance, yet it receives too little attention from many therapists who tend to work solely at their own pace and level of intensity rather than that of their clients. From the therapist's point of view, it is often inconvenient that clients differ so much and that a fifty-minute session once a week or once a fortnight does not suit them all. Particularly for clients in an acute crisis, successful therapy might require the therapist to give a great deal of time and support – though not necessarily in the form of therapy sessions, since telephone calls will often be adequate. On the other hand, some clients will find the pace too hot, indicating this by failing to attend sessions or to complete tasks set by the therapist.

Needless to say, the solution to differences in pacing lies in discussing them directly with the family, as part of a regular review of the progress of therapy in general and of the impact of the therapist's interventions in particular (see chapter 1). Similarly, as part of our contractual approach, we negotiate the frequency of the sessions from meeting to meeting, and especially in the latter stages of work when we typically move from fortnightly or monthly meetings to sessions six to twelve weeks apart. (See Palazzoli, 1980, for a full discussion of the time interval between sessions.)

Has the therapist been suitably creative in designing tasks?

Often therapy gets stuck because the timing of a session has gone astray, so that there is little time left at the end to design an adequate task. Badly designed tasks which, for theoretical or practical reasons (or both), cannot induce change seem to be a common cause of stuckness. A task that they find trivial or too complicated will cause the clients to lose confidence in their therapist. Unfortunately, as we have cautioned throughout, their failure to achieve it may be compensated by the therapist labelling the family as un-cooperative or resistant.

Haley (1976, p. 64) recommends that when clients fail to do tasks the therapist should express regret that they missed an opportunity to change. Similarly, Anderson and Stewart (1983, p. 105) state that 'Failure to perform tasks is always a resistance', although they do go on to acknowledge that the 'resistance' may well be caused by 'therapist error'. Our position is that task failure is always the therapist's mistake, since it was her responsibility to design and set a task which her clients could achieve. (There is one exception to this rule: occasionally a task may be set which the clients are expected to fail: this is a 'strategic' task, designed to illustrate, for example, the folly of a particular form of destructive behaviour.)

Dryden and Hunt (1985, p. 153) remind us that it is the therapist's job first to help her clients see the *relevance* of the homework task – to demonstrate how implementing it will bring them closer to their goals – and secondly, to help them execute the task as efficiently as possible. They reviewed studies by Maluccio (1979) and Silverman (1970) which suggested that therapists typically gave clients little explanation of the value of talk as the medium for change, and hence did not establish the relevance of communication or talking tasks for achieving their goals.

In addition to the failure to explain relevance, other common errors in task setting are that the task

1 was not adequately explained and/or important details were left out,
2 was expressed in negative terms only – what the clients should *not* do, rather than what they should do,
3 omitted important members of the system,
4 was too ambitious.

Despite apparently believing in clients' resistance, Anderson and Stewart (1983) agree with us concerning the advantages of the therapist's admitting mistakes in task setting. By doing so, and by setting a more appropriate task, the therapist not only enhances her credibility but also prevents her clients feeling blamed and/or foolish for not being able to do the task.

The first step is to evaluate the task with the couple or family in terms of its relevance to them. If they accept its relevance, the therapist should review their efforts to undertake the task, in order to establish what precisely went wrong. Having accepted responsibility, there are, as Anderson and Stewart suggest, a number of different options for the therapist:

1 Asking the clients if they would like to try the task once more

– in effect, giving them a second chance to test their own motivation for change. It is wise to make some small variations in the instruction, thus saving them any possible embarrassment.

2   Setting an easier or more specific task. This is preferable to abandoning the idea of a task, something which would probably decrease the clients' confidence in the therapist. The task can be limited in scope, or the time available for its completion extended. On the other hand, the original task may have been too vague and far too easy to achieve; a more challenging and focused task would be indicated.

3   Give the clients the choice of repeating the original task or undertaking a new one. Anderson and Stewart suggest putting the onus for change on one part of the system on the grounds that this part might be ready to move before the others. For example, the parents might be asked to implement some changes in their relationship, irrespective of their children.

Finally, we would add that the therapist can question the clients' commitment by stating that she had erred in over-estimating their readiness to change and consequently pushing them too hard. Whilst some clients will agree, others will take this as a challenge and respond by protesting their motivation and undertaking the task.

Conclusion

In this chapter we have argued that to talk simply of 'resistant' families or even 'resistant' therapists is unhelpful. When we get the sinking feeling about a couple or family turning up again for yet another session of 'therapy' we try to re-frame this positively. The sinking feeling reflects our stuckness and demands that we examine the situation in great depth rather than temporizing and taking yet another pointless session.

It is only when stuckness has been recognized and adequately assessed that it becomes appropriate to think of new tactics. In this chapter we have attempted to define stuckness in situations where it is caused by either inadequate systemic formulation or faulty methods of therapy or both. Consideration of all the factors related to these two dimensions will identify whether secure foundations have been laid for successful therapy.

However, secure foundations do not guarantee that a building will be successfully completed. Even if the therapeutic system has been correctly formed it may yet become stuck. In the next chapter we explore forms of stuckness which can be more directly related to the therapeutic system and the structure of supervision and support within which the therapist works. To attempt to overcome this stuckness is, we contend, the therapist's responsibility.

Further Reading

Andolfi, M. (1979) *Family Therapy*. Chapter 4 offers a useful classification of tasks.

Crowe, M. (1985) 'Marital therapy. A behavioural-systems approach: indications for different types of intervention', in W. Dryden (ed.), *Marital Therapy in Britain*, vol. I. Presents a progression of therapeutic interventions from behavioural to strategic and indications for their use with increasingly difficult problems.

Dimmock, B. and B. Dungworth (1985), 'Beyond the family: using network meetings with statutory child-care cases', *Journal of Family Therapy*, 7, 45–68. Guidelines for network meetings with the 'problem system'.

Furniss, T. (1983), 'Mutual influence and interlocking professional–family process in the treatment of child sexual abuse and incest', *Child Abuse and Neglect*, 7, 207–23. Discussion of mirroring and 'conflict by proxy' in the problem system, with a powerful case example.

8

Stuckness in the Therapeutic and Supervisory Systems

In the previous chapter we considered 'stuckness' arising from the therapist's failure to understand the context in which therapy is taking place and to have made a clear contract with her clients. We also discussed stuckness as a result of the therapist's method and style. In this chapter we move on to an examination of the therapeutic and supervisory systems. First, looking at the therapeutic system we note that if the therapist is not part of the solution then she is almost certainly part of the problem. She may either have been 'sucked in' to the dynamics of her clients' conflicts or problems, or 'locked out' from making any impact at all. Secondly, we note that whilst supervision and consultation are set up as safeguards against stuckness and in order to help find solutions to the problems of therapy, the supervisory system itself may become stuck.

Sucked In or Locked Out? – The Loss of Manoeuvrability

In the same way that a client's 'attempted solutions' become the 'problem' (Watzlawick et al., 1974), so too may their therapist's attempted solutions. Their therapist may persist with repeated doses of the same medicine ('more of the same'), creating a repetitive cycle of interaction and ensuring that no change will take place. The therapist becomes a homeostatic part of the system, part of the problem rather than part of the solution, losing all her therapeutic leverage or 'manoeuvrability' (Fisch et al., 1982, ch. 2).

This concept of 'manoeuvrability' seems to us to be particularly useful in understanding the therapist's experience of being stuck. Many couples and families come to therapy because they are stuck: stuck in repetitive cycles of behaviour, thoughts and feelings and unable to find a way out. If their therapy is to be successful, then they must encounter a therapist who has at her disposal a wide range of skills and the ability to make use of *herself* in a variety of ways. Haley (1980, p. 273) has described the situation in the following way:

> Sometimes [s]he must take charge; at other times [s]he must be helpless so that others will take charge. [S]he must be serious but at times introduce humour; [s]he must be flirtatious at one moment and distant at another. One of the therapist's tasks is to be intensely involved in a situation at one moment and to sit on the periphery of it the next. Sometimes the therapist must be repetitive, insisting over and over on the same behaviour; at other times [s]he must be changeable . . .

However, as he also states, 'to be both human and a professional expert is a difficult task for some therapists'. In our experience this problem, which we have all encountered, applies particularly to beginning therapists. It is graphically described by Coulshed (1981): 'I did not manage to convince the family that I was more human than otherwise.' It is difficult not to be wooden and immovable when learning new skills. Once they have been mastered, then, as Minuchin and Fishman (1981, p. 1) advise in the introduction to their book *Family Therapy Techniques*, the books should be given away.

Therapists, then, can be stuck in the rigidity of their learning. They can also be stuck within the limitations of their use of self. In this section we examine some of the technical and personal aspects of the loss of manoeuvrability. Following Haley and Minuchin and Fishman, we consider that successful therapy requires flexibility and invention. As Minuchin and Fishman put it: 'Any technique may be useful, depending on the therapist, the family and the moment' (1981, p. 31).

Sucked In?

Is the Therapist Stuck in the System?

The therapist must have an understanding of the system as a whole, and within the structural model this is gained by mobilizing joining skills which at the same time allow the couple or family to 'absorb' the therapist temporarily. She can then experience the family's properties, understand its rules and intervene from within (for example, through 'unbalancing') and without (for example, by means of 'restructuring' and 'boundary making') as Minuchin and Fishman (1981) point out.

However, the therapist may become stuck *in* the system, for example by being in conflict with one member and yet in sympathy with the others. Alternatively, she may take the side of the 'powerless, sick victim' (for example that of the child against the apparent victimizers, the parents (Carr, in press)). As we suggested in the previous chapter, this is usually indicated by 'linear thinking': 'Mr Smith is a chauvinist pig', 'Mrs Smith has a schizoid personality disorder', or more subtly 'Jimmy is just their scapegoat'.

Typically, the therapist takes on a role: she may, for example, try to be a 'surrogate' mother, either because she feels that the real mother does not have the capacity herself, or in order to detour conflict.

□ A therapist had become stuck in the role of conflict-detourer between mother and daughter on behalf of the father (and the family). The family, consisting of parents and twenty-one-year-old daughter, had been referred because of the daughter's heroin addiction. The family had been seen some half dozen times, during which period the therapist felt he had lost therapeutic direction and manoeuvrability. He brought the case for consultation to a team with whom he worked regularly. It became clear to the group and the therapist that he had allowed the father to continue detouring conflict while apparently trying to arbitrate difficulties between the two female family members. This effectively prevented mother and daughter from sorting out their differences, since communication was routed via father. It also protected the parents from ever dealing with each other as spouses.

The therapist was instructed by his colleagues to ask the mother (who had a drink problem) and her daughter to discuss what they had in common, namely their respective addiction problems. In doing this, and in keeping the father out of this discussion, the therapist adopted the father's conflict-detouring position, intervening to smooth over any difficulties and disagreements as they arose. The therapist had merely substituted for the father and no real change had taken place. The father was able to tolerate exclusion on those terms, but as the therapist became more effective at encouraging greater emotional closeness between the mother and daughter, the father became more intrusive. It was necessary for the therapist to alter the seating, to place daughter alongside mother and to sit next to the father himself in order to emphasize the importance of the two women talking together without interference from the two men (father and therapist). From that point, the affective level of the session changed, although it remained necessary for the consulting team to monitor the therapist's tendency to be drawn in. □

Haley (1980, p. 45), with his particular focus on triangles, is alert to the situation in which the therapist will substitute for one party in order to 'stabilize' the other two. For example, the therapist may 'detach' an adolescent from the triangle with his parents only to find herself taking his place. The parents, who were previously united only in their concern about their child's behaviour, now come together in relation to the therapist, often in a similar pattern of love and hate. The difficult task for the therapist is then to free herself without either attracting the adolescent back or involving a younger sibling as a replacement. This requires her to use her position within the triangle to effect change in the parents' relationship before she withdraws.

The same process occurs in marital therapy, although it is less obvious because there is not such a clear substitution (Haley, 1976, ch. 6). Nevertheless, many marital conflicts are stabilized by a third party who, if not a child, may be a parent, a sympathetic neighbour or another professional. The therapist may become stuck through having taken over this person's role when the couple entered therapy. Alternatively, as in the following example, the therapist may become locked in competition for the triangulated position.

□ A psychiatrist referred a woman and her husband for marital therapy. However, in making the referral she indicated that a major part of the problem, as she saw it, was the unhelpful involvement of a retired social worker who had taken on the role of confidante and advocate for the wife. They had crossed swords most recently when the social worker had discouraged the wife from taking medication which the psychiatrist had prescribed, and had accused the (female) psychiatrist of not caring enough. There was, however, no disagreement between them on the question of who was to blame for the marital difficulties – the husband.

The marital therapist invited all four members of the problem system to attend a meeting, although the husband failed to turn up. He was reported by the wife as having said that he had no intention of going along to be criticized by three women. It soon became apparent to both the social worker and the psychiatrist that their coalition with the wife against her husband was unhelpful in that it prevented any change in the marital relationship. Any attempt the wife made to talk with her husband ended in a row about her professional allies. (Previously, the couple's rows had been about the wife's mother, but these stopped when she died.) The competing therapists were both able to acknowledge that they had become substitutes for the deceased mother and their personal dispute merely made matters worse, since it placed the wife in a conflict of loyalties with her two 'supporters'. The marital therapist was then able to make a contract in which both psychiatrist and social worker agreed to withdraw in order to give marital therapy a chance. A new effort to engage the husband (by inviting him to an initial individual interview and assuring him of the therapist's neutrality) was successful, and the difficulties between the couple were eventually resolved. □

Transference and Countertransference

The psychoanalytic literature uses the terms transference and countertransference (Skynner, 1979; Stierlin, 1975; Whitaker et al., 1965) to describe the process of substitution which we have been describing. For example, Dare (1981, p. 293) states that in family therapy,

> ... the therapist can be observed responding to aspects of the family in ways that are identical to those defined by countertransference. That is to say, the therapist tends to be put into a relationship with the family that represents not just the professional functioning of the therapist, nor the open wishes of the family to get help, but are the outcome of the

family finding a role for the therapist which is in keeping with their habitual ways of functioning. This process is known as affiliation, and it both endangers the professional (and therapeutic) activities of the therapist, but, if identified, is a rich source of understanding of the nature of the family.'

This is seen by authors such as Whitaker et al. (1965) and Ferber et al. (1972) as an inevitable, two-way process. As the family or couple try to find a role for the therapist in terms of their own past and present experiences, so does the therapist respond in ways which relate to her own family. Ferber et al. (1972, p. 441) describe this as the inevitable, secret presence of the therapist's own family in the therapy room.

For those therapists who work from a psychoanalytic or an object-relations base, working with transference and countertransference remains the central focus of therapy. (The classic book on marital therapy is by Dicks (1967), but more recently Scharff and Scharff (1987) have outlined a form of object-relations family therapy.) But, as Feld (1982) remarks, even if we take as given the existence of the unconscious, and therefore of transference and countertransference, is it always nècessary to uncover and deal with these phenomena in order to provide successful therapy? Because we do not work from a psychoanalytic position our answer is essentially pragmatic – you need to pay attention to such reactions when you get stuck.

Bowen's model of family therapy (Bowen, 1966) takes the minimal position that the therapist should avoid triangulation, defined by his followers Guerin and Guerin (1976, p. 99) as being '... emotionally locked into the process in the family in such a way that you seem a victim and a villain. It means that the issues being raised by the family trigger something in you [as therapist] so that you behave vis-à-vis the family or one of its members in a way that demonstrates you are reactive to their toxic behaviours.' They go on to note (1976, p. 100) that, 'One good indication that you have been caught in the system is that you notice that you don't have any more questions or any more thoughts, or a sense of where you want to move with the family.' This is as good a description of the loss of manoeuvrability as you will find!

According to Bowen's model, the therapist's task is to stay 'detriangulated', and whilst this is not the overall strategy we advocate, Guerin and Guerin's ideas on recovering this detriangulated

position are of considerable interest. Most importantly, they stress
the therapist's monitoring of her own 'personal triggers' – that is,
the behaviours of the family members that activate an emotional
response in the therapist. 'Is someone talking too much? not talking
at all? contradicting everyone in sight? or invalidating what I think
is going on?' In other words, the therapist steps back from her
concern with tracking the *content* of the interview and pays attention
to its *process*.

Not surprisingly, even though his theoretical emphasis is very
different, Sluzki makes the same recommendation (Sluzki, 1978, p.
389). As he elaborates, '. . . cease paying attention to content, and
observe verbal patterns, sequences, gestures and postures, and/or
observe your own emotions, attitudes or postures'. Consequently,
in order to regain her perspective it is the *therapist* who must
change *her* behaviour.

Guerin and Guerin (1976, p. 100) suggest feeding back to the
family a question related to the therapist's personal trigger (as
identified above): '. . . I assume that if the behaviour is bugging me,
then there's a good possibility that it also bugs some family members.'
Thus, if the trigger is the husband's vagueness, the question posed
to his wife might be, 'What do you do when faced with your husband's
vagueness?'

A possible difficulty with this method, however, is that it may
be experienced unhelpfully as a form of blaming in that it attributes
the problem to a member of the family. As we have argued earlier,
if the therapist is stuck with the family then they too are stuck with
her: if she thinks the husband is being vague and defensive then
the likelihood is that he is experiencing her just as he experiences his
wife – that is, as attacking and unsympathetic. Our recommendation
therefore is that the therapist completes this intervention by adding
in the other side of the coin and asking the husband how he usually
deals with his wife's complementary behaviour.

The essential conceptual skill in marital and family therapy is the
ability to see both sides of the coin and to understand what is going
on from the various points of view of the different participants.
Most therapists are able to retrieve this perspective once they realize
that they have been sucked in. The difficulty, as we have stressed
frequently, is in recognizing the stuckness and stopping, and not
ploughing on with the same 'solutions'. It is because recognition is
difficult that many family therapists, as we discuss later, work with
a live consultant or supervisor either in the room or behind a one-

way screen. If, however, the therapist is unable to acknowledge her loss of perspective then she will certainly have to pay attention to her countertransference reactions by examing the resonances in her personal life of the couple or family's behaviour. This is, in our view, essential if she is frequently 'caught' in certain roles or with certain types of family.

Is the Therapist Frequently 'Caught' in Certain Roles or with Certain Types of Family?

If the answer to this question is affirmative, then, as we have been discussing, it is most likely that the 'problem' is related to a 'personal agenda' or 'unfinished business' that the therapist brings to the situation.

Pascoe (1980) notes that therapists use specific labels such as 'depressed, 'chaotic' and 'irresponsible' when describing what they consider to be their problem clients. He insists that therapists usually deny that they possess these characteristics themselves, and recommends as a useful exercise that they should identify with a quality they dislike and claim it as 'part' of themselves: 'Once claimed as a characteristic of self, the therapist is asked how being depressed, manipulative, irresponsible or weak is useful in their personal lives and would they brag or boast about this characteristic. Having claimed this piece of themselves experientially, they are able to arrive at a new understanding . . . and use it.' (Pascoe, 1980, p. 222)

Additionally, we would recommend that all therapists should consider the implications of their experiences as members of their own families for those families with whom they work. A simple co-counselling exercise which can be done in a training session or supervision group is to invite participants to consider a time in their lives when the search for a solution to a family difficulty might have benefited from the intervention of an outside person – in other words, a time when their family was 'stuck'. They are then asked to reflect on whether there would have been 'resistance' to help offered and by which member or members of the family the resistance would have been most clearly expressed. Most participants are able to identify such a situation and are successful in relating it to difficulties they experience in working with couples and families.

Feld (1982) points out that countertransference reactions may be to one person (for example, the father, as though he were her own father), to a process of communication (for example, arguing), to a pervasive feeling (such as fear), as well as to the system as a whole (as in a therapist's response to a family in which sexual abuse or violence has been taking place). In our experience, it has been important to identify the 'personal triggers' as closely as possible. It is not usually sufficient for the therapist to declare, 'Men like that drive me mad!' Instead, a colleague or supervisor should help her to define what it is about particular men, in terms of their behaviour, their physical appearance and the feelings they engender, that provoke the therapist's response.

□ A male therapist described in a supervision group how he became paralysed in therapy sessions if a father verbally attacked one of his children. Encouraged to recall his feelings when this happened, he described anger and fear and, with the supervisior's prompting, he was able to recognize these as emotions he had frequently experienced as a child when humiliated by his articulate and controlling father.

His father had in fact died some years before, but the therapist was able to undertake some personal work in order to discover a sense of his own power, which enabled him to deal with further parental attacks in therapy sessions. □

Broderick (1983) lists some further examples of therapists' past experiences which can develop strong countertransference reactions:

1 Therapists who have experienced abusive violent relationships in their own background may find it very difficult to deal with violent or bullying clients because the resonances are just too powerful.
2 Therapists who were neglected, treated unfairly or taught that they were of no value as children may find it difficult when faced with a client having a similar background.
3 Therapists who are competent and well organized but have spent a significant part of their lives being frustrated by incompetent, unreliable, self-centred relatives may have a lot of difficulty with passive clients who recapitulate these situations.
4 Therapists who have grown up in the shadow of more beautiful, talented or accomplished siblings may have trouble dealing with clients who exhibit these same characteristics.

Bowen (1974) developed a model of therapy in which individuals are coached in self-differentiation through the resolution of family conflicts by making direct contact with their families of origin. Carter and Orfanidis (1976, pp. 209–14) recount a beautiful example of a therapist dealing with countertransference problems by this method:

□ A twenty-five-year old family therapist would, when bogged down in therapy, react in a way which inevitably exacerbated the stuckness. She became an 'over-responsible do-gooder' who placated and tried to make everything 'nice' in the family. Her efforts to offer sweet reason only served to render them less and less able to deal with the difficulties which confronted them. However, as she gained an understanding of her own family (through a process of contacting her relations) she began to appreciate and then relinquish her own role within the family as the even-tempered mediator and emotional caretaker. By losing this role in her own family she was able to allow her therapy families to work out their own problems. □

We should stress that countertransference reactions can involve the therapist's present circumstances as well as those in her past. As Gurman (1984) notes in a discussion of marital therapy, '. . . it is nearly impossible for most therapists not to encounter, in their own current intimate relationships, the painful issues involved in the relationships of patient couples . . .' This point is elaborated by Broderick (1983), who remarks that if a therapist's own marriage is in disrepair and she feels a degree of instability, loneliness, self-pity or lack of a sexual relationship, then there may be a hazard in working closely with a couple which has an attractive member who might become a source of emotional support and nurturance. The other half of this process, of course, involves the husband or wife seeing in the therapist someone who is so much more warm, understanding, sensitive and attractive than their partner!

Finally, we should note that countertransference reactions do not occur only with individual therapists. We will therefore return to this topic later in the chapter when we discuss co-therapy.

Locked Out?

Is the Therapist Stuck as a Peripheral Member of the Therapeutic System?

A therapist can lose manoeuvrability by being stuck within the couple or family system, but alternatively she could find herself stuck at its periphery. There are probably two reasons for this latter kind of stuckness: (a) that she is afraid of exposing something in the system that makes her uncomfortable; (b) that her formulation and strategy are 'wrong', or rather, 'unhelpful', and yet she is insisting on them.

Is the Therapist Afraid of Exposing Something in the Family that Makes her Uncomfortable?

If her clients sense that their therapist is unhappy to discuss certain problems, for example violence and sexuality, then they usually co-operate in avoiding these subjects because they make them feel uncomfortable too. The content of the sessions then settles down to 'safe' topics such as child rearing, the state of the country today or the impossibility of living with the presenting client (so long as this is just a theoretical discussion). Ironically, such discussions leave both clients and therapist feeling stuck and frustrated that they are not 'getting down to the real business'.

In the first instance, we would recommend that the therapist ask herself what she feels most anxious about when in the presence of the couple or family. Usually this will be a distressing or taboo subject such as violence, separation, sexuality (especially homosexuality and incest), and death. We suggest that she then confront these issues directly on the assumption that their exposure and subsequent resolution will be the core of the therapy. Again, for the therapist to take responsibility is often the best tactic: for example, 'I've not helped you to get down to what I expect is really bothering you.'.

In earlier chapters we have considered how to tackle problems associated with violence and incest. Similarly, one of the outcomes of the therapist raising the issue of stuckness in this way is for one member of the couple or family to make a telephone call or to ask for a private word with the therapist – a topic we discussed earlier in the chapter on secrets. With regard to taboo subjects such as sexuality and death, it is essential that the therapist conveys that she is ready to discuss them and that she will not make judgements. Furthermore, she should emphasize that her clients' thoughts and feelings are not bizarre and are understandable in terms of their context. A useful formula is: 'Given X, I could quite understand it if you felt like doing/thought Y' (for example, 'Given the stress that you were under at the time, I could quite understand it if you had felt really quite pleased when he killed himself'; 'Given your strict family upbringing, I could quite understand it if you felt revulsion at the thought that you might be homosexual.'). Note that this formula is couched in terms of a possibility – 'if' – and does not insist that this is the way that a client is thinking or feeling. Needless to say, an immediate denial does not necessarily mean that the hypothesis is wrong: people usually need time to digest such an intervention. However, once the thoughts or feelings have been acknowledged, the clients may need some gentle pushing to examine them in more detail.

To this end, Paul (1976) has used 'stressor tapes', recordings of couples and families discussing emotionally-charged subjects, especially repressed grief-reactions and sexuality. He played these tapes to clients in therapy, encouraging them to empathize with the speakers and then to remember and discuss similar experiences in their own lives. Alternatively, clients can be asked to bring photographs to the session.

☐ An elderly couple had been engaged for some months in marital therapy, but – after some initial progress – the work had lost momentum. The therapist, reflecting on what it was that she was most anxious to avoid, realized that she had been making considerable efforts not to refer to the husband's physical disabilities – he had lost both legs in World War II.

In the following session, the therapist invited the couple to discuss the effects of the husband's disability. However, this request was anxiously brushed aside by the wife, who said that it had happened so long ago that it was now part of their life and of no relevance to their present difficulties. Nevertheless, she confirmed that she still had some old pre-War photographs from their wedding and agreed to bring these to the next meeting.

The photographs, showing the handsome, upright figure of her young husband, provided the means by which they were able to unblock not only a great emotional dam of past hurts but also the path to an open discussion of their present feelings. He was able to express frustration at his wife's acting only as his 'nurse' and not as his partner. She retorted that it was the only way she knew to cope with the overwhelming feeling that she had 'lost' her husband during the War. Over the course of the next few months they were able to renew their relationship, including re-establishing sexual relations for the first time in over thirty years. □

Finally, like Pascoe (1980) we recommend that therapists should periodically ask themselves what types of couple or family and what kinds of issues they specifically fear. Having done so, they should relate these fears to their own families of origin and procreation, as suggested in the previous section.

Is the Therapist's Formulation and Strategy Unhelpful?

There is of course a stage beyond which simple persistence is unhelpful: the more the therapist insists on a particular formulation or intervention, the more the family insist that she is wrong. It is then insufficient to label the family as 'resistant' because they deny her expertise (Solomon, 1969). Coleman (1985, p. 347) suggests that many failures in therapy are associated with theoretical oversights or omissions, and offers a checklist of questions for the therapist to consider in assessing her formulation. This includes:

1 What theoretical framework is being used?
2 Are hypotheses formulated and do these include the presenting problem?
3 Are life-cycle issues included?
4 Are inter-generational issues included?
5 Is the history of the family of procreation included? This might reveal the loss of a child, significant separations, previous medical and psychological problems and treatment etc.
6 Are all systems levels assessed: family as a system, marital system and each individual as a psychological sub-system and a biological sub-system?

Obviously, different theoretical approaches to marital and family therapy will stress different questions more rigorously than others and, as we have indicated, we do not consider that any one has the monopoly of the truth (cf. Kaffman, 1987, and Rakoff, 1984).

In looking for an alternative formulation or set of hypotheses, the help of colleagues in a supervision group is invaluable and should be sought if at all possible. It is essential for the therapist to remember that she should not be trying to defend her own ideas but rather to hear and assess as many alternatives as possible. If supervision is not available, then a lot of progress can be made by imagining the responses of well-known proponents of different marital and family therapy schools – namely, 'What would Pincus/Ellis/Satir/Minuchin/Haley etc. have to say?'

According to Coleman's analysis of family therapy failures (Coleman, 1985, pp. 347–50) a number of issues typically received only minimal attention or were omitted altogether. Most striking of these was separation and loss which was embedded in seventy-five per cent of all cases studied, a finding which would hardly surprise Rakoff (1984) who has remarked on the tendency of many therapists to divorce a family from its history. Similarly, issues of power were considered to present severe problems in two-thirds of the cases and to have received inadequate attention. In particular these involved hierarchical inversions – where one sub-system, a child or children, exercised power inappropriate to the stage of the life cycle – and cross-generational coalitions in which a parent and child were in coalition against another adult. (See Haley, 1976, ch. 4 for a full discussion of these concepts.)

Discussion of the influence of intergenerational patterns on present behaviour was conspicuous by its absence from Coleman's cases. We agree with her that although such patterns are not given much significance in many theoretical models, in complex cases intergenerational processes are too important to be overlooked.

Finally, recalling the example quoted in chapter 1, we should reiterate the importance of biological factors in assessing the adequacy of a formulation. Johnson (1987) and Coyne (1987) have emphasized their significance, especially in relation to adult psychiatric problems. There is consistent evidence that a combination of psychotherapeutic and medical approaches offers the best results. On the other hand, a straightforward medical assessment may be sufficient in itself. As Lask (1987, p. 212) pleads, 'Can we allow a child to have an asthma attack because of a chest infection?'

The error of over-elaborate theorizing which Lask highlights is termed by Rakoff (1984, p. 209) the 'Schliemann error', after the nineteenth-century archaeologist who managed to miss the levels of Homer's Troy in his digging because they were much nearer the surface than he thought. His 'Troy' turned out to be the remains of a prehistoric village many levels below. As Rakoff remarks, 'The Troy we want to enter for therapeutic purposes may be available at a more obvious level than some of the more esoteric models of family functioning suggest.'

Having reassessed her formulation, the therapist is in a position to re-design her therapeutic strategy remembering that interventions can be made at a number of different levels (as discussed in chapter 1). If, however, no new ideas of merit are forthcoming or the clients are reluctant to explore them, the therapist can consider two remaining approaches. The first is to switch from a focus on *problems* to a focus on *goals*; the second invites the clients to resume responsibility for change, on the assumption that it has been appropriated by the therapist.

A Focus on Goals

Kaffman (1987) has described how an intensive and persistent preoccupation with the presenting clients' problems and symptoms can become the most important and absorbing issue in the life of the family. The problem and the reactions to it, he suggests, '. . . become a kind of prison, whose high walls isolate the family and therapist from the surrounding world' (1987, p. 318). The therapist too becomes an additional source of energy which fuels the problem.

The alternative approach, as Kaffman suggests, is for the therapist to divert the energy that the couple or family have been wasting in brooding on their problems into more constructive channels, so that they can start to live again. He proposes two steps (1987, p. 320): (1) a 'moratorium' of six months in which there is no discussion of, or action around, the complaint, and (2) planning for the whole family, and for the presenting client in particular, an appropriate programme of constructive 'competing activities' that will replace preoccupation with the problem.

☐ A sixty-seven-year-old man had been referred with his wife following unsuccessful medical treatment for depression and severe, persistent headaches which were so bad he was unable to go out of the house. Following an initial preoccupation with the search for a medical solution, the couple agreed to treat it 'as if' it were a psychological problem (see previous chapter). However, in spite of detailed analysis of the psychological aspects and situational contexts of the problem, including the keeping of a diary, little progress was made. When it emerged that an adult daughter, a nurse who lived many miles away, had regular discussions about the problem with her mother by phone, she too was invited to the sessions. It became clear that the whole family was obsessed by the father's problem, to the exclusion of any other topic of conversation.

After hearing from the daughter at great length, the therapist was able to persuade them all to agree to a moratorium and to engage in planning for the future. She was able to achieve the moratorium by convincing them that all known medical approaches had been tried, and had failed, and that they would have to do their best to help the father carry on living in spite of his disability.

The future plan was drawn up over two sessions plus 'homework' and was spelt out in great detail. It involved all aspects of the family's life, including finding a hobby (tapestry) for the husband, while his wife went out to develop her own interests, and arrangements for the daughter and her family to visit. At the end of the six months, the husband reported that he still had the headaches from time to time, but that they were shorter in duration and less severe. More importantly, he felt much more interested and alive. □

Responsibility for Change

Lask (1986), in an article entitled 'Whose responsibility?' (which we will discuss more fully in the final chapter), reminds us that, in the final analysis, change is the client's responsibility. This remains so even if the therapist has statutory duties. She can spell out what will happen if things remain the same (for example, a probation officer can emphasize the likely consequences if offending continues), and she can even present unnegotiable demands (for example, a social worker can point out that if a child is neglected or ill-treated she will take Care proceedings). She can also stress the probable consequences if the present situation continues (such as that anorexia can lead to death). But, as the proverb says, you can take a horse to water, but you cannot make it drink.

Therapists will do well to remember that they cannot make their clients change. Highlighting the advantages and disadvantages of change for their clients is, therefore, a useful way of emphasizing that change is not the therapist's responsibility.

☐ A therapist was stuck with a couple who, although divorced, continued to live in the same house. Both parties declared their relationship to be finished and argued bitterly at home and in the therapy sessions. They expressed their concern as being for the damaging effects these rows had on their young children, as evidenced by nightmares, bed-wetting and other symptoms of anxiety. The therapist had agreed with them the goal of their separating and making arrangements to share the parenting of their children. However, all discussion of how to effect these changes inevitably became bogged down in acrimonious dispute and any suggestion made by the therapist was immediately rejected as impractical. He was left feeling like a helpless spectator.

After consultation, the following intervention was made: 'It isn't easy to separate after twelve years of marriage. During that time you've gone through a great deal together and learnt each other's strengths and weaknesses. It is not surprising that, in spite of the tremendous difficulties you are having at the moment, you still care greatly about each other. You know each other better than I could ever do. You have told me that, before you were married, you were both lonely people. You both knew, therefore, how terrible life would be for John on your own. Jill, you still care enough not to wish such loneliness on him. Again, John knows how lonely and unsupported you will feel alone in the house with two demanding and upset children. It is obvious that I have made a great mistake in trying to push you into separating when you are not yet ready. The consequences of separation are still too difficult to contemplate, yet obviously you cannot remain living together as though nothing has happened. Difficult and painful though it may be, especially for the children, to continue arguing about leaving is inevitable – at least until you are ready to change.'

The father in fact left home the following weekend, although it should be pointed out that this was not necessarily the therapist's goal. Indeed, by framing the difficulty in terms of 'readiness' to separate, the intervention is designed to give the couple a choice. Both parents returned for a series of conjoint and individual sessions and for sessions of one parent and children – all with a focus on the re-structuring of the family following separation. These sessions led to a successful termination and an encouraging follow-up a year later. □

However, even if clients do not return, such a termination is preferable to an eventual breakdown in therapy which implicitly labels the couple or family as 'resistant'. As we have argued throughout, if the family do not change then it is best to assume that they are either unable, not yet ready, or have a good reason for not changing.

This approach obviously requires a sound understanding of the clients' predicament. If that is lacking then we have found that an honest statement that we do not know what is going on or what we should do can frequently produce the most creative developments in therapy. Typically, this allows the clients to take back their share of the responsibility for change. It is not only inexperienced therapists who fall into a pattern of 'becoming a nag in pushing for change' (Coulshed, 1981). Indeed, the more experienced and 'clever' we become, the more prone we may be to the sin of 'therapeutic arrogance', assuming that no one else has either the motivation or the ability to produce change.

As Pascoe (1980, p. 219) affirms, 'If the therapist perceives that the total solution lies narcissistically within him he will preclude the tremendous ability and at times a higher degree of capacity which lies within the family as a whole . . .'. In other words, acknowledging that we are stuck is not merely a therapist's ploy: just as a therapist can help her clients in seeking out new solutions, so too can she hinder them.

Stuck Supervision

The value of supervision and support in dealing with problems in therapy has been recognized for a long time. However, such solutions, adopted by the therapist to solve the problems of stuckness, may become a source of stuckness themselves.

Co-therapy: Solution or Problem?

There is a large literature on the use of co-therapy work with families (see, for example, Holt and Greiner, 1976). One of the advantages most frequently claimed is that it provides a solution to the problem of being 'overwhelmed' by the family. As Haley (1962) described it, 'Just as many swimmers who are uneasy about drowning will associate with a life preserver, so do many family therapists prefer company when they dive into a family.' Thus, Whitaker (Napier and Whitaker, 1978) uses his co-therapists as a lifeline as he enters the family system, and in so doing is able to exert a considerable influence within it whilst retaining, with assistance, the possibility of moving out.

Other advantages claimed for co-therapy are that it enhances transference, facilitates identification and provides a model relationship for the family. It is not surprising therefore that, as Holt and Greiner (1976) point out, it has been most enthusiastically practised and developed by therapists of a psychoanalytic orientation: such processes are grist to the analyst's mill.

The psychoanalytic approach, as described by Byng-Hall et al. (1982) and Daniell (1985), involves the two therapists, preferably male and female, allowing themselves, and their relationship, to be 'sucked in' to the client system, so mirroring the pathological aspects of the marital relationship. This countertransference is an unconscious process, the effects of which can be seen in the co-therapists' interaction with each other in the session or in their subsequent discussion. The therapists are trained to pay particular attention to the times when they behave 'out of character' and then, usually with the help of a supervisor or supervision group, they try to make explicit the unconscious fears and assumptions of their clients. The supervisor or group helps them to explore the dynamics of their own relationship, and this frees them to offer an interpretation to the couple in the next session. As Daniell (1985, p. 177) puts it, '. . . only when the therapists have solved their "quarrel" can the clients start to solve theirs.'

It is probably inevitable that co-therapy enhances transference, encourages identification and provides an influential model relationship, particularly in conjoint marital therapy and especially with a male and female team. It is not surprising, therefore, that the Milan group of family therapists (Palazzoli et al., 1978) abandoned this method as they moved away from their psychoanalytic roots. What is essential for one method is at least an unnecessary complication and usually a handicap in another. As Mackay (1985, p. 233) points out in discussing behavioural approaches, 'Given the directive chairmanlike [*sic*] role envisaged for the behavioural marital therapist, most authorities maintain that co-therapy teams introduce an unnecessary complication to the therapeutic process.' This is apparently the case, even though it means that behavioural therapists have to sacrifice the opportunity for using a standard method of social learning – modelling.

Unfortunately, however, as one of us has observed previously (Carpenter, 1984b, p. 191), all too often co-therapy is seized upon either as a convenient solution to the problem of providing work for two therapists (for example, doctor and social worker) assigned to a case for organizational reasons (for example, to ensure that both medical and social viewpoints are seen to be represented), or as an (inappropriate) means of providing support (hand-holding) for inexperienced therapists. The relationships so formed are often on an *ad hoc* basis, and with little or no commitment to examining their dynamics or development, let alone using their relationship as part of the therapeutic process. The co-therapists, therefore, take all their own unresolved problems and difficulties into the formation of a therapeutic system. It is hardly suprising if the resulting therapy is unsuccessful.

Difficulties in co-therapy relationships have been investigated by Rice and his colleagues, who considered the effects of differing levels of experience (Rice et al., 1972) and problems of sharing power and control and of status and sex role inequality (Rice and Rice, 1974). Coleman's review of failed cases concluded that 'Not one of the co-therapy teams appeared to benefit the family. Even more critical is the fact that co-therapy may have contributed substantially to the ultimate treatment failures.' (Coleman, 1985, p. 356)

Echoing Rice's work, Coleman identified unequal status as a problem, and L'Abate and Baggett (1985, p. 238) suggest that in their case this prevented the development of a coherent therapeutic style. As Wynne and Green (1985, p. 148) observe in discussing their presentation,

> One of the hazards of a loosely-structured co-therapy relationship is that it is all too easy for the therapists to evade dealing with differences and responsibility about what should be done.

Each therapist can unwittingly assume that the other will take responsibility, resulting in a lack of effective leadership by either. In effect, the avoidance of divergence constitutes a pseudomutual co-therapy relationship.

The co-therapy relationships investigated by Rice and reviewed by Coleman were in fact relatively straightforward in that they comprised colleagues or trainer and trainees from the same agency and profession. However, in many instances the co-therapists are not only members of different professions with different status and of different sex, but they may also work for different employers.

For example, the co-therapy 'team' may consist of a male psychiatrist and female social worker working in a psychiatric hospital or child guidance clinic. The social worker may be expected to receive supervision from her senior officer; the psychiatrist, especially if he is a consultant, will probably receive none at all. Again, these co-therapists are, because of their different backgrounds and training, likely to have important, but hidden, theoretical positions that may surface when the therapy becomes 'stuck'. Thus, typically, the psychiatrist may pull 'rank' and 'sex' and define the problem as being caused by one member's psychiatric condition (for example, a schizoid personality disorder or a 'masked' depression) and therefore as being exclusively within his province. The social worker may retaliate by refusing to accept his re-definition, and may involve her supervisor in order to add weight to her position. However, the supervisor, who may already be in conflict with the psychiatrist over other issues, will probably find herself in an ambiguous hierarchical position and the conflict impossible to resolve. At the other extreme, such may be their sensitivity to differences that an incapacitating pseudomutuality develops. In all unresolved cases it is the therapy and therefore the family which suffers; furthermore, they can even be blamed for 'causing' the problems in the first place.

Similarly, it is important to note that Rice and Coleman did not study co-therapists who used a psychoanalytic approach to family and marital therapy. As we suggested above, it is probably inevitable that co-therapy enhances transference, encourages identification and provides an influential modelling relationship. Because these processes are part and parcel of the psychoanalytic approach we may assume that they are managed properly. If, on the other hand, the co-therapists are using a different theoretical framework in which transference and countertransference is not examined, we would recommend that attention be paid to these processes when therapy becomes stuck. Bearing in mind that the co-therapists bring into therapy not just themselves but also their relationship with each other, they should at the very least ask the question, 'What model does our relationship offer to our clients?'

In particular, the co-therapists should examine what model they provide of sex-role and power relationships (for example, does a male therapist dominate his female partner), of acknowledging, discussing and resolving conflicts and of valuing and supporting each other's contributions. A simple, yet very common, example will make this clear.

□ A co-therapy team presented a 'stuck' marital case for consultation, bringing a videotape recording of the previous therapy session. The middle-aged couple in therapy comprised a successful business executive and his wife, who had been referred for agoraphobia. The co-therapists were a young male clinical psychologist and a middle-aged psychiatric nursing sister. The nurse had brought the case for consultation, even though her partner said that he knew what they should do next.

It is easy to see how the co-therapists' behaviour 'mirrored' that of the couple, with the female partner in each case feeling stuck and wanting outside help. However, detailed analysis of the videotape showed clearly that the husband had become more and more confident and assertive as the male therapist had taken charge of the interview. The female therapist, on the other hand, had shown her discomfort by her gestures and posture, and had said very little, making only two half-hearted attempts to involve the subdued wife in the discussion.

Further exploration by the consultant revealed that the co-therapists had worked together on a number of cases and in all of these the same pattern of assertive male psychologist and submissive yet uncomfortable nurse had been in evidence. Although more experienced than her younger colleague, the nurse considered him to be more capable and knowledgeable than her. In addition, she said that in her own family of origin, as in her present marriage, she had always deferred to men and, in particular, to her younger, brighter, brother. Furthermore, she had learnt never to challenge men in public. In symmetrical fashion, the psychologist was the only child of a successful academic, for whom he had to 'shine' if he was to receive any attention, and a mother who indulged him and acceded to all his requests.

With the consultant's help, the co-therapists were able to appreciate that the relationship which they had brought into therapy with their clients was one characterized by sexual inequality and pseudomutuality in which conflicts were neither recognized nor resolved. Such a relationship provided a highly inappropriate model for the couples with whom they worked, especially for those couples for whom inequality and conflict-avoidance were important issues. The co-therapy relationship made matters worse, not better. □

An interesting example of countertransference reactions in co-therapy is discussed by Feld (1982), who remarks on the developing relationship between the therapists. It does seem to be true in our experience that, somewhat perversely, therapists skilled in helping marital and family relationships, rarely pay much attention to the development of their own co-therapy relationships. However, as Brent and Marine (1982), Coleman (1977), Skynner (1976) and Sonne and Lincoln (1965) have pointed out, co-therapy relationships, like marital relationships, typically go through stages. Brent and Marine characterize these as: encounter; the struggle for power and control; the development of intimacy; and separation. It is easy to see how the stage of the co-therapy relationship can influence the therapy itself: as one of us remembers saying many years ago to a new female colleague at the end of a conjoint session, 'That was a really terrific piece of co-therapy! – I'm going to enjoy working with you.' The family, however, failed to return. The therapists had been so preoccupied with the excitement of their own 'encounter' that they had paid little attention to the needs of their clients.

In summary, therefore, we have to question the use of co-therapy as a solution to the problem of the therapist becoming stuck in the family system. Moreover, we consider that in the event of co-therapists being stuck, they should carefully examine what their own relationship has brought into the therapeutic system. It may be that the problem (the stuckness) between them 'mirrors' that of the family (see Dowling, 1979, pp. 178 ff) but it may also be serving as a 'model'.

At this point our discussion inevitably touches on the issue of personal work. Family therapists do not agree about the significance of personal work, but our own view is fairly straightforward. Our model involves our working closely with families and couples so we assume whether we like it or not (or whether or not we are fully aware of it) that all sorts of emotional processes are stirred up between us. It is therefore our duty as therapists to take responsibility for trying to establish the nature of the unfinished business which we bring to our work. Lieberman (1979) has made a number of useful suggestions for working on such material. He suggests, for instance, that family therapy training should include a 'family therapy training analysis' which would require a trainee and her supervisor working together for between ten and twenty hours. The content of the analysis would be centred on a transgenerational analysis of the trainee's family background. The process begins with the construction of a detailed genogram which enables family processes to be explored. Subsequent sessions involve the supervisor acting as a problem-solving resource for the trainee, who seeks to work out strategies for dealing with areas of unfinished business which continue to cause difficulties.

Lieberman's approach can be adapted to suit co-therapists who can use a co-counselling format to explore mutually their family backgrounds and work out ways of supporting each other while they work on any unfinished business that requires attention. The approach is essentially similar to the format that Lieberman suggests for group trainees who work in pairs under the supervision of a trainer. Co-therapists can elect to work more intimately, just with each other but possibly calling upon help from a colleague if they cannot find ways of helping each other to resolve difficulties.

Live Supervision – a Solution not Without its Problems

An alternative approach to problems of stuckness is the use of live supervision (which, in the case of peers working together, is more accurately termed 'live consultation'). This may be provided either from behind a one-way screen (cf. Cade and Cornwell, 1985; Montalvo, 1973) or with the supervisor present in the room (Smith and Kingston, 1980). In either procedure, the supervisor is able to monitor the process and not just the content of the interview, and therefore to assist in rescuing the therapist when she loses manoeuvrability. Also, the supervisor can help plan interventions and tasks to be agreed during interludes in the session.

Of course, the provision of live supervision does not elminate stuckness. Differences in therapeutic orientation and in values are still relevant to discord between therapist and supervisor, even if issues of hierarchy and sex-role modelling are controlled. For example, a supervisor and a therapist with different views on marriage (one perhaps recently married, the other going through divorce proceedings) will almost inevitably disagree when issues of marriage and separation are raised by a family. (They may even be at a disadvantage to co-therapists in these circumstances in not having the opportunity within the interview itself to acknowledge and work through these differences. A post-session review is therefore essential.) Nevertheless, such differences of opinion can be used imaginatively and creatively in presenting alternative views to the family (as in Papp's use of the 'Greek Chorus'; Papp, 1980).

It is important to note that different models of family therapy have developed their own distinctive methods of live supervision (Carpenter, 1984b). In our experience, problems often arise out of theoretical confusion and because the 'ground rules' have not been agreed by the participants. Thus, the structural approach, described in a seminal paper by Montalvo (1973), assumes that the therapist in the room will be drawn into the family's pattern of organization, but that she should retain sufficient manoeuvrability to change it. The supervisor's task is to prevent her colleague being drawn away from her function as agent of change, and, when necessary, to help her recover control and direction. Montalvo emphasizes the sensitivity required by the supervisor, who must not inhibit the therapist's freedom too greatly. The suggestions she makes must be tailored to the therapist's personal style and be neither too frequent, too vague or too equivocal. Most crucially, the supervisor must 'empower' the therapist to do her job effectively, just as the therapist must empower the family. It is therefore a serious mistake for a supervisor to burst into the therapy room and 'take over' the work, making the therapist appear incompetent. On the contrary, Montalvo asserts that the supervisor's task, at its unintrusive best, is to suggest a course of action for the therapist which will reveal new aspects of her clients' behaviour in such a way that the therapist can react usefully. Thus, the therapist is helped to regain her effectiveness and the family helped to change.

The Milan approach, on the other hand, requires the therapist to take a distant joining position (see chapter 3); it does not assume that the therapist will actively try to change the family in the session. The therapeutic method rests on the creation of systemic hypotheses, on the technique of circular questioning and on interventions usually delivered at the end of the session in the form of a prescription (Palazzoli et al., 1980b). As practised in many settings (for example, Campbell and Draper, 1985; Procter and Stephens, 1984; Speed et al., 1982), this is in effect a team approach in which 'the therapist', the person in the room with the clients, is not an independent agent and has exclusive responsibility only for asking questions. Indeed, it is probably more accurate to describe the therapist in this method as the 'interviewer', thereby stressing that she is but part of the team which, as a whole, has the responsibility for effecting change.

The obvious danger in this team approach is if the therapeutic system flounders because the couple or family begin to experience 'their' therapist as less than genuine or as a puppet controlled from behind the screen. (This is a potential hazard of the use of 'ear bugs' which can cause the therapist's eyes to glaze over and/or can become so intrusive as seriously to disrupt the relationship.) Even more serious, however, is the apparent tendency of some teams to become embroiled in covert conflict with their clients, so that therapy is seen as a contest in which 'resistance' has to be defeated, an issue we considered at length in chapter 1. The point to stress here, perhaps, is that 'teamwork' can exacerbate inter-group conflict, or as the newspaper columnist Katherine Whitehorn once said, 'The question about teamwork is, who are they playing *against*?' *

Of course, as Breunlin and Cade (1981) have pointed out, the members of the team behind the screen can intervene in order to unbalance both the family system *and* the therapeutic system. They can disagree with the therapist, triangulating the family, therapist and themselves. Alternatively, the therapist and team member can, by prior agreement, each side with different members of the family in order to highlight the dilemmas of change. (The development of team approaches in strategic family therapy is described by Cade and Cornwell, 1985.)

Team approaches are certainly very popular in family therapy

* Annual Conference of the British Association of Social Workers, 1986.

centres (although as with co-therapy, there is no evidence that they are any more effective than solo therapy (Gurman et al., 1985, p. 572)). The main reasons are probably that family therapists have found that they enjoy working together and that teams provide good opportunities for doing so. We will now consider the most frequent problems which are the result of the different perspectives of therapist and supervisor – differences which reflect both the strengths and weaknesses of supervision as a method of working.

When stuck, the therapist typically feels that her supervisor behind the screen does not really understand 'her' family or appreciate what is going on in the room, and in particular, is insensitive to their distress. The supervisor on the other hand feels that the therapist has been sucked in to the family system and has lost her objectivity. As Kingston and Smith (1983) remark, the success of live supervision requires that both therapist and supervisor believe that the supervisor's 'meta' position confers an advantage in terms of planning the course of therapy. However, with the best intentions, it is often difficult for the therapist to accept the validity of this belief, especially when it concerns change.

In our experience of supervising many marital and family therapists in a variety of agencies, one of the most common failings is therapists' inability to see change taking place before their eyes. Therapists are much better at identifying 'resistance', noting for example their clients' failure to communicate, than at acknowledging change, as in their attempts to talk. Indeed, as Berger and Dammann (1982) observe, one of the supervisor's tasks is to ensure that the therapist does not undo change once it has occurred.

☐ A young female therapist was working with an adolescent and his parents. The parents' complaint was that the boy would not join in with the family: the more they tried to persuade him, the less involved he had become, to the extent that they now just attacked him. In a family session, the therapist had commended the parents on their wish to include him and sympathized with their difficulties. She also succeeded in getting them to talk together about their expectations of a family holiday. However, when this discussion broke down with the father accusing his son of not wanting to go with them, the therapist made her exasperation clear, looking at the father with her criticism thinly veiled. He responded by reminding her how 'impossible' the boy was.

From the supervisor's more detached position, the family's effort to change by talking together was quite striking – in spite of the fact that a dispute had ensued. It was also clear that the therapist's criticism had begun to undo this change. The supervisor, therefore, telephoned the therapist asking her to ask the family members to 'have another go'. Unfortunately, the therapist's request was made without apparent enthusiasm and the discussion broke down in the same way as before, with both therapist and parents looking disgruntled.

The problem in this case was that the supervisor had not convinced the therapist that change was taking place – from the latter's point of view, the instruction to repeat the discussion was to persist with a failed strategy. The solution to this impasse came when the therapist was asked to take 'time out' with the supervisor. The supervisor complimented her on the initial success of her effort to get the parents and child to talk together, pointing out that this was the first time they had achieved any two-way discussion in all the sessions so far. That they had not managed to resolve all their problems in a few minutes was not a failure! Once the therapist was able to feel positive about her own efforts, she was ready to recognize the family's achievements and to convey this to them. When affirmed rather than criticized by the therapist, the family members could recommence their attempts to change. □

Berger and Dammann (1982) comment that:

The predictable difficulty for the supervisor in live supervision arises from the failure to take into account the difference in perspective of the supervisor and the therapist. This can result in the supervisor pushing the therapist to move faster than the family can tolerate or in the supervisor proposing a tactic that the therapist knows will not work with a particular family at that particular time.

As in the above example, when supervision becomes stuck, it is essential for the therapist to have 'time out'. Berger and Dammann recommend that it is essential in such discussions that the therapist have an immediate opportunity to give the supervisor her impressions of the family members' feelings about the therapy. Only if the therapist feels that her supervisor understands what is going on in the room will she be amenable to efforts to resolve the impasse. Similarly, the supervisor is well advised to listen to how the therapist herself feels. In the same way that the therapeutic alliance between family and therapist has to be sustained, so does that between therapist and supervisor.

A common problem in live supervision is creating a cascade of blame or criticism. For example, the supervisor may criticize the therapist, who then criticizes the family; or family members may blame the therapist for lack of progress and she then blames her supervisor. These cascades may even include the supervisor's own supervisor! (Wright and Coppersmith, 1983) There is, of course, considerable potential for triangulation in these disputes, and a particular danger arises when the supervisor sides with the family against the therapist – for example, constantly interrupting the therapist whenever she challenges the family members, by sending in 'supportive' messages to them. Supervisors can easily become over-intrusive and covertly critical of the therapist who, in turn, resents the intrusion at the same time as 'inviting' it by her helpless behaviour (Westheafer, 1984). As Wright and Coppersmith (1983) remind us, it is essential to be clear about the different systems levels involved in supervision, and this is especially important when supervisors are themselves being supervised. The supervision of supervision does not involve the supervision of the therapy itself, but supervision of the supervisory process.

Consultation: a Help or a Hindrance?

When a therapist and her clients are stuck, a consultation with another therapist (or therapists in a supervision and support group) may be helpful. But it is very important to consult a therapist who not only understands the model of therapy being used but is also familiar with the agency context in which it is practised. In our experience, consultation has been most unhelpful when we have presented our difficulties to multi-agency support groups whose members have offered advice from a bewildering variety of therapeutic orientations without any reference to the constraints and liabilities of our own agencies. This is a recipe for increased confusion and stuckness.

Most crucially, as we have argued in these chapters, the consultant must appreciate that the task is to focus on the *therapeutic system* as a whole and not just on the 'resistant' family or the 'unmotivated' or 'mixed-up' therapist.

☐ For example, let us suppose that a male therapist presents a case in which he has become stuck with a family comprising a single-parent mother and three children. Suppose also that he is employed by a social services department and is 'key worker' to the family, the mother being suspected of abusing one of the children.

If the consultation is to be helpful then it must include a consideration of the social and legal context, including the facts that the family is a 'compulsory' client and that the social worker has the role of both therapist and inspector in relation to the family and that of liaison in relation to other involved professionals. It may also be assumed, if the therapist has become stuck in the family, that he has taken on a role within that system. For example, one might hypothesize that he has become to some extent a substitute husband or father: a role that may be implicitly sanctioned by his agency, who see him as providing 'social work support' but about which he nevertheless feels uncomfortable. The consultant's task must be to provide help to this new system: an exclusive focus on the family with no regard to the therapist's position will be both inaccurate and, as experienced by the therapist, insensitive. He might therefore resent and resist the consultant's attempts to push his family around, leading to no helpful change. ☐

In our experience, stuckness can usually be resolved by means of a consultation which systematically addresses the questions posed in these two chapters. This can be achieved either in one-to-one discussion with the therapist, or through the use of sculpting or choreography (Papp, 1976). However, unlike Papp, we do include the therapist as part of the choreography either with the family themselves or with colleagues acting as substitutes. This method not only allows the identification of the influence of other actors in the drama, but also gives an indication of the therapist's manoeuvrability or lack of it. Through the identification of where she is stuck, within or on the periphery of the therapeutic system, we can look at what she might do to become 'unstuck'.

In some instances it may be possible for the consultant to intervene directly in the therapeutic system by interviewing the family and therapist together. This procedure, which is described by Garfield and Schwoeri (1981) and van Trommel (1984) is, in our opinion, to be considered when the therapist has become stuck in the system. It is not so appropriate when the stuckness is a result of contextual and contractual aspects of therapy. If the stuckness is a consequence of the couple or family's relationships with other systems, then a focus on the therapeutic system rather than the whole problem system can lead to a mis-assessment. In this case a network meeting would be appropriate.

Campbell (1985, p. 200) warns that a common pitfall in consultation interviews is covert competition between therapist and consultant. It is essential for the consultant to remember that her task is to enable the therapist to regain her manoeuvrability so that she can work more effectively with her clients. The temptation to take over the role of the therapist is irresistible to some consultants, particularly those visiting experts called in to give live demonstrations of their skills. Such consultations can easily provoke premature termination of the contract when the expert fails to hand back responsibility in a manner which emphasizes confidence in the original therapist (Neilsen and Kaslow, 1980).

Garfield and Schwoeri (1981) describe the consultant's task as 'entering' by establishing a relationship with the therapist and 'exiting' by returning the therapeutic authority at the close of the interview. It is essential, therefore, that the therapist and consultant meet before the interview with the couple or family in order to discuss the stuckness from the therapist's point of view, to establish the goals of the consultation and to decide how the therapist will present the consultation to her clients. (The purpose should always be described by the therapist to her clients as 'to help me to help you'.)

The focus of the consultation interview is, as we have indicated, the working of the therapeutic system. In other words, it is not appropriate, in our opinion, for the consultant to begin an exploration of the dynamics of the family system, still less to intervene directly in that system. To do so would give a covert message that the therapist was incompetent. Rather, the consultant should ask about how and why the couple or family came to therapy, how the therapist and her clients had experienced their work together, why the therapist had sought a consultation and what had been her clients' reactions to this proposal. By reviewing the working of the therapeutic system in this way, the consultant can identify the causes of stuckness and recommend solutions along the lines suggested earlier in this chapter. Like van Trommel (1984) we do think it essential that the therapist remains with her clients during any 'time out' from the session, lest they think that the therapist and consultant are ganging up against them. However, we do not agree that this 'neutrality' should be extended outside the session so that the consultant declines to discuss any forms of intervention with the therapist. The latter may indeed have been 'part of the problem' but does not mean that the problem has to be solved by the consultant. Therapists, like their clients, need to be empowered, and one of the crucial ways this can happen is through their being able to rely on the open-handed help of experienced consultants who are willing to give therapists the benefit of their skills in the same way as therapists are willing to give the benefit of their skills to families.

Conclusion

In these two chapters we have extended the analysis of 'stuckness' first presented in articles in the *Journal of Family Therapy* (Treacher and Carpenter, 1982; Carpenter et al., 1983). We have offered a framework within which to understand stuckness in terms of the context of therapy, the contract between the therapist and her clients, the therapist's skills and the working of the therapeutic and supervisory systems. In so doing, we have tended to concentrate on the problems of 'middle therapy', for this is when therapy usually gets stuck. However, the final stage of therapy can also be problematic – not just when therapist and family are unable to part company, but also when therapy ends in apparent failure. These topics are the concern of our final chapter.

Further Reading

Cade, B. and M. Cornwell (1985), 'New realities for old: some uses of teams and one-way screens in therapy', in D. Campbell and R. Draper (eds), *Applications of Systemic Family Therapy*. A review of uses in strategic family therapy.

Kingston, P. and D. Smith (1983), 'Preparation for live consultation and live supervision', *Journal of Family Therapy*, 5, 219–33.

A valuable article which suggests questions for co-workers to consider in preparing to work together.

Mattinson, J. (1975), *The Reflection Process in Casework Supervision*. A classic paper concerned with the effect of the client/therapist relationship or the therapist/supervisor relationship.

Whiffen, R. and J. Byng-Hall (eds) (1982), *Family Therapy Supervision: Recent Developments in Practice*. A 'mixed bag' of conference papers including helpful contributions from trainees.

Wynne, L. C. et al. (eds) (1986), *Systems Consultation: A New Perspective For Family Therapy*. Consultation methods in many settings. Consultation to stuck therapeutic systems is described by Todd (chapter 5) and Penn and Sheinberg (chapter 7), who offer clear frameworks for assessment and intervention. Consultation to problem systems is described by Anderson and Goolishian (domestic violence) and Imber-Black.

9

Endings – Successful and Unsuccessful

There is relatively little written about ending marital and family therapy. This is especially true for family therapy – perhaps because, as Combrinck-Graham (1981) suggests, the end-point is difficult to define since families are always changing. It is also true that family therapists tend to place an emphasis on the family finding the 'answers' to their problem amongst themselves: this inevitably tends to play down the significance of the relationship with the therapist, so that termination is not seen as very important. Nevertheless, our own experience has led us to believe that when and how to end therapy is often more of a problem than is commonly acknowledged. Interestingly, Hunt's (1984) study of marriage guidance counselling has illustrated that counselling rarely comes to a smooth conclusion: more than half of her sample ended therapy by default, either by cancelling or failing to attend appointments.

In this chapter we will explore termination problems and briefly consider related issues such as burn-out and failure.

When Enough is Enough

It is sometimes difficult to know when to finish working with a couple or family. It may be that they continue to attend sessions willingly but the therapist feels that no further progress is being made. Alternatively, one member may ask whether they 'need' to come any more, leaving the therapist unsure whether or not to try and persuade them to continue. In either case the problem has arisen because the therapist has no clear idea about how to review and evaluate their work together.

To a considerable extent a therapist's decision about the success or otherwise of therapy depends on the goals she sets and consequently on the model she uses. Whilst some schools emphasize the importance of profound personality-change or individual and family growth to 'maturity', others are much less ambitious and are satisfied with the remission of symptoms or the resolution of the presenting problems.

One important question in considering termination is: who is responsible for deciding whether or not the goals have been achieved? Again the answer depends very much on the model used: in general, the more ambitious the goals, the more likely it is that the therapist will decide – on the grounds, apparently, that she knows best whether sufficient change has taken place. This can lead to problems when the clients disagree, and a covert struggle ensues with the therapist trying to restrain them from leaving. At the other extreme, some strategic therapists (for example, Fulweiler, in Haley and Hoffman, 1967, pp. 95–6) seem to be most pleased when their clients, without any reference to the therapist, decide to end therapy themselves, after pronouncing it irrelevant. Whilst this has the advantage of leaving clients feeling in charge of their own destiny, it also inhibits any follow-up and the chance of their going back to therapy should the need arise. Our contractual approach lies somewhere between these two extremes.

Evaluating Change

In chapter 1 we discussed the importance of negotiating a contract with the couple or family and stressed that this process was one which should be repeated throughout the course of therapy. Accordingly, our model requires therapist and clients to plan the ending together. The first step is to evaluate the extent to which change has taken place. This is achieved by asking the following questions:

1 What has happened to the presenting problem? Has it disappeared, been reduced to a level which is now found acceptable or been successfully re-framed so that it is no longer seen as a problem?
2 What changes have taken place in the structure of marital and family relationships?
3 What changes have taken place in individual and family beliefs,

particularly those concerned with the problems discussed in therapy?

Any changes should be evaluated in the light of the goals set at the beginning of therapy. As we noted earlier, the clients' goals may be more limited than those of the therapist and may be concerned with the presenting problem rather than with relationships. Nevertheless, both levels are important. A therapist who concludes by saying that 'The parents are much more together, but the problem remains' is like the apocryphal surgeon who said, 'The operation was successful but the patient died'.

A further crucial question for evaluating whether termination is on the agenda involves asking how the couple or family have dealt with any further problems that may have cropped up. To what extent have they managed the ups and downs of everyday life between sessions, without relying on the therapist to provide the answers?

If the answers to the above questions are positive, then the task facing the therapist is to disengage from the therapeutic alliance and for the couple or family once more to own the responsibility for determining the course of their lives. For this to happen, the therapist and her clients must first recognize change, as the following example illustrates.

☐ A married couple, both with physical disabilities, had been in conjoint therapy for six months. The presenting problem was 'depression' in both partners and serious marital rows which concluded in a succession of overdoses of medication by the wife, and admission to hospital.

Therapy had focused on finding new ways of resolving conflicts between the couple – conflicts which were exacerbated by their physical problems and mutual dependence. It had been successful to the extent that the depressions were now seen not as psychiatric disorders but as moodiness or sulking – part of the marital warfare; the rows no longer ended in hospital and, instead, the couple had successfully resolved several major problems in recent therapy sessions. However, when invited by the therapist to review progress the couple were despondent: they announced that they had barely spoken to each other for the previous three days and then launched into a recapitulation of their usual themes of mutual blame and recrimination.

The therapist's initial intention was to attempt once more to end the dispute using the successful negotiating tactics employed previously. However, just in time, he recognized the danger of his becoming an indispensable part of their conflict-resolving strategy – the couple would disagree, cease talking to each other and wait for the therapist, in true parental fashion, to 'knock their heads together', remind them that they loved each other and negotiate a resolution. What he and they had 'forgotten' was that before the previous session the couple had resolved a problem *on their own*. Change had indeed taken place; what was missing was due recognition of the fact. Rather than display a lack of confidence in their ability by staying to resolve the dispute for them, the therapist left the room, returning only when they had done it themselves. As they discussed later, they no longer needed a therapist, just some neutral ground on which to talk. □

In this case, the review of therapy took place as a result of a crisis in the therapeutic system. It was concluded that sufficient change had indeed been made. In most circumstances a pre-arranged structured review is undertaken. This involves asking the family and ourselves as therapists the following questions:

1   *What is different?*   In answering this question we seek to evaluate changes at the three levels described earlier. It is important to listen carefully to the clients' review of how they feel things have changed. Sometimes clear-cut goals have not been entirely achieved but they feel more confident about their ability to live with their problems. This is a commonplace of families with adolescents. Often the presenting problems may not have changed significantly but parents are able to see that their children's behaviour is not that bad and that stepping back is the best solution. Careful monitoring (at follow-up) will reveal whether this level of change is sufficient to allow the family to move through the transition of the children leaving home.

2   *Why is it different?*   Here we are concerned with the clients' understandings about change. In our view, it is essential that the couple or family acknowledge what they have done and can explain it. After all, it was they who changed, not the therapist, and the sense of control must be securely in their hands if they are to deal with the inevitable problems of living without returning for help each time. Furthermore, they must know *how* they resolved their

problem, so that, should the need arise, they can do so again.

Following on from this last consideration, it is our practice to anticipate future stresses and problems, such as the next stage in the family life-cycle and possible future crises like illness or unemployment. If the clients know how they resolved the earlier problems (for example, by mother and father pulling together rather than pushing apart) then they can create guidelines for resolving new ones. We often ask them to rehearse solutions through asking them 'What if X should occur?' (X can be any one of a number of hazardous events). Minuchin has talked about leaving the 'ghost of the therapist' behind when he finishes working with a family; if they have really benefited from therapy they will demonstrate new problem-solving capabilities, and this is what such questions monitor. Obviously, the purpose of this line of questioning is to confirm their strengths, and this intention can be expressed more directly by inviting them to discuss their long-term goals, for themselves as individuals and for their family as a whole. But if things do go wrong then they can always return. In any case, it is our policy to offer clients a follow-up appointment, a topic which we will discuss later.

Problems

1   The Family or Couple who are Reluctant to Finish Therapy

Occasionally we have experienced families or couples who are reluctant to terminate despite our assessment that they are more or less ready to do so. This reluctance can take many forms, but it is unusual in our experience for all family members to adopt the same position. Usually one wants to continue but other members do not. This is especially difficult with couples who have presented with symptoms such as depression. It is usually the woman who is the symptom-bearer, with the man being overprotective and overbearing (see Treacher, 1985, for a detailed description of the dynamics of this type of relationship). Despite the therapist's best efforts to maintain an alliance with both partners, the woman often idealizes the therapist, because he or she has been able to respond to her in an entirely different way from her husband, who can see only her weaknesses. If the situation has been further complicated by the therapist undertaking individual therapy – for example, to teach cognitive behaviour therapy self-help skills – then it is not surprising that termination runs into difficulties.

□ Despite a series of family and marital therapy sessions which had achieved the agreed goals, it became obvious that Mrs S's depression persisted and was being aggravated by the very success of her older children leaving home. Mr S was supportive, but was experiencing difficulties at work since his firm was being taken over by another company. After negotiation with the couple, it was decided that individual work should be offered so that Mrs S could learn to fight her own 'depresso-genic' tendencies. A series of six cognitive behaviour therapy sessions was undertaken. It was difficult for Mrs S to unravel some of her deep self-downing and perfectionist scripts. A fortuitous visit by her mother enabled the therapist to work on some of these scripts directly by getting Mrs S to confront her mother on such issues as her continual criticizing and moralizing about her daughter's behaviour. The work was intense but successful and a review session with both partners revealed considerable progress. However, the issue of termination was not handled with any sensitivity. The therapist was feeling quite drained and exhausted, was due to go on holiday and so was pleased to close the case.

A few days later Mrs S phoned up and insisted on arranging a brief session because she felt that she had not been allowed to say what she wanted at the last meeting which had, unusually, been supervised by a team. The therapist agreed to the session with some trepidation, but Mrs S handled it with great skill insisting that the goodbye had been too abrupt. A six-month follow-up by telephone was duly negotiated, but in fact Mrs S returned (by arrangement) a few months later as she was still struggling with her perfectionism. The therapist asked a colleague to join him for this session as he felt he needed an extra pair of eyes to evaluate what was happening. The session was very positive, with Mrs S using both workers to check out the progress she had made. Her ability to use self-help skills were now quite remarkable and she shared examples of her self-designed homework tasks. Termination was finally agreed. Subsequent telephone calls recorded the family's progress and Mrs S's depression has not returned. Mr S is now much more settled at work and has become much more involved with his trade union. The marital relationship has flowered and the couple now actively seek time together away from their remaining children. □

2 The Family or Couple Wish to Withdraw but the Therapist is Reluctant

Sometimes the family or couple wish to withdraw from therapy but the therapist is reluctant to terminate because she feels that only superficial change has occurred. From a client's point of view the most popular way to terminate is just not to turn up. There are also cases where the family or couple do still come to sessions (because they have a good relationship with the therapist), albeit dragging their feet.

As Heath (1985) points out, the reasons for disagreement between the clients and the therapist may reflect their assumptions about therapy. For many, if not most, clients, an end to their presenting problem is the be all and end all. So if they feel they have benefited from therapy because the problem has disappeared then it is only natural that they should want to leave. A psychodynamically orientated therapist who believes that therapy should involve not just symptom relief but also some developments in the family's habitual ways of responding may well get into a tangle at this point. Our own position lies somewhere in between these two. We feel it is an error to adopt only problem resolution as a criterion for termination. We have had some disappointing experiences of families discharging themselves only to return within months or even weeks with either the same problem or another very similar one.

Faced with a family or couple who want to discharge themselves and yet all the indications are that no major structural change has occurred, we attempt to slow their departure from therapy by sharing our experience with them. For example, (in Aesopian fashion) we share case examples of families who have worked with us previously to warn them that Rome was not built in a day. If they still persist in wanting to discharge themselves we will do our best to set a follow-up session rather than passively waiting for something to turn up. We will share our pessimism with them while commending their optimism. In a sense, therefore, the intervention is a challenge – they may in fact go out of their way to disprove our pessimism. So much the better! If, on the other hand, our pessimism is justified then at least we retain our credibility as therapists and our chance of building the therapeutic alliance with them is likely to be increased.

☐ Mr and Mrs W were reluctant to enter therapy and yet their daughter Helen had recently attempted suicide by jumping off a very high cliff, surviving only by chance because she landed on some bushes. Her parents wondered if they needed some help, even though the attempt had been some months previously and everything seemed to have gone back to 'normal'. However, their therapist was not convinced and attempted to talk to them about other important matters. The therapeutic alliance remained shaky and the therapist feared that the family would unilaterally abandon therapy.

However, the situation was radically changed by the news that Helen was pregnant. She attempted to have an abortion but her obstetrician refused to proceed and so she had to carry on with her pregnancy. Her baby was delivered prematurely at about seven months. At this point the family wished to withdraw from therapy; they felt that things had sorted themselves out and that they could cope.

The therapist, however, was very concerned that Helen would reject her baby who was being looked after in a Special Care Baby Unit. He was also concerned about the role adopted by Mr and Mrs W. They had taken it for granted that they would take care of Helen and her baby rather than negotiating a clear-cut role with Helen on an adult-to-adult basis. With some difficulty they were encouraged to attend sessions in the Special Care Baby Unit while Helen was visiting her daughter. Helen only wished to come to see her daughter two or three times a week, but both the staff of the unit and the therapist believed that it was necessary for her to come each day. Helen gradually changed her position and attended the unit five or six times a week. When the baby was discharged from the unit the family once again did not want to attend therapy.

The therapist was still convinced that many important issues remained unresolved. He suggested that it would be helpful to have a follow-up meeting four weeks later, so that he could reassure himself that things were okay and that the family's confidence that they could solve their own problems was well founded. The family reluctantly agreed.

At follow-up the therapist was able to discuss some of the difficulties they had had in the previous month and some of the stormy arguments that had arisen about the care of the baby daughter. In fact, the therapist's intuition that deeper issues needed resolving was confirmed, since the family changed its position and agreed to a clearly-defined contract for the first time. Therapy terminated successfully about a year later following a series of regular sessions. ☐

There are other difficult examples. In marital therapy it is quite often the case that one partner is more reluctant than the other to end therapy. Usually it is the man who wants to terminate and the woman who wants to continue (reflecting an original scenario of her dragging him reluctantly to therapy). Certainly there are often other extenuating circumstances that feed the man's reluctance — for example, difficulty in getting time off work, financial pressures or both. Again the best approach is to understand and sympathize with his desire to leave, but also warn him that the problem may well get worse without his participation. If this does not work then it is probably best to settle for individual marital therapy rather than agreeing to end therapy altogether.

In any situation where an individual wants to finish therapy, the first step is obviously to evaluate why that individual wishes to leave. If it is a parent who is wishing to finish family therapy, this is a crisis and careful evaluation of the therapeutic alliance is required. If it is a teenager or a child then the problem is usually less acute. Sometimes teenagers who are at a 'leaving home' stage do not want to attend sessions — this can be valuable, since it may well create a model for other teenagers who are enmeshed. But there can be a trap involved. If the potential non-attender is, in fact, still heavily involved with the family then it is best either to try and encourage future attendance or, if this is impossible, at least negotiate a review session which enables the therapist to evaluate the impact of the non-attendance on the progress of therapy.

3   The Therapist Needs to Finish Because She is Leaving the Agency

At the time of writing this book, one of us (A. T.) was in the process of leaving to take up a new job. For some of his clients the situation has been entirely beneficial, as they have had to face the reality that their therapist will no longer be around. In other cases the effects have been less beneficial because the clients have had to transfer to other therapists in mid-therapy. This 'forced' termination is painful, but it is worth considering some of the scenarios that have arisen.

In some cases, transfer has been achieved by agreeing that the original co-therapist involved in the case should continue working with the couple or family. The 'termination' session has therefore involved reviewing the work so far and exploring whether the clients would like a replacement for the departing therapist.

☐ One particularly difficult case (involving some forced mourning work) has required transfer to a therapist in another health district because both therapists were leaving at more or less the same time. Sadly, this transfer did not take place according to plan because the departure of myself (A. T.) unfortunately and unexpectedly coincided with the change-over therapist going on holiday for three weeks. In the event, the clients arrived at their first interview with their new therapist without the advantage of having their 'old' therapist present. To make matters worse, this interview took place in exactly the same room as a previous interview (about a year before) with a therapist who had left the clients feeling labelled and stigmatized. Fortunately, the new therapist rose to the challenge very well and was able to cope with the feelings of anger and rejection the clients brought with them to the first interview. ☐

This case clearly demonstrates the necessity for a proper change-over session to be organized (as we discussed in chapter 2). I should have made a special effort to be at the session rather than using the excuse of a new job to avoid my responsibility. In fact such a meeting, although difficult to organize, was feasible. In a case where transfer is impossible then a special de-briefing session needs to be devised so that the 'terminating' therapist can explore with her clients all their feelings and fears about the transfer.

4 It is Difficult to Say Goodbye

Obviously, one of the reasons why families and couples have difficulties ending therapy is that previous 'exits' in the experience of both the family and the therapist have been traumatic. According to Nelsen (1983, p. 255), 'in successful endings, clients and practitioners often go through a progression of stages similar to those through which people pass in dealing with death'. This is an over-statement, but in particular cases, where intense work has been undertaken over a long time, it is likely that Nelsen's view has some relevance. Patterson and Eisenberg (1983) have postulated that people who enter the caring professions may be especially high in unsatisfied needs for gaining acceptance, giving nurturance, achieving intimacy and receiving recognition of their competence. Whether this is true of marital and family therapists is an open question – it is possible that family therapists are not needy in all these dimensions, since one of the apparent attractions of family therapy is its instrumentality and 'technique' orientation. But it may be true that different schools of family therapy attract different types of people. The crux of the issue, however, is that therapists need to 'own' their difficulties in termination otherwise they will run into difficulties for which they are not prepared (cf. Goodyear, 1981).

This discussion clearly overlaps quite strongly with that of transference and countertransference in the previous chapter. If a therapist repeatedly runs into difficulties at the termination stage of therapy then she owes it to herself and her clients to seek help from a consultant in order to examine the problem. It may even be appropriate to enter therapy herself rather than to be continually stressed by such situations.

Goodyear (1981) has pointed out that there are several aspects of termination which may affect the therapist. Termination may: (a) signal the end of a significant relationship; (b) arouse conflicts within the therapist about her own level of individuation; (c) prompt guilt-feelings about her ineffectiveness; and (d) threaten her professional self-concept.

□ Some time ago I (A. T.) began to notice that my termination sessions were too abrupt and not appropriately paced to suit the families or couples I had in therapy. One particular case caused me much concern.

Discussion with colleagues was helpful in establishing that my family style of saying goodbye was very abrupt and probably reflected the rather disengaged style that was the hallmark of my family of origin, particularly on my father's side. I also came to realize that I had not come to terms with the loss of two important people in my family – my maternal grandmother and my sister. My grandmother died at a time when I was very estranged from my parents, while my sister was killed in the Hither Green train crash. I did not attend my grandmother's funeral, and although I did attend my sister's I still had difficulty, at times, in realizing she was dead – probably because I never saw her body. My abruptness in terminating was obviously a defence against the emotional feelings that were still being carried. I resolved to change my practice and to prepare both myself and my clients much more meticulously for termination. □

5   Not Quite the End of the Road: Marital Therapy Turns Into Divorce Therapy

Woody (1981) has summarized the difficulties involved when marital therapy turns into divorce therapy. She points out that dealing with the transition is complicated by such factors as: (a) the therapist's own values regarding divorce; (b) her feelings about the couple and their efforts to achieve change in marital therapy; (c) her degree of clarity regarding the professional's helping function when divorce becomes the choice. These issues can be translated into a series of salient questions that need to be asked of the therapist:

1 Is there a tendency for her to see divorce as a sign of personal failure or of her own failure to give sufficient help?
2 Does the therapist hold a balanced view of divorce, seeing it as the difficult and painful and yet potentially growth-producing process that may be the healthy choice for some people?
3 Do her own personal experiences of divorce (or lack of them)

influence the way she defines her way of helping couples decide to divorce?

Solutions

At a practical level, Woody (1981) suggests that the initial first step when divorce emerges as an issue in therapy is to attempt to slow the process down by gaining permission to convene at least one more session. The couple may well be insisting that they want to divorce immediately, but this may be a gesture of despair because therapy has not achieved longed-for changes in the relationship. A contractually-convened session which enables the pros and cons of divorce to be discussed openly can be effective in bringing out the often suppressed reasons for the decision. The therapist's task is to try and stay 'out' of the process in order to register and evaluate the possibilities for either continuing marital work or pressing for divorce work to commence.

Obviously, enormous ethical problems arise at this point: is the therapist to continue to try and help the couple to pull together or is she to act as a catalyst for creating a split? Different therapists handle this issue differently, but our own preference is to give straight answers to straight questions. We do not hold back if a couple asks us for our advice. If our experience of them during the last few sessions is that the marriage is not working and that this really reflects an impasse between them, then we are frank about this. But our usual preference is to suggest a trial separation rather than proceeding directly to divorce therapy. Sometimes the couple are emphatic that this is not necessary (often they have already tried it without success). If they want to proceed with divorce then it is useful to have some of Woody's guidelines in mind when approaching such work. She makes eight suggestions:

1   Explore the reasons for the decision to divorce and precisely how the couple arrived at it. To what extent are they assuming genuine mature responsibility for the decision, and how far is it just a grandiose gesture which will not lead to serious action?

2   Explore the extent to which *both* partners want to go through with the divorce. If the decision is one-sided, with one partner feeling betrayed, coerced or convinced that it is wrong, these feelings need to be explored, otherwise it is likely that they will cloud all the future relationships with the ex-partner.

3   Explore any actions that the couple have taken collectively or individually to start divorce proceedings. The degree of rationality (as opposed to emotionality) involved in the couple's action are crucial in influencing their adjustment to the divorce.

4   Explore each partner's hopes, fears and even fantasies about what divorce means for them as individuals. If their answers are quite concrete and specific, it is clear that they have begun to adjust.

5   If the couple has children, focus discussion on the impact that the divorce will have on the children and how the parents would like them to be told. Confronting the reality of these details enables them to begin to come to terms with some of the most painful facets of divorce. At the same time they will begin to express both their feelings and the degree of understanding of the tasks that lie ahead. Through this process it is possible to evaluate their abilities to cope.

6   Anticipate and discuss the typical reactions which people experience as they go through a divorce. If children are involved, this discussion must be extended to include their likely reactions. The couple must understand that the quality of their continuing relationship with the children is the most decisive factor in influencing how the children will respond.

7   Introduce discussion of the realities of divorce that couples either avoid or approach irrationally. For example, some partners refuse to deal with economic issues by saying they just want to leave. While such feelings are perfectly understandable, they need to be confronted otherwise irrevocable decisions about money and possessions will be taken, leaving behind a bitter sense of injustice.

8   Give the couple feedback about how they will adjust. Emphasize the healthy and positive aspects of divorce while insisting that the powerful feelings of loss, sadness and helplessness experienced are themselves positive (since they enable separation to take place) and are a prelude to moving into a phase of acceptance and planning for the future.

Woody's list is formidable, and in practice it is very difficult to tackle more than two or three of these issues in a single conjoint session. After this session has taken place we usually work with each partner separately but negotiate occasional conjoint sessions with the other partner to discuss specific issues such as their parenting of the children. If co-therapists have been working with the couple it is possible to assign one to each partner after the decision to part, but it is important to negotiate an agreement that the therapists should not confer unless they have explicit permission from both partners to do so.

If we are working with a single partner (because the couple have already separated before arriving for therapy) we have found it very useful to propose an agenda-making session as a preliminary to conjoint sessions – that is, both partners are invited to attend solely to agree an agenda. The therapist's role in this session is to keep them to task and prevent any discussion of *substantive* issue. The effect of such a session (which is usually brief) is to create a feeling of security – that the couple *can* meet in a business-like fashion and avoid conflicts. This usually makes subsequent sessions easier to handle from the therapist's point of view and less punishing from the couple's. Modelling and achieving co-operation, albeit in the confines of an ('artificial') session can have knock-on effects in helping the couple relate better in their everyday dealings with each other.

□ Mick and Jean had parted company after a long, bitter marriage. Jean brought her problems to a therapist – these involved difficulties with her two children (who were experiencing a lot of sadness at Mick's departure) and unresolved financial problems involving alimony. Jean agreed to meet Mick and the therapist but was very anxious as she feared reprisals from Mick. The session began with the therapist asking both parties to accept the ground rule that no substantive discussion would take place at the session – the only discussion was to be of agenda items. The session was brief but productive. Four agenda items were agreed and a time for the next appointment was fixed.

A subsequent session with Jean revealed that she had gained a great sense of relief because the therapist was able to keep the session to the point and had prevented old wounds from being opened. The subsequent negotiating session between the two ex-partners went well and important agreements were negotiated. □

Following Up Therapy

Often when we finish therapy with a couple or family we have a feeling of exhaustion (perhaps shared by our clients too), so we feel no incentive to use a follow-up imaginatively. Indeed, we often slip into gross bad practice and either rely on a perfunctory telephone call or neglect the follow-up altogether. The latter is particularly true if therapy has been successful, and yet there is absolutely no reason why successful cases should be neglected. As therapists, we need feedback about the success of therapy; but there may well be shocks for us when we follow up 'successful' cases.

☐ While training at the Family Institute, Cardiff, one of us (A. T.) followed up a 'successful' case after three months. The family had apparently responded very positively during the seven-session period of therapy, and termination seemed to arise organically. At follow-up the whole situation had reverted back to square one with the presenting problem (stealing) being even worse. The shock of this failure was a crucial learning experience, since it made me much more cautious about terminating cases without a phased period of withdrawal. It seemed from the follow-up that the family was able to function better while under pressure from their therapists, but their motivation collapsed directly the therapists withdrew. ☐

One obvious way around such a problem is a phased withdrawal: weekly sessions become fortnightly, fortnightly sessions monthly. If a three- or six-month follow-up is then built in at the point of termination it is much more likely that the therapist will achieve her goal in ensuring that therapy is not a seven-day wonder but the source of sustained changes.

Follow-ups themselves fit into four categories:

1   *The safety net*   A family may be dubious about whether they have achieved sufficient change but the therapist is reluctant to continue working because sessions have become too entertaining or social and she feels that the family is attending for personal reasons (for example, liking the therapist) rather than in order to get down to business. The offer of a safety net follow-up helps the family overcome its reluctance to launch itself back into life unregulated by a therapist.

2 *The 'MOT' follow-up* This is a more matter-of-fact follow-up along the lines 'Let's meet up again in six months just to check out what's been happening'. A couple that worked with one of us actually drew up an MOT-type test card on which they recorded a number of dimensions of family and marital functioning which they considered significant. Both partners evaluated changes on these dimensions – they then awarded a pass certificate to themselves (as they concluded that they had done rather well) and brought the 'documentation' to the follow-up session.

3 *The research follow-up* Sometimes families are reluctant to agree to a follow-up for various reasons. In this situation we suggest to them that it would be useful for us to carry out the follow-up because *we* need to know whether we are effective or ineffective. This is a genuine request on our part, but it also opens up the possibility of maintaining contact with otherwise reluctant clients. If at follow-up there are clearly grounds for concern, these need to be shared with the couple or family and a new contract negotiated if they are willing.

4 *Failure follow-ups* Earlier in the book we explored what to do when a family or couple drops out of therapy. It is important to reiterate our belief that if this happens it is essential to try and make contact with the family. Given our stress on joining clients and building the therapeutic alliance, it is both puzzling and even punishing for us as therapists to go through the experience of a couple or family breaking off contact without explanation. In practice such an experience is rare, but we nevertheless like to complete the process by actively seeking contact ourselves. This can best be achieved by telephone, but if this is not possible a letter should be sent. Alternatively, an unannounced home visit can be made. Often it is difficult to find the family at home, but our experience of making such visits has been rewarding. We have never been turned away and have always gained useful feedback about why they broke off contact with us. In some cases a new contract has been negotiated and the family has successfully returned to therapy. In every case the family or couple has given us useful ideas about how to undertake our therapy differently and we feel that our subsequent work has benefited from these failures.

Failure

Throughout this book we have (we hope) presented an optimistic picture of what therapists can do to help their clients open up new possibilities for themselves. We have stressed that this task requires high levels of commitment, resourcefulness and compassion; but it is, nevertheless, important to recognize the limits of our responsibilities. Some schools of therapy seem at times to be carried away by their sense of powerfulness and inventiveness and lose sight of who is ultimately responsible for achieving change.

Kaffman (1987) has explored the issue of failure in some depth. He argues that there are four identifiable major stages in the development of any therapeutic method. In the first (pioneering) stage, the initiator or small group of 'founding fathers' (*sic*) seek to make room for their idea by means of workshops and publications which have a clearly proselytizing edge to them. The pioneers typically report clinical work based on a small number of patients, all of whom exhibit significant improvement thanks to the new therapy. In the second stage, the circle of adherents to the new therapy expands since the pioneers are joined by trainees and others. Greater therapeutic success is reported as non-practitioners participate in the work. The third stage is marked by omnipotence since the disciples of the original founders not only report an ever-growing number of successful outcomes but become convinced that the new therapy model may be used with almost every type of clinical problem.

Kaffman suggests that these three stages typically span successive ten-year periods, but that the fourth decade is marked by a sobering-up stage. The first self-critical comments begin to appear – these deal with the constraints and limitations of what has effectively become a new orthodoxy, and gradually papers appear which actually document failure. Kaffman (1987) suggests that there is a parallel between Freud's famous paper 'Analysis terminable and interminable' (1937, in Kaffman) and Coleman's *Failures in Family Therapy* (1985), to which we have referred in previous chapters. Both publications appeared approximately thirty-five years after the founding of the new therapeutic approach with which they are concerned.

In our opinion Kaffman makes too much of the three decades

idea, and clearly his figure of thirty-five years should not be taken too seriously. (For example, in his analysis he overlooks Gurman and Kniskern (1978a) who published an important paper, 'Deterioration in marital and family therapy', seven years before Coleman's book.) Nevertheless, the general thrust of his argument is important. We feel that family therapy has indeed entered a new phase of self-criticism and self-examination, and we hope that our book is part of this process. Pioneering therapists are especially prone to ignore their failures, so it is entirely just that we should, by way of contrast, be very concerned about them. The previous two chapters of the book have concerned themselves with forms of failure which are mostly not immutable. There are, however, categories of failure which are far more fundamental. Kaffman, together with Coleman (1985) and Lask (1986), has explored these important categories which we need to examine as the final section of this chapter.

Kaffman's position is eloquently put in the following passage from his paper (1987, pp. 308–9):

> We know well enough that there is no one method of treatment that is omnipotent. There are some clinical problems that are inaccessible, not only to family therapy but to any form of therapy practised at the present time. One should be cautious of falling into a folie à deux where both the therapist and the family join forces with the aim of reaching unattainable aims .... If a therapist really believes in [her] omnipotence, [she] must have forgotten what [she] was taught in [her] school history class about the Roman emperors ... who had a slave whose sole function was to whisper from time to time into his master's ear the warning 'Remember – you are not a god'.

Equally, Coleman (1985) echoes Kaffman's point when she compares the treatment of medical and psychological disorders (pp. 368–9):

> Those in the medical profession know that some diseases cannot be cured .... [They] know that their treatment with some will probably fail and although they may continue to experiment with non-traditional approaches long after the more usual ones have proven useless there is a point where it must be conceded that nothing can save the patient. Similarly one might wonder if there are certain intrinsic factors that render family therapy hopeless.

Bryan Lask, the editor of the *Journal of Family Therapy*, has similarly drawn attention to some of the dilemmas of failure in an editorial entitled 'Whose responsibility?' (Lask, 1986, p. 205):

Family therapists seem to go to extraordinary lengths in their attempts to help their clients, taking on the most apparently unhelpable families, working at any hours that families demand, using wonderfully impressive high technology equipment and large numbers of people behind one-way screens to provide teams, supervisors, and even "choruses". The term resistance has become a dirty word: to say a family is impossible is a heresy! We are expected to devise strategies to help families overcome their natural disinclination to change, however strong that may be.

We have argued in this book that 'resistance' is not a useful term, but we nevertheless accept the essence of what Lask says. We can offer to help a family or couple and make sure that the offer is made in such a way that they are *genuinely* informed about how we will work with them, and we can do our best to build a therapeutic alliance with them, but we should avoid taking away their right to stay as they are if there is a genuine consensus to do so. We agree with Lask's main conclusion – that we need to approach work with families realistically and within a framework which does not usurp the family's right to maintain its responsibility for solving its own problems. Lask concludes his argument with a basic plea for realism (1986, p. 206):

We may ... recognize a family's need to be cared for, or an inability to take decisions, but it is not our responsibility to take over in these respects but rather to help the family recognize its difficulties and start seeking solutions. Whilst therapists may decide to accept responsibility for providing a setting, establishing and maintaining a therapeutic alliance, and offering observations and suggestions, those who take considerably greater responsibility for change are diluting what energy and motivation the family might have, as well as being likely candidates for burn-out ....

The time has come to allow the pendulum to return to the

middle. Therapists may be consultants to families, facilitators, catalysts for change but for their own sakes and that of their families (personal and client) only if the law is being broken or life or health is in danger, need they take as much responsibility as is currently in vogue.

Clearly, it is important to respect this position: only careful research into failure will ultimately clarify our understanding of which families and couples cannot change and why. But we must also beware of blaming the victim. One of us (J. C.) worked in a community mental health centre which provided a broad spectrum of therapeutic approaches to clients. One interesting result of this policy meant that families and couples who did not do well in family or marital therapy could return to the centre for other forms of treatment. These therapy 'failures' were interesting to follow up – the majority of clients reported to their new therapists that they felt blamed by their former therapists. This finding came as a shock since the family therapists themselves felt that they did, in fact, conscientiously attempt to avoid blaming their clients. Such a contradiction in perceptions obviously requires careful researching, but the most obvious answer is that both sets of respondents are correct. The therapists probably did avoid *overt* blaming but this does not mean that they avoided the trap of *covert* blaming. Terkelsen (1983), in a challenging paper concerned with schizophrenia, has pointed out that any form of sociogenic hypothesis about the causation of schizophrenia carries the risk of creating intractable problems between the therapists and the families they work with.

Terkelsen argues that when either therapist or family harbour the belief that schizophrenia is caused by personal experience with family members then a therapeutic misalliance is bound to be created. Originally trained to accept a sociogenic hypothesis about schizophrenia, he found that his work with schizophrenic families had disastrous outcomes. He now proposes an iatrogenic hypothesis to explain the unusual interactional patterns that are observed in schizophrenic families (1983, p. 196): '. . . [These] unusual forms . . . and also unusual interactions between family members and outside observers result from the family realization that an authority regards the family's way of being with each other as the source of the illness.'

Clearly, such a position is highly problematic. For example, is Terkelsen implying that the unusual patterns of communication observed by professionals in such families do not exist prior to contact with such professionals? If so, his hypothesis is probably untestable. But where does this leave therapists who work with such families? The importance of Terkelsen's work is his stress that therapists must adopt an explicitly non-blaming framework, and this seems to be borne out by research since it is precisely the group that stress non-blaming who claim the most success with schizophrenia (Falloon et al., 1984; Leff et al., 1982).

Our conclusion from this type of work takes us back to many of the themes of chapter 3. Our model stresses the paramount importance of the therapeutic alliance in determining the success of therapy. We are therefore very sympathetic to Terkelsen's work because it once again draws attention to the fact that therapeutic success cannot be achieved if the therapist and her clients are not in step. Obviously, our position is vulnerable to criticism since it is based on our experience of working with couples and families rather than on well-executed independent research, but we are by no means unique in arguing for such a position. Strategic therapists may well disagree with us but we would retort that, first, the evidence for the effectiveness of strategically-orientated family therapy is by no means impressive, and secondly, the ethics of such approaches are questionable (see Treacher, 1987, for a more extensive discussion of this point).

Terkelsen's work, together with our own experiences of failure in trying to help families and couples, leads us to conclude that a great deal of careful research work needs to be undertaken before we can be certain about the causes of failure. Above all else, we need to share our failures openly with our colleagues rather than concealing them. But we also need to re-open the debate concerning the indications and contra-indications for family and marital therapy.

The earlier pioneers of family therapy (and especially Haley, who was amongst the most influential opinion makers in the field) tended to stress that there were no indications or contra-indications for such an approach since it was essentially problem-solving. Such a stance clearly encouraged practitioners to test out whether their work could be developed to deal with almost every clinical problem they encountered, but it should now be possible to be clearer about the types of situation which cause some approaches to fail and some to succeed. This leads inexorably to the still unfashionable and often avoided issue – how can therapists (and their therapies) be suitably matched with clients and their problems? Alternatively, is it possible to devise an integrated model of marital and family therapy which draws upon many strands, and which will therefore be sufficiently rich to cater for the needs of a broad spectrum of families and couples that enter therapy? Unfortunately, such a discussion requires more space than we have room for here, so we can only invite you to look at some of the integrated models that are already on offer to see whether they have solved this problem (see Treacher, 1988, for further reading on this point).

6. Burn-out

Finally, before closing our discussion of failure it is necessary to look at its cost to the therapist. In particular we will examine the effects of failure on over-conscientious therapists.

An over-conscientious therapist who believes *she* has responsibility for solving families' problems will inevitably pay an enormous price for adopting such a position. Friedman (1985) in his useful short review of burn-out in family therapy cites several studies which link burn-out to over-dedication and over-commitment (Edelwich, 1980; Freudenberger, 1980; Sullivan 1979). Again, Bermak (1977) studied psychiatrists' work-related emotional problems and identified a group of therapists who had a great need to help and rescue others. If this need was thwarted, they felt helpless. In other words, professionals can be their own worst enemies.

Solutions

Friedman has devised a series of guidelines for preventing burn-out, which he has defined as 'a significant loss of interest, motivation, energy, satisfaction and effectiveness in connection with the work' (Friedman, 1985, p. 549). We have selected the five most important of these guidelines from Friedman's list.

1 *Responsibility for change* This rests with the family, not the therapist.

2 *Expectations and goal-setting* Both the therapist and the family or couple bring different expectations about what will happen in the session, as well as different views about the nature of the problem and different overt and covert agendas. Careful contract-making is therefore an essential antidote to burn-out, since it prevents the therapist from wittingly or unwittingly taking on tasks and responsibilities which are unrealistic and unobtainable.

3   *Role definition*   It is essential to avoid the trap of being
cast in the role of the all-knowing, all-powerful expert because
functioning in this way destroys the agency of the family. If the
therapist answers all the questions and becomes the sole advice-
giver then inevitably the family or couple become passive. The
whole thrust of therapy must therefore be to engage clients in a
search for solutions which *they* desire and carry out.

4   *Expressing feelings*   A therapist is human too and has every
right to express her feelings, or as Friedman says eloquently (1985,
p. 551):

> At times I may feel puzzled, angry, defeated, discounted, or
> anxious during a therapy session ... [so it] is often helpful
> for me to share these feelings openly, in a non-hostile way. By
> so doing, I relieve pressure on myself and can thus be more
> objective. At the same time I validate myself to the family as
> a real person with real feelings. The family, in turn, is presented
> the opportunity and need to cope with the therapist's feelings.
> This process may serve to clarify interaction between the
> therapist and the family and to define session content. Issues
> of transference and countertransference may also become
> explicit.

Friedman is careful to insist that any sharing of feelings must avoid
a destructive 'dumping' process which involves the therapist
punishing her clients for causing her distress or disturbance. Many
therapists (particularly those influenced by Haley) may well part
company with Friedman on this point, but we have found such an
approach liberating for both us and the families with whom we
have been struggling.

5   *Permitting the clients to keep the problem*   Clients must have
the right to keep their problems and not to change. Notable
exceptions to this rule are situations involving suicide, endangering
others, or sexual abuse. A therapist who is able to communicate
this basic message when working with a family or couple that is
stuck and not moving opens up possibilities for her clients rather
than closing them off. The clients may well respond with anxiety
if the therapist insists on recognizing their right not to change and
begins to initiate termination. They may well protest and, through
the process of exploring their anxiety, it may prove possible to
negotiate a transfer to another therapist. Alternatively, they may

accept a consultative session with a colleague of the therapist so that both the therapist and the clients can see where things have gone wrong. Above all else, this approach counteracts the therapist's grandiosity and enables her to let go of a hazardous experience which can lead to damaging experiences for both her clients and herself.

Surprisingly, Friedman does not directly discuss support and consultancy. He seems to write from the stance of a lone practitioner, but usually it is possible for a practitioner to gain support either from colleagues or a support group. If the practitioner is really stretched and out of her depth then it is obviously necessary to gain regular consultancy, although this, in turn, is not without its hazards as we pointed out in the last chapter. However, it is also true that if a therapist repeatedly gets stuck with certain types of client then it is essential that she should seek help for her problem. Otherwise she risks burn-out or becomes fearful and avoids working with certain couples or families.

Conclusion

As therapists, we have a responsibility for freeing ourselves as best we can from the scripts which influence the way we work. We need to ensure that we work in such a way that our clients retain responsibility for solving their problems. This means that we must free ourselves from the pernicious inclination to snatch responsibility away from them. We can provide support, skills, energy and hope from our side of the fence but if a therapeutic alliance cannot be forged then we have to acknowledge that therapy is not on the agenda. Either other ways and means of helping our clients need to be found or we need to retire gracefully and respectfully from the field, leaving them to get on with their lives in ways that they think are best. We are, therefore, sympathetic to Ryder (1987) who has argued in favour of an essentially modest approach to therapy, one which casts the therapist in the role of a gentle midwife rather than an aggressive *accoucheur*.

Further Reading

Ending Therapy

Barker, R. L. (1984), *Treating Couples in Crisis*. Offers some useful ideas about follow-up to marital therapy.

Epstein, N. and D. Bishop (1981), 'Problem-centred systems therapy of the family', in A. S. Gurman and D. Kniskern (eds), *Handbook of Family Therapy*. The McMaster model of family therapy offers a structured approach in four stages: a review of the contract; summary of treatment; the setting of long-term goals and optimal follow-up. Similar in many respects to the method outlined in this chapter.

Heath, A. (1985), 'Ending family therapy: some new directions', *Family Therapy Collections*, 14, 33–40. Advocates a consumerist position, likening therapy to private medical practice. Clients should be able to opt in and out of therapy as they choose; the therapist should be 'always there' providing input sparingly and only when necessary.

Kramer, C. (1980), *Becoming a Family Therapist*. Includes an excellent chapter on ending family therapy.

Parkinson, L. (1987), *Separation, Divorce and Families*. A practical guide to post-divorce therapy and conciliation.

Success and Failure

Calof, D. (1984), 'An exchange of identities', *Family Therapy Networker*, 8 (4), 47–53. Discusses the questionable means used in therapy to achieve 'successful ends'.

Coleman, S. (ed.) (1985), *Failures in Family Therapy*. An illuminating text in which prominent marital and family therapists discuss cases in which they failed. Concludes with an analysis which seeks to draw out important themes and suggests avenues for future research.

Ryder, R. G. (1987), *The Realistic Therapist: Modesty and Relativism in Therapy and Research*. A powerful argument to the effect that modesty is in professionals' self-interest. Chapter 10 is delicately called 'Minimal Therapy' and likens therapy to midwifery: the therapist helps to deliver but this help is useless if the baby is not already pressing to be born.

References

Ahmed, S. (1986), 'Cultural racism in work with Asian Women and Girls', in S. Ahmed et al. (eds), *Social Work with Black Children and Families*. London: Batsford.

Ainley, M. (1984), 'Family therapy in probation practice', in A. Treacher and J. Carpenter (eds) (1984).

Anderson, C. M. and S. Stewart (1983), *Mastering Resistance: A Practical Guide to Family Therapy*. New York: Guilford Press.

Anderson, S. A. et al. (1985), 'Dropping out of marriage and family therapy: intervention strategies and spouses' perception', *American Journal of Family Therapy*, 13, 39–54.

Andolfi, M. (1979), *Family Therapy*. New York: Plenum Press.

Ballard, R. (1979), 'Ethnic minorities and the Social Services: What type of service?', in V. S. Khan (ed.), *Minority Families in Britain*. London: Macmillan.

Barker, P. (1981), *Basic Family Therapy*. London: Granada.

Barker, R. L. (1984), *Treating Couples in Crisis*. New York: Free Press.

Barot, R. (1988), 'Social anthropology, ethnicity and family therapy', *Journal of Family Therapy*, 10, 271–82.

Barragan, M. (1976), 'The child-centred family', in P. J. Guerin (ed.), *Family Therapy: Theory and Practice*. New York: Gardner Press.

Bavington, J. and Majid, A. (1986), 'Psychiatric services for ethnic minority groups', in J. Cox (ed.), *Transcultural Psychiatry*. London: Croom Helm.

Beck, A. et al. (1979), *Cognitive Therapy of Depression*. New York: Guilford Press.

Bennun, I. (1985), 'Unilateral marital therapy', in W. Dryden (ed.), *Marital Therapy in Britain*, vol. 2. London: Harper and Row.

Bentovim, A. (1981), 'The rejected scapegoated child', in A. S. Gurman (ed.), *Questions and Answers in the Practice of Family*

Therapy. Vol. 1, New York: Brunner/Mazel.

Bentovim, A., A. Elton and M. Tranter (1987), 'Prognosis for rehabilitation after abuse', *Adoption and Fostering*, 11, 26–31.

Berg, B. and N. Rosenblum (1977), 'Fathers in family therapy: a survey of family therapists', *Journal of Marital and Family Therapy*, 3, 85–91.

Berger, M. (1975), 'A note on luring a resistant spouse into marital therapy', *Journal of Marriage and Family Counselling*, 1, 387–8.

Berger, M. and C. Dammann (1982), 'Live supervision as context, treatment and training', *Family Process*, 21, 337–44.

Berger, M., G. J. Jurkovic et al. (1984), *Practicing Family Therapy in Diverse Settings*. San Francisco: Jossey Bass.

Bermak, G. (1977), 'Do psychiatrists have special emotional problems?', *American Journal of Psychoanalysis*, 37, 141–6.

Bloch, D. (1976), 'Including the children in family therapy', in P. J. Guerin (ed.), *Family Therapy: Theory and Practice*. New York: Gardner Press.

Bogdan, J. L. (1984), 'Family organisation as an ecology of ideas: an alternative to the reification of family systems', *Family Process*, 23, 375–88.

Bordin, E. (1979), 'The generalizability of the psychoanalytic concept of the working alliance', *Psychotherapy Theory, Research and Practice*, 16, 252–60.

Bordin, E. (1983), 'Myths, realities and alternatives to clinical trials.' Paper delivered at the International Conference on Psychotherapy, Bogota, Columbia.

Bowen, M. (1966), 'The use of family theory in clinical practice', *Comprehensive Psychiatry*, 7, 345–74.

Bowen, M. (1974), 'Toward the differentiation of a self in one's family of origin', in F. Andres and J. Lorio (eds), *Georgetown Family Symposia*, a collection of selected papers, I. Washington DC.

Bowen, M. (1978), *Family Therapy in Clinical Practice*. New York: Jason Aronson.

Brent, D. and E. Marine (1982), 'Developmental aspects of the cotherapy relationship', *Journal of Marital and Family Therapy*, 8, 69–75.

Breunlin, D. and B. Cade (1981), 'Intervening in family systems with observer messages', *Journal of Marital and Family Therapy*, 7, 453–60.

British Medical Journal (1979), 'Subacute sclerosing panencephalitis', 3 November.

Britton, R. (1981), 'Re-enactment as an unwitting professional response to family dynamics', in S. Box et al. (eds), *Psychotherapy with Families*. London: Routledge & Kegan Paul.

Broderick, C. (1983), *The Therapeutic Triangle: A Source Book on Marital Therapy*. Beverly Hills: Sage.

Brown, G. and T. Harris (1978), *Social Origins of Depression: A Study of Psychiatric Disorder in Women*. London: Tavistock.

Brown, R. et al. (1985), *Social Workers at Risk: The Prevention and Management of Violence*. London: Macmillan.

Burnham, J. (1986), *Family Therapy*. London: Tavistock.

Byng-Hall, J. (1973), 'Family myths used as a defence in conjoint family therapy', *British Journal of Medical Psychology*, 46, 239–50.

Byng-Hall, J. (1980), 'Symptom bearer as marital distance regulator', *Family Process*, 19, 355–65.

Byng-Hall, J. et al. (1982), 'Evolution of supervision: an overview', in R. Whiffen and J. Byng-Hall (eds) (1982).

Cade, B. and M. Cornwell (1985), 'New realities for old: some uses of teams and one-way screens in therapy', in D. Campbell and R. Draper (eds) (1985).

Calam, R. and P. Elliott (1987), 'Why are we too busy? Problems of practitioner research in family therapy', *Journal of Family Therapy*, 9, 329–38.

Calof, D. (1984), 'An exchange of identities', *Family Therapy Networker*, 8 (4), 47–53.

Campbell, D. (1985), 'The consultation interview', in D. Campbell and R. Draper (eds) (1985).

Campbell, D. and R. Draper (eds) (1985), *Applications of Systemic Family Therapy: The Milan Approach*. London: Grune and Stratton.

Carl, D. and G. Jurkovic (1983), 'Agency triangles: problems in agency–family relationships', *Family Process*, 22, 441–51.

Carpenter, J. (1984a), 'Child guidance and family therapy', in A. Treacher and J. Carpenter (eds) (1984).

Carpenter, J. (1984b), 'Working together', in A. Treacher and J. Carpenter (eds) (1984).

Carpenter, J. (1987a), 'For the good of the family', in S. Walrond-Skinner and D. Watson (eds), *Ethical Issues in Family Therapy*. London: Routledge & Kegan Paul.

Carpenter, J. (1987b), 'Has family therapy gone 'over the top'? Reflections on the state of family therapy in the UK', *Journal of Family Therapy*, 9, 217–30.

Carpenter, J. and A. Treacher (1982), 'Structural family therapy in context – working with child-focused problems', *Journal of Family Therapy*, 4, 15–34.

Carpenter, J. and A. Treacher (1983), 'On the neglected but related arts of convening and engaging families and their wider systems', *Journal of Family Therapy*, 5, 337–58.

Carpenter, J., A. Treacher, H. Jenkins and P. O'Reilly (1983), '"Oh no! Not the Smiths again!' An exploration of how to identify and overcome 'stuckness' in family therapy', part II: 'Stuckness in the therapeutic and supervisory systems', *Journal of Family Therapy*, 5, 81–96.

Carr, A. (in press), 'Countertransference and child abuse', *Journal of Family Therapy*.

Carter, E. and M. Orfanidis (1976), 'Family therapy with one person and the family therapist's own family', in P. J. Guerin (ed.), *Family Therapy: Theory and Practice*. New York: Gardner Press.

CIBA Foundation (1984), *Child Sexual Abuse within the Family*. (R. Porter, ed.) London: Tavistock.

Clark, T., T. Zalis and F. Sacco (1982), *Outreach Family Therapy*. New York: Jason Aronson.

Coleman, S. (1977), 'A developmental stage hypothesis for non-marital dyadic relationships', *Journal of Marital and Family Counselling*, 3, 71–6.

Coleman, S. (ed.) (1985), *Failures in Family Therapy*. New York: Guilford Press.

Coleman, S. and Gurman, A. S. (1985), 'An analysis of family therapy failures', in S. Coleman (ed.) (1985).

Combrinck-Graham, L. (1981), 'Termination in family therapy', in A. S. Gurman (ed.), *Questions and Answers in the Practice of Family Therapy*. New York: Brunner/Mazel.

Combrinck-Graham, L. (ed.) (1986), *Treating Young Children in Family Therapy*. Rockville, MD: Aspen.

Cook, D. and Frantz-Cook, A. (1984), 'A systemic treatment approach to wife battering', *Journal of Marital and Family Therapy*, 10, 83–93.

Coulshed, V. (1981), 'Engaging in family therapy: problems for the inexperienced, uninvited therapist', *Journal of Family Therapy*, 3, 51–8.

Cox, J. (ed.) (1986), *Transcultural Psychiatry*. London: Croom Helm.

Coyne, J. (1987), 'Depression, biology, marriage and marital therapy', *Journal of Marital and Family Therapy*, 13, 393–407.

Coyne, J. and T. Widiger (1978), 'Towards a participatory model of psychotherapy', *Professional Psychology*, 9, 700–10.

Crowe, M. (1985), 'Marital therapy. A behavioural systems approach: indications for different types of intervention', in W. Dryden (ed.), *Marital Therapy in Britain*, vol. I. London: Harper and Row.

Dale, P. et al. (1986), *Dangerous Families. Assessment and treatment of child abuse*. London: Tavistock.

Daniell, D. (1985), 'Marital therapy. The psychodynamic approach', in W. Dryden (ed.), *Marital Therapy in Britain* vol. I. London: Harper and Row.

Dare, C. (1981), 'Psychoanalysis and family therapy', in S. Walrond-Skinner (ed.), *Developments in Family Therapy*, 281–97. London: Routledge & Kegan Paul.

Dare, C. and C. Lindsey (1979), 'Children in family therapy', *Journal of Family Therapy*, 1, 253–69.

Dell, P. (1982), 'Beyond homeostasis: toward a concept of coherence', *Family Process*, 21, 21–41.

Deschner, J. (1984), *The Hitting Habit: Anger Control for Battering Couples*. New York: Free Press.

de Shazer, S. (1984), 'The death of resistance', *Family Process*, 23, 11–21.

Dicks, H. V. (1967), *Marital Tensions*. London: Routledge & Kegan Paul.

Dimmock, B. (1984), 'Family counselling in general practice', in A. Treacher and J. Carpenter (eds) (1984).

Dimmock, B. and D. Dungworth (1983), 'Creating manoeuvrability for family/systems therapists working in social service departments', *Journal of Family Therapy*, 5, 53–69.

Dimmock, B. and D. Dungworth (1985), 'Beyond the family: using network meetings with statutory child care cases', *Journal of Family Therapy*, 7, 45–68.

Dingwall, R. et al. (1983), *The Protection of Children: State Intervention and Family Life*. Oxford: Blackwell.

Doctor, R. M. and E. M. Singer (1978), 'Behavioural intervention strategies with child abusive parents: a home intervention program', *Child Abuse and Neglect*, 2, 57–68.

Doherty, W. J. (1981), 'Involving the reluctant father in family therapy', in A. S. Gurman (ed.), *Questions and Answers in the Practice of Family Therapy*. New York: Brunner/Mazel.

Doherty, W. J. and M. A. Baird (1983), *Family Therapy and Family Medicine*, ch. 9. New York: Guilford Press.

Dowling, E. (1979), 'Co-therapy: a clinical researcher's view', in S. Walrond-Skinner (ed.), *Family and Marital Psychotherapy*. London: Routledge & Kegan Paul.

Dryden, W. and P. Hunt (1985), 'Therapeutic alliances in marital therapy', 1: Pre-therapy influences, 2: Process issues, in W. Dryden (ed.), *Marital Therapy in Britain*. vol. I. London: Harper and Row.

Dungworth, D. (1982), 'Family therapy and Social Services Departments: a field work perspective', Personal Social Services Fellowship Study Report. Bristol University (unpublished).

Edelwich, J. (1980), *Burn-out: Stages of Disillusionment in the Helping Professions*. New York: Human Sciences Press.

Ely, P. and D. Denny (1987), *Social Work in a Multi-Racial Society*. Aldershot: Gower.

Epstein, N. and D. Bishop (1981), 'Problem-centred systems therapy of the family', in A. S. Gurman and D. Kniskern (eds), *Handbook of Family Therapy*. New York: Brunner/Mazel.

Falloon, I., J. Boyd and C. McGill (1984), *Family Care of Schizophrenia*. New York: Guilford Press.

Farrar, N. and I. Sicar (1986), 'Social work with Asian families in a psychiatric setting', in V. Coombs and R. Little (eds), *Race and Social Work*. London: Tavistock.

Feld, B. (1982), 'Countertransference in family therapy', *Group*, 6, 3–13.

Ferber, A. et al. (1972), *The Book of Family Therapy*. New York: Science House.

Fisch, R., J. H. Weakland and L. Segal (1982), *The Tactics of Change: Doing Therapy Briefly*. San Francisco: Jossey Bass.

Fisher, L. (1981), 'Helping parents get resistant adolescents into family therapy', in A. S. Gurman (ed.), *Questions and Answers in the Practice of Family Therapy*. New York: Brunner/Mazel.

Freudenberger, H. (1980) with G. Richardson, *Burn-out: The High Cost of High Achievement*. New York: Doubleday.

Friedman, R. (1985), 'Making family therapy easier for the therapist:

burn-out prevention', *Family Process*, 25, 549–53.

Furniss, T. (1983), 'Mutual influence and interlocking professional–family process in the treatment of child sexual abuse and incest', *Child Abuse and Neglect*, 7, 207–23.

Furniss, T. (1985), 'Conflict avoiding and conflict regulating patterns in incest and child sexual abuse', *Acta Paedopsychiatrica*, 50, 6.

Gaines, T. (1978), 'Factors influencing a failure to show for family evaluation', *International Journal of Family Counselling*, 6, 57–61.

Garfield, R. and L. Schwoeri (1981), 'A family consultation model: breaking the therapeutic impasse', *International Journal of Family Psychiatry*, 2, 251–67.

Gelles, R. J. and C. P. Cornell (1985), *Intimate Violence in Families*. Beverly Hills: Sage.

Giarretto, H. (1982), 'A comprehensive child sexual abuse treatment program', *Child Abuse and Neglect*, 6, 263–78.

Goldner, V. (1985), 'Feminism and family therapy', *Family Process*, 24, 31–47.

Goodyear, R. (1981), 'Termination as a loss experience for the counselor', *Personnel and Guidance Journal*, 59, 347–50.

Gorell Barnes, G. (1984), *Working with Families*. London: Macmillan.

Greenberg, I. M. et al. (1964), 'Family therapy: indications and rationale', *Archives of General Psychiatry*, 10, 7–25.

Guerin, P. J. and K. Guerin (1976), 'Theoretical aspects and clinical relevance of the Multigenerational Model of family therapy', in P. J. Guerin (ed.), *Family Therapy: Theory and Practice*. New York: Gardner Press.

Gurman, A. S. (1981), 'Integrative marital therapy: towards the development of an interpersonal approach', in S. Budman (ed.), *Forms of Brief Therapy*. New York: Guilford Press.

Gurman, A. S. (1984), 'Transference and resistance in marital therapy', *American Journal of Family Therapy*, 12, 70–3.

Gurman, A. S. and D. Kniskern (1978a), 'Deterioration in marital and family therapy: empirical, clinical and conceptual issues', *Family Process* 17, 3–19.

Gurman, A. S. and D. Kniskern (1978b), 'Research on marital and family therapy', in S. Garfield and A. Bergin (eds), *Handbook of Psychotherapy and Behavior Change*. New York: Wiley.

Gurman, A. S. and D. Kniskern (1981), 'Family therapy outcome research: known and unknown', in A. S. Gurman and D. Kniskern, *Handbook of Family Therapy*. New York: Brunner/Mazel.

Gurman, A. S. and D. Kniskern (1986), 'Commentary', *Family Process*, 25, 51–62.

Gurman, A. S., D. Kniskern and W. Pinsof (1985), 'Research on the process and outcome of marital and family therapy', in S. Garfield and A. Bergin (eds), *Handbook of Psychotherapy and Behavior Change* (3rd edn). New York: Wiley.

Hafner, R. et al. (1983), 'Spouse-aided versus individual therapy in persisting psychiatric disorders: a systematic comparison', *Family Process*, 22, 385–99.

Haley, J. (1962), 'Whither family therapy?', *Family Process*, 1, 69–100.

Haley, J. (1967), *Advanced Techniques of Hypnosis and Therapy: Selected Papers of Milton H. Erickson, M.D.* New York: Grune and Stratton.

Haley, J. (1976), *Problem Solving Therapy*. San Francisco: Jossey Bass.

Haley, J. (1980), *Leaving Home: The Therapy of Disturbed Young People*. New York: McGraw-Hill.

Haley, J. and Hoffman, L. (1967), *Techniques of Family Therapy*. New York: Basic Books.

Hare-Mustin, R. (1978), 'A feminist approach to family therapy', *Family Process*, 17, 181–94.

Haynes, R. B., D. W. Taylor and D. L. Sackett (eds) (1979), *Compliance in Health Care*. Baltimore: Johns Hopkins University Press.

Heath, A. (1985), 'Ending family therapy: some new directions', *Family Therapy Collections*, 14, 33–40.

Hoffman, L. (1981), *Foundations of Family Therapy: A Conceptual Framework for Systems Change*. New York: Basic Books.

Hoffman, L. and L. Long (1969), 'A systems dilemma', *Family Process*, 8, 211–34.

Holt, M. and D. Greiner (1976), 'Co-therapy in the teatment of families', in P. J. Guerin (ed.), *Family Therapy: Theory and Practice*. New York: Gardner Press.

Hornung, C. et al. (1981), 'Status relationships in marriage: risk factors in spouse abuse', *Journal of Marriage and the Family*, 43, 679–92.

Hudson, P. (1980), 'Different strokes for differen olk a comparative examination of behavioural, structural and paradoxical methods in family therapy', *Journal of Family Therapy*, 2, 181–97.

Humphrey, F. (1981), 'Treatment of extra-marital sexual affairs', in A. S. Gurman (ed.), *Questions and Answers in the Practice of Family Therapy*, vol. I. New York: Brunner/Mazel.

Hunt, P. (1984), 'Response to marriage counselling', *British Journal of Guidance and Counselling*, 12, 72–83.

Jackson, D. D. (1957), 'The question of family homeostasis', *The Psychiatric Quarterly Supplement*, 31, 79–90.

Jenkins, H. and Donnelly, M. (1983), 'The therapist's responsibility: a systemic approach to mobilising family creativity', *Journal of Family Therapy*, 5, 199–218.

Johnson, H. (1987), 'Biologically based deficit in the identified patient: indications for psychoeducational strategies', *Journal of Marital and Family Therapy*, 13, 337–48.

Kaffman, M. (1987), 'Failures in family therapy: and then what?', *Journal of Family Therapy*, 9, 307–28.

Karpel, M. (1980), 'Family Secrets: I. Conceptual and ethical issues in the relational context; II. Ethical and practical considerations in therapeutic management', *Family Process*, 19, 295–306.

Keeney, B. P. (1983), *Aesthetics of Change*. New York: Guilford Press.

Kempe, R. S. and C. H. Kempe (1978), *Child Abuse*. London: Fontana.

Kingston, P. (1977), 'Family therapy and material aid', *Family Service Unit Quarterly*, December, 1–23.

Kingston, P. (1979), 'The social context of family therapy', in S. Walrond-Skinner (ed.), *Family and Marital Psychotherapy*. London: Routledge & Kegan Paul.

Kingston, P. (1984), ' "But they aren't motivated ..." Issues concerned with encouraging motivation for change in families', *Journal of Family Therapy*, 6, 381–403.

Kingston, P. and Smith, D. (1983), 'Preparation for live consultation and live supervision', *Journal of Family Therapy*, 5, 219–33.

Kramer, C. (1980), *Becoming a Family Therapist*. New York: Human Sciences Press.

L'Abate, L. (1975), 'Pathogenic role rigidity in fathers: some observations', *Journal of Marital and Family Therapy*, 1, 69–79.

L'Abate, L. and M. Baggett (1985), 'A failure to keep the father in family therapy', in S. Coleman (ed.) (1985).

Lask, B. (1986), 'Editorial – Whose responsibility?', *Journal of Family Therapy*, 8, 205–6.

Lask, B. (1987), 'Cybernetico-epistobabble, the emperor's new clothes and other sacred cows', *Journal of Family Therapy*, 9, 207–15.

Lau, A. (1984), 'Transcultural issues in family therapy', *Journal of Family Therapy*, 6, 91–112.

Lau, A. (1986), 'Family therapy across cultures', in J. Cox (ed.), *Transcultural Psychiatry*. London: Croom Helm.

Le Fave, K. (1980), 'Correlates of engagement in family therapy', *Journal of Marriage and Family Counselling*, 6, 75–81.

Leff, J. et al. (1982), 'A controlled trial of social intervention in the families of schizophrenic patients', *British Journal of Psychiatry*, 141, 121–34.

Lerner, B. (1972), *Therapy in the Ghetto*. Baltimore: Johns Hopkins University Press.

Lerner, R. and G. Spanier (1978), *Child Influences on Marital and Family Interaction: A Life-cycle Perspective*. New York: Academic Press.

Lewis, C. and M. O'Brien (eds) (1987), *Reassessing Fatherhood: New Observations on Fathers and the Modern Family*. London: Sage.

Liddle, H. A. (1985), 'Five factors of failure in Structural-Strategic Family Therapy: a contextual comparison', in S. Coleman (ed.) (1985).

Lieberman, S. (1979), *Transgenerational Family Therapy*. London: Croom Helm.

Lindow, V. (1986), 'The social consequences of seeing a psychiatrist', unpublished PhD. thesis. University of Bristol.

Littlewood, R. and M. Lipsedge (1982), *Aliens and Alienists: Ethnic Minorities and Psychiatry*. Harmondsworth: Penguin.

Liverpool, V. (1986), 'When backgrounds clash', *Community Care*, 2 October, 19–21.

Lorion, R. P. (1978), 'Research on psychotherapy and behavior change with the disadvantaged', in S. Garfield and A. Bergin (eds), *Handbook of Psychotherapy and Behavior Change*. New York: Wiley.

McDermott, J. and W. Char (1974), 'The undeclared war between child and family therapy', *Journal of the American Academy of Child Psychiatry*, 13, 422–36.

McGoldrick, M. et al. (1982), *Ethnicity and Family Therapy*. New York: Guilford Press.

Mackay, D. (1985), 'Marital therapy. The behavioural approach', in W. Dryden (ed.), *Marital Therapy in Britain*, vol. I. London: Harper and Row.

Magagna, J. and D. Black (1985), 'Changing roles for men and women: implications for marital therapy', in W. Dryden (ed.), *Marital Therapy in Britain*, vol. I. London: Harper and Row.

Maluccio, A. (1979), *Learning from Clients: Interpersonal Helping as Viewed by Clients and Social Workers*. New York: Free Press.

Maluccio, A. and Marlow, W. (1974), 'The case for the contract', *Social Work*, 19, 28–36.

Maruyama, M. (1968), 'The second cybernetics: deviation-amplifying mutual causal processes', in W. Buckley (ed.), *Modern Systems Research for the Behavioural Scientist*. Chicago: Aldine.

Mattinson, J. (1975), *The Reflection Process in Casework Supervision*. London: Institute of Marital Studies.

Mattinson, J. and I. Sinclair (1979), *Mate and Stalemate: Working with Marital Problems in a Social Services Department*. Oxford: Blackwell.

Minuchin, S. (1974), *Families and Family Therapy*. London: Tavistock.

Minuchin, S. (1984), *Family Kaleidoscope*. Cambridge, MA: Harvard University Press.

Minuchin, S. and C. Fishman (1981), *Family Therapy Techniques*. Cambridge, MA: Harvard University Press.

Minuchin, S., B. Rosman and L. Baker (1978), *Psychosomatic Families: Anorexia Nervosa in Context*. Cambridge, MA: Harvard University Press.

Montalvo, B. (1973), 'Aspects of live supervision', *Family Process*, 12, 343–59.

Montalvo, B. and J. Haley (1973), 'In defence of child therapy', *Family Process*, 12, 227–44.

Moore, J. (1985), *The ABC of Child Abuse Work*. Aldershot: Gower.

Myerstein, I. and P. Dell (1985), 'Family therapy versus schizophrenia and the psychiatric-legal establishment', in S. Coleman (ed.) (1985).

Napier, A. and C. Whitaker (1978), *The Family Crucible*. New York: Harper and Row.

National Council for Voluntary Child Care Organisations, (1987) Family Centre Conference Report. London: NCVCCO.

Neilson, E. and F. Kaslow (1980), 'Consultation in family therapy', *American Journal of Family Therapy*, 8, 35–42.

Nelsen, J. (1983), *Family Treatment: An Integrative Approach*. Englewood Cliffs, NJ: Prentice-Hall.

Nichols, M. P. (1984), *Family Therapy: Concepts and Methods*. New York: Gardner Press.

O'Brien, A. and P. Loudon (1985), 'Redressing the balance – involving children in family therapy', *Journal of Family Therapy*, 7, 81–98.

O'Connor, P. (1974), 'Coalition formation in conjoint marriage counselling', unpublished PhD. thesis. University of California, Department of Sociology.

Osborne, K. (1983), 'Women in families: feminist therapy and family systems', *Journal of Family Therapy*, 5, 1–10.

Palazzoli, M. S. (1980), 'Why a long interval between sessions? The therapeutic control of the family–therapist suprasystem', in M. Andolfi and I. Zwerling (eds), *Dimensions of Family Therapy*. New York: Guilford Press.

Palazzoli, M. S. (1983), 'Emergence of a comprehensive systems approach', *Journal of Family Therapy*, 5, 165–77.

Palazzoli, M. S. et al. (1980a),'The problem of the referring person', *Journal of Marital and Family Therapy*, 6, 3–9.

Palazzoli, M. S. et al. (1980b), 'Hypothesizing-circularity-neutrality: three guidelines for the conductor of the session', *Family Process*, 19, 3–12.

Palazzoli, M. S., G. Cecchin, G. Prata and L. Boscolo (1978), *Paradox and Counterparadox*. New York: Jason Aronson.

Palazzoli, M. S. and G. Prata (1982), 'Snares in family therapy', *Journal of Marital and Family Therapy*, 8, 443–50.

Papp, P. (1976), 'Family choreography', in P. J. Guerin (ed.), *Family Therapy: Theory and Practice*. New York: Gardner Press.

Papp, P. (1980), 'The Greek chorus and other techniques of paradoxical therapy', *Family Process*, 19, 45–57.

Papp, P. (1983), *The Process of Change*. New York: Guilford Press.

Parkinson, L. (1987), *Separation, Divorce and Families*. London: Macmillan.

Parloff, M., I. Waskow and B. Wolfe (1978), 'Research on therapist variables in relation to process and outcome', in S. Garfield and A. Bergin (eds), *Handbook of Psychotherapy and Behavior Change*. New York: Wiley.

Pascoe, W. (1980), 'Overcoming blocks to creativity in family treatment', *Journal of Family Therapy*, 2, 211–14.

Patterson, L. and S. Eisenberg (1983), *The Counselling Process*. Boston: Houghton Mifflin.

Paul, N. (1976), 'Cross confrontation', in P. J. Guerin (ed.), *Family Therapy: Theory and Practice*. New York: Gardner Press.

Pestrak, V. A. et al. (1985), 'Extra-marital sex: an examination of the literature', *International Journal of Family Therapy*, 7, 107–15.

Pilalis, J. and J. Anderton (1986), 'Feminism and family therapy – a possible meeting point', *Journal of Family Therapy*, 8, 99–114.

Pimpernell, P. and A. Treacher (in preparation), 'Overcoming clients' reluctance to engage in family therapy – a review of the literature and a report of a videotape project.'

Pincus, L. and C. Dare (1978), *Secrets in the Family*. London: Faber and Faber.

Pittman, F. and K. Flomenhaft (1970), 'Treating the doll's house marriage', *Family Process*, 9, 143–55.

Procter, H. and T. Stephens (1984), 'Developing family therapy in the Day Hospital', in A. Treacher and J. Carpenter (eds) (1984).

Rack, P. H. (1982), *Race, Culture and Mental Disorder*. London: Tavistock.

Rakoff, V. (1984), 'The necessity for multiple models in family therapy', *Journal of Family Therapy*, 6, 199–210.

Ransom, D. C. (1982), 'Resistance: family or therapist generated?', in A. S. Gurman (ed.), *Questions and Answers in the Practice of Family Therapy*, vol. 2. New York: Brunner/Mazel.

Rapoport, R., M. Fogarty and P. Rapoport (eds) (1982), *Families in Britain*. London: Routledge & Kegan Paul.

Reder, P. (1983), 'Disorganised families and the helping professions: "Who's in charge of what?"', *Journal of Family Therapy*, 5, 23–36.

Rees, S. and A. Wallace (1982), *Verdicts on Social Work*. London: Edward Arnold.

Rice, D., W. Fry and J. Kepecs (1972), 'Therapist experience and style as factors in co-therapy', *Family Process*, 11, 1–12.

Rice, D. and J. Rice (1974), 'Status and sex role issues in co-therapy', in A. S. Gurman and D. Rice (eds), *Couples in Conflict: New Directions in Marital Therapy*. New York: Jason Aronson.

Roberts, J. (1984), 'Antidotes for secrecy. Treating the incestuous family', *Family Therapy Networker*, 8, 49–54.

Rutter, M. and N. Madge (1976), *Cycles of Disadvantage*. London: Heinemann.

Ryder, R. G. (1987), *The Realistic Therapist: Modesty and Relativism in Therapy and Research*. Newbury Park: Sage.

Sager, C. (1981), 'Marital contracts', in G. P. Sholevar (ed.), *The Handbook of Marriage and Marital Therapy*. Lancaster: MTP Press.

Sager, C. et al. (1968), 'Selection and engagement of patients in family therapy', *American Journal of Orthopsychiatry*, 38, 715–23.

Scharff, D. and J. Scharff (1987), *Object Relations Family Therapy*. Northvale, NJ: Jason Aronson.

Scheflen, A. (1978), *Levels of Schizophrenia*. New York: Brunner/Mazel.

Scott, D. and P. Ashworth (1967), '"Closure" at the first schizophrenic breakdown: a family study', *British Journal of Medical Psychiatry*, 40, 109–45.

Segal, L. and Watzlawick, P. (1985), 'On window-shopping or being a noncustomer', in S. B. Coleman (ed.) (1985).

Sgroi, S. M. (1975), 'Sexual molestation of children: the last frontier in child abuse', *Children Today*, 4, 18–21.

Shackman, J. (1985), *The Right to be Understood*. Cambridge: National Extension College.

Shah, I. (1975), *The Pleasantries of the Incredible Mullah Nasrudin*. London: Pan.

Shapiro, R. (1974), 'Therapist attitudes and premature termination in family and individual therapy', *Journal of Nervous and Mental Disease*, 159, 101–7.

Shapiro, R. and S. Budman (1973), 'Defection, termination and continuation in family and individual therapy', *Family Process*, 12, 55–67.

Silverman, P. (1970), 'A re-examination of the intake procedure', *Social Casework*, 51, 625–34.

Simon, F., H. Stierlin and L. Wynne (1985), *The Language of Family Therapy: A Systemic Vocabulary and Source Book*.

New York: Family Process Press.

Skinner, A. and R. Castle (1969), *78 Battered Children: A Retrospective Study*. London: National Society for the Prevention of Cruelty to Children.

Skynner, A. C. R. (1976), *One Flesh, Separate Persons*. London: Constable.

Skynner, A. C. R. (1979), 'Reflections on the family therapist as family scapegoat', *Journal of Family Therapy*, 1, 7–22.

Skynner, A. C. R. (1981), 'An open-systems, group analytic approach to family therapy', in A. S. Gurman and D. P. Kniskern (eds), *Handbook of Family Therapy*. New York: Brunner/Mazel.

Slipp, S., S. Ellis and K. Kressel (1974), 'Factors associated with engagement in family therapy', *Family Process*, 13, 413–27.

Sluzki, C. (1978), 'Marital therapy from a systems theory perspective', in T. J. Paolino and B. S. McCready (eds), *Marriage and Marital Therapy*. New York: Brunner/Mazel.

Smith, D. and P. Kingston (1980), 'Live supervision without a one-way screen', *Journal of Family Therapy*, 2, 379–87.

Solomon, M. (1969), 'Family therapy drop-outs: resistance to change', *Canadian Psychiatric Association Journal*, 14, 21–9.

Sonne, J. and Lincoln, G. (1965), 'Heterosexual co-therapy team experiences during family therapy', *Family Process*, 4, 177–97.

Spark, E. (1974), 'Grandparents and intergenerational family therapy', *Family Process*, 13, 225–37.

Speed, B. (1987), 'Over the top in the theory and practice of family therapy', *Journal of Family Therapy*, 9, 231–40.

Speed, B. et al. (1982), 'A team approach to therapy', *Journal of Family Therapy*, 4, 271–84.

Speer, A. (1970), 'Family systems: morphostasis and morphogenesis', *Family Process*, 9, 259–78.

Sprenkle, D. and C. Weis (1978), 'Extra-marital sexuality: implications for marital therapists', *Journal of Sex and Marital Therapy*, 4, 279–91.

Stanton, M. (1980), 'Marital therapy from a structural/strategic viewpoint', in E. Sholevar (ed.), *Marriage is a Family Affair: A Textbook of Marriage and Marital Therapy*. New York: Spectrum.

Stanton, M. and T. Todd (1981), 'Engaging 'resistant' families in treatment', *Family Process*, 20, 261–93.

Stierlin, H. (1975), 'Countertransference in family therapy with adolescents', in M. Sugar (ed.), *The Adolescent in Group and*

Family Therapy. New York: Brunner/Mazel.

Stratton, P. (1988), 'Circles and spirals: the contribution of developmental psychology to family therapy', *Journal of Family Therapy*, 10, 207–31.

Street, E. (1985), 'From child-focused problems to marital issues', in W. Dryden (ed.), *Marital Therapy in Britain*. vol. II. London: Harper and Row.

Sullivan, R. (1979), 'The burn-out syndrome', *Journal of Action Development and Disorder*, 9, 112–26.

Summit, R. C. (1983), 'The child sexual abuse accommodation syndrome', *Child Abuse and Neglect*, 7, 177–93.

Szapocznik, J. et al. (1982), 'One person family therapy', in W. O'Connor and B. Lubin (eds), *Ecological Approaches to Clinical and Community Psychology*. New York: Wiley.

Teismann, M. (1980), 'Convening strategies in family therapy', *Family Process*, 19, 393–400.

Terkelsen, K. (1983), 'Schizophrenia and the family. II. Adverse effects of family therapy', *Family Process*, 22, 191–200.

Treacher, A. (1983), 'On the utility or otherwise of psychotherapy research', in D. Pilgrim (ed.), *Psychology and Psychotherapy: Current trends and issues*. London: Routledge & Kegan Paul.

Treacher, A. (1985), 'Working with marital partners – systems approaches', in W. Dryden (ed.), *Marital Therapy in Britain*, vol. I. London: Harper and Row.

Treacher, A. (1986), 'Invisible patients, invisible families – a critical examination of some technocratic trends in family therapy', *Journal of Family Therapy*, 8, 267–306.

Treacher, A. (1987), ' "Family therapists are potentially damaging to families and their wider networks." Discuss.', in S. Walrond-Skinner and D. Watson (eds), *Ethical Issues in Family Therapy*. London: Routledge & Kegan Paul.

Treacher, A. (1988), 'Family therapy – an integrated approach', in E. Street and W. Dryden (eds), *Family Therapy in Britain*. Milton Keynes: Open University Press.

Treacher, A. and J. Carpenter (1982), ' "Oh no! Not the Smiths again!" An exploration of how to identify and overcome "stuckness" in family therapy. Part I: Stuckness involving the contextual and technical aspects of therapy', *Journal of Family Therapy*, 4, 285–305.

Treacher, A. and J. Carpenter (eds) (1984), *Using Family Therapy*. Oxford: Blackwell.

Triseliotis, J. (1986), 'Transcultural social work', in J. Cox (ed.), *Transcultural Psychiatry*. London: Croom Helm.

Van Trommel, M. (1984), 'A consultation method addressing the therapist–family system', *Family Process*, 23, 469–80.

Walker, L. E. (1979), *The Battered Woman*. London: Harper and Row.

Watzlawick, P., J. Weakland and R. Fisch (1974), *Change: Principles of Problem Formation and Problem Resolution*. New York: Norton.

Weitzman, J. (1985), 'Engaging the severely dysfunctional family in treatment: basic considerations', *Family Process*, 24, 473–85.

Wells, R. and Y. Giannetti (1986), 'Individual marital therapy: a critical reappraisal', *Family Process*, 25, 43–51.

Westheafer, C. (1984), 'An aspect of live supervision: the pathological triangle', *Australian and New Zealand Journal of Family Therapy*, 5, 169–75.

Whiffen, R. and J. Byng-Hall (eds) (1982), *Family Therapy Supervision: Recent Developments in Practice*. London: Academic Press.

Whitaker, C. et al. (1965), 'Countertransference in the family treatment of schizophrenia', in I. Boszormenyi-Nagy and J. Framo (eds), *Intensive Family Therapy*. New York: Harper and Row.

Wilcoxon, S. and S. Gladding (1985), 'Engagement and termination in marital and family therapy: special ethical issues', *American Journal of Family Therapy*, 13, 65–71.

Wilden, A. (1980), *System and Structure: Essays in Communication and Exchange* (2nd edn). London: Tavistock.

Will, D. and D. Baird (1984), 'An integrated approach to dysfunction in inter-professional systems', *Journal of Family Therapy*, 6, 275–90.

Woody, J. D. (1981), 'Transition from marital therapy to divorce adjustment therapy', in A. S. Gurman (ed.), *Questions and Answers in the Practice of Family Therapy*. New York: Brunner/Mazel.

Wright, L. and E. Coppersmith (1983), 'Supervision of supervision: how to be 'meta' to the metaposition', *Journal of Strategic and Systemic Therapies*, 2, 40–50.

Wynne, L. and R. Green (1985), 'A truant family', in S. Coleman

(ed.), *Failures in Family Therapy*. New York: Guilford Press.
Wynne, L. C. et al. (eds) (1986) *Systems Consultation: A New Perspective for Family Therapy*. New York: Guilford Press.
Zilbach, J. (1986), *Young Children in Family Therapy*. New York: Brunner/Mazel.

Subject Index

Note: references in bold include case examples; a reference followed by (fig.) indicates material in a figure or table.

Index by Margaret Hardwidge

Author Index

Note: references in bold indicate location of substantial quotation from that author, or significant use of that author's ideas.

CARMARTHENSHIRE COLLEGE OF TECHNOLOGY AND ART
AMMANFORD CAMPUS
LIBRARY

Index by Margaret Hardwidge